T0132726

INTERNET OF MEDICAL THINGS IN SMART HEALTHCARE

Post-COVID-19 Pandemic Scenario

INTERNET OF MEDICAL THINGS IN SMART HEALTHCARE

Post-COVID-19 Pandemic Scenario

Edited by
Saravanan Krishnan, PhD
Aboobucker Ilmudeen, PhD

First edition published 2024

Apple Academic Press Inc.
1265 Goldenrod Circle, NE,
Palm Bay, FL 32905 USA

760 Laurentian Drive, Unit 19,
Burlington, ON L7N 0A4, CANADA

CRC Press
2385 NW Executive Center Drive,
Suite 320, Boca Raton FL 33431

4 Park Square, Milton Park,
Abingdon, Oxon, OX14 4RN UK

© 2024 by Apple Academic Press, Inc.

Apple Academic Press exclusively co-publishes with CRC Press, an imprint of Taylor & Francis Group, LLC

Library and Archives Canada Cataloguing in Publication

Title: Internet of medical things in smart healthcare : post-COVID-19 pandemic scenario / edited by Saravanan Krishnan, PhD, Aboobucker Ilmudeen, PhD.
Names: Saravanan, Krishnan, 1982- editor. | Ilmudeen, Aboobucker, editor.
Description: First edition. | Includes bibliographical references and index.
Identifiers: Canadiana (print) 20230471951 | Canadiana (ebook) 20230471978 | ISBN 9781774913253 (hardcover) | ISBN 9781774913260 (softcover) | ISBN 9781003369035 (ebook)
Subjects: LCSH: Internet in medicine.
Classification: LCC R859.7.I58 I58 2024 | DDC 610.285—dc23

Library of Congress Cataloging-in-Publication Data

....

CIP data on file with US Library of Congress

....

ISBN: 978-1-77491-325-3 (hbk)
ISBN: 978-1-77491-326-0 (pbk)
ISBN: 978-1-00336-903-5 (ebk)

About the Editors

Saravanan Krishnan, PhD
Assistant Professor,
Department of Computer Science and Engineering,
College of Engineering, Guindy,
Anna University, Chennai, Tamil Nadu, India

Saravanan Krishnan PhD, is working as an Associate Professor in the Department of Computer Science and Engineering at the College of Engineering, Guindy, Anna University, Chennai, Tamil Nadu, India. He has an ME in Software Engineering and a PhD in Computer Science Engineering. His research interests include cloud computing, software engineering, Internet of Things, and smart cities. He has published 14 papers at international conferences and 27 papers in international journals. He has also written 14 book chapters and edited eight books with international publishers. He has done consultancy work for several municipal corporations and smart city schemes. He is an active researcher and academician. Also, he is reviewer for many reputed journals published by Elsevier, IEEE, etc. He is a member of the Indian Society for Technical Education, The Institution of Engineers (India), Indian Science Congress Association, Association for Computing Machinery, among others.

Aboobucker Ilmudeen, PhD
Senior Lecturer in Management and IT,
Department of Management and IT, Faculty of
Management and Commerce, South Eastern
University of Sri Lanka, Oluvil, Sri Lanka

Aboobucker Ilmudeen, PhD, is working as a Senior Lecturer in Management and Information Technology in the Department of Management and Information Technology of the Faculty of

Management and Commerce, South Eastern University of Sri Lanka. His research areas are managing IT investment, IT governance, healthcare applications, big data, IT capabilities, and innovation. He has 15 indexed research articles published in various reputed journals of Elsevier, Springer, Emerald, and Taylor and Francis. In addition, many of his book chapters have been published in book series of popular publishers such as Elsevier, Springer, CRC Press – Taylor and Francis, IGI Global, and De Gruyter. He has received PhD in Management: majoring in Management Science and Engineering, and MSc in IS.

Contents

Contributors

Anushree Acharya
Assistant Professor, Hospital Administration, SGT University, Haryana, India

T. Amudha
Department of Computer Applications, Bharathiar University, Coimbatore, Tamil Nadu, India

Jose Anand
Department of ECE, KCG College of Technology, Karapakkam, Chennai, Tamil Nadu, India

Trishit Banerjee
Department of Basic Engineering and Sciences, Netaji Subhash Engineering College,
Techno City Garia Kolkata, India

R. Dhanalakshmi
School of Computer Science and Engineering, Vellore Institute of Technology (VIT), Chennai, India

S. Jijitha
Department of Computer Applications, Bharathiar University, Coimbatore, Tamil Nadu, India

E. Kaliappan
Professor, Department of Electrical and Electronics Engineering, Easwari Engineering College,
Chennai, Tamil Nadu, India

P. Kathirvel
Assistant Professor, Department of Electronics and Instrumentation Engineering,
Dr. Mahalingam College of Engineering and Technology, Pollachi, Tamil Nadu, India

T. Kesavan
Assistant Professor, Department of Electrical and Electronics Engineering,
Easwari Engineering College, Chennai, Tamil Nadu, India

Bantu Kovela
Student, Department of ECE, BVRIT Hyderabad College of Engineering for Women, Hyderabad, India

C. Muralidharan
Department of Computing Technologies, SRM Institute of Science and Technology, Kattankulathur,
Tamil Nadu, India

Varalakshmi Perumal
Madras Institute of Technology, Anna University, Chennai, Tamil Nadu, India

A. Ponmalar
Department of CSE, Sri Sai Ram Institute of Technology, Chennai, Tamil Nadu, India

G. Lakshmi Prabha
PhD Scholar, Department of Computer Science and Engineering, College of Engineering, Guindy,
Anna University, Chennai, Tamil Nadu, India

Mandipalli Sai Preethi
Student, Department of ECE, BVRIT Hyderabad College of Engineering for Women, Hyderabad, India

Sakthi Jaya Sundar Rajasekar
Melmaruvathur Adhiparasakthi Institute of Medical Sciences and Research, Melmaruvathur, Tamil Nadu, India

Banala Rajitha
Student, Department of ECE, BVRIT Hyderabad College of Engineering for Women, Hyderabad, India

Swamynathan Ramakrishnan
Amity University Dubai, Dubai International Academic City, Dubai, UAE

L. Sai Ramesh
CEG Campus, Anna University, Chennai, India, Tamil Nadu

K. Rameshkumar
Assistant Professor, Department of Electrical and Electronics Engineering, Dr. Mahalingam College of Engineering and Technology, Pollachi, Tamil Nadu, India

Kunal Rawal
Senior Faculty Hospital Administration, SGT University, Gurugram, Haryana, India

Kusa Sushmi Reddy
Student, Department of ECE, BVRIT Hyderabad College of Engineering for Women, Hyderabad, India

S. Sabena
Anna University Regional Centre, Tirunelveli, Tamil Nadu, India

K. Saravanan
Associate Professor, Department of Computer Science and Engineering, College of Engineering,Guindy, Anna University, Chennai, Tamil Nadu, India

K. Selvakumar
National Institute of Technology, Trichy, Tamil Nadu, India

Y. Mohamed Sirajudeen
Assistant Professor, School of Computer Science and Engineering, VIT-AP University, Amaravati, Andhra Pradesh, India

S. Sivaranjani
Assistant Professor, Department of Electrical and Electronics Engineering, Sri Krishna College of Engineering and Technology, Coimbatore, Tamil Nadu, India

R. Somasundaram
Faculty of Engineering and Technology, Sri Ramachandra Institute of Higher Education and Research, Chennai, Tamil Nadu, India

Shweta Soni
Assistant Professor, SGT University, Gurugram, Haryana, India

Swarnalingam Thangavelu
Melmaruvathur Adhiparasakthi Institute of Medical Sciences and Research, Melmaruvathur, Tamil Nadu, India

Santhosh Kumar Veeramalla
Associate Professor, Department of ECE, BVRIT Hyderabad College of Engineering for Women, Hyderabad, India

Abbreviations

ACID	atomic, consistent, isolated, and durable
ACO	ant colony optimization
AI	artificial intelligence
ANN	artificial neural networks
AUC	area under the curve
BAN	body area network
BCE	binary cross entropy
BGV	Brakerski-Gentry-Vaikuntanathan
BSC	base station controller
CAD	computer-aided diagnosis
CC Score	COVID criticality score
CDS	clinical decision support
CE	cross-entropy
CLI	command-line interface
CNN	convolutional neural network
CoEWS	COVID early warning score
COVID-19	coronavirus disease 2019
CRF	conditional random fields
CT	computed tomography
CXR	chest x-ray
DA	data augmentation
DEWS	deep early warning system
DK	declarative Knowledge
DL	deep learning
DMS	decision-making system
DNN	deep neural networks
DRL	deep reinforcement learning
DSS	decision support system
DTL	deep transfer learning
EC	edge computing
ECG	electro-cardiogram
ED	emergency department
EMG	electromyography

EMR	electronic medical records
FM	free modeling
GA	genetic algorithms
GPR	Gaussian process regression
GPS	global positioning system
GSM	global system for mobile
GUI	graphical user interface
HAR	human activity recognition
HCPs	health care professionals
HER	electronic health record
HIE	health information exchange
HRV	heart rate variability
IoMT	Internet of Medical Things
IoT	Internet of Things
IR sensor	infrared sensor
IT	information technology
KR	knowledge representation
KRR	kernel ridge regression
LIMS	laboratory information management system
M2M	machine-to-machine
MEWS	modified early warning score
ML	machine learning
MPN	multilayer perception network
nCoV	novel coronavirus
NEWS	national early warning score
NLP	natural language processing
NLTK	natural language tool kit
NLU	natural language understanding
NN	neural networks
NTUH	National Taiwan University Hospital
OTP	one-time password
PACS	picture archiving and communication systems
PACT	private automated contact tracing
PEPX	projection-expansion-projection-extension
PK	procedural knowledge
PMD	programmer monitor device
PoS	parts of speech
PPE	personal protective equipments

PRESEP	prehospital early sepsis detection
QoS	quality of service
RAN	radio access network
REM	rapid eye movement
REMS	rapid emergency medicine score
RFID	radio-frequency identification
RNN	recurrent neural network
rPPG	remote photoplethysmography
RT-PCR	reverse transcription polymerase chain reaction
SA	simulated annealing
SARS-CoV-2	severe acute respiratory syndrome coronavirus 2
SDK	software development kit
SEIR	susceptible-exposed-infectious-removed
SIR	susceptible -infectious removed
SK	structural knowledge
SMS	short message service
SSML	speech synthesis markup language
SVM	support vector machine
TBM	template-based modeling
VUI	voice user interface
WHO	World Health Organization
WSN	wireless sensor network

Preface

Improving healthcare services is vital for human livelihood. There are several technologies such as IoT, Artificial Intelligence, Robotics, Big Data, and wearable devices used in healthcare applications worldwide today. These technical advantages help the Internet of Medical Things (IoMT) achieve precision in diagnosis, improved healthcare systems, extended lifetime for the patients, reduced cost for treatments, minimal efforts for physicians, and controlled and secure health ecosystem for hospitals.

IoMT plays a major role during pandemic periods, in which a huge population gets affected and requires treatment. These diseases, e.g., COVID-19 will spread to people nearby at a rapid rate if proper practices are not followed. Physicians and hospitals will face difficulties in handling such diseases and situations. In such cases, modern healthcare IoMT applications can greatly help in diagnosis and monitoring the patients without much human intervention. Wearable healthcare sensors can continuously monitor the patient's health status 24x7 and send emergency alert notifications to the hospital staff.

The Internet of Medical Things (IoMT) has proven to be a viable solution for integrating and sharing data between healthcare devices. This book provides an overview of modern wearable healthcare devices, principles, and architectures, IoMT COVID-19 real world applications, real use cases, IoMT-based healthcare system development, etc. This book also targets recent applications, state-of-the-art developments in the healthcare domain, IoMT experiments, and sensor-based systems. The COVID-19 epidemic has helped expand the function of IoMT in healthcare at an exponential rate. Several rapidly emerging innovations are convergent and will impact the IoMT's trajectory in healthcare.

This book offers the reader a comprehensive exploration and presentation of IoMT in the post-COVID-19 pandemic scenario in the healthcare domain. Accordingly, the readers will understand the practical applications, development of healthcare systems, architectural frameworks, and modern design elements of healthcare systems. This book will be beneficial for students (undergraduate and post-graduate), researchers, academicians, practitioners, healthcare professionals, healthcare developers, and policymakers.

CHAPTER 1

IoMT-Based Telemedicine Monitoring Machine for COVID Patients

T. KESAVAN,[1] E. KALIAPPAN,[2] S. SIVARANJANI,[3] K. RAMESHKUMAR,[4] and P. KATHIRVEL[5]

[1]*Assistant Professor, Department of Electrical and Electronics Engineering, Easwari Engineering College, Chennai, Tamil Nadu, India*

[2]*Professor, Department of Electrical and Electronics Engineering, Easwari Engineering College, Chennai, Tamil Nadu, India*

[3]*Assistant Professor, Department of Electrical and Electronics Engineering, Sri Krishna College of Engineering and Technology, Coimbatore, Tamil Nadu, India*

[4]*Assistant Professor, Department of Electrical and Electronics Engineering, Dr. Mahalingam College of Engineering and Technology, Pollachi, Tamil Nadu, India*

[5]*Assistant Professor, Department of Electronics and Instrumentation Engineering, Dr. Mahalingam College of Engineering and Technology, Pollachi, Tamil Nadu, India*

ABSTRACT

With this pandemic situation going on, it has become difficult for the public to visit a doctor for a regular health checkup. Even with online video calls, the doctors may not be available all the time to pick them up. It will be difficult for the doctors to check on the patients physical

Internet of Medical Things in Smart Healthcare: Post-COVID-19 Pandemic Scenario.
Saravanan Krishnan, PhD and Aboobucker Ilmudeen, PhD (Eds.)
© 2024 Apple Academic Press, Inc. Co-published with CRC Press (Taylor & Francis)

as well. With this pandemic situation going around, more importance is given to the covid patients, and all the doctors are provided with a full-time duty to monitor these patients and revive them from their sick beds. People with regular sickness and other illness are not prioritized. Hence, they have to rely on home medications and the internet suggestions without no accurate checks and measurements of their health parameters. Though there are other health monitoring machines available, they are only provided to patients who are bedridden and have difficulty in mobility, the other people are left out. Therefore, there are no immediate proper consulting services for sick patients. All these methods of self-medication are highly dangerous, with no proper medical consolations these actions can lead to severe risk or danger to health. This chapter proposed Internet of Medical Things-based monitoring machine COVID-19 affected people.

1.1   INTRODUCTION

This chapter aims to give access for the patients who find it difficult to get a doctor's consultations during this pandemic situation. The patient in need can access the module registered to their locality. The basic parameters such as the blood pressure, heart rate, and SpO2 level are measured and are updated to the database of the hospital to which the module is linked. The user will be provided with a list of symptoms from which they can choose and the related sickness will be shortlisted [1]. With the inputs provided by the user, based on his selection of symptoms, and using AI, his sickness will be found out with the predefined instruction loaded in the system, and accordingly the prescription details are printed [2]. The data collected from the user is stored in the hospital's database in the cloud to keep a record and for the referral purpose of his next visit. There are several types are followed in the medical field. In this chapter, we have discussed three important telemarketing system [3].

Interconnected IoT contraptions give a lot of information that should be gainfully overseen by providers. That would be a major test. The interaction for beating this test and dissecting itemized data The Internet of Things Analytics (Particle) is initiated. Unrefined information is being transformed into important and helpful importance Information that utilizes strategies like information extraction and information examination. Indeed, this was normal. By 2020, a larger number of than 50–55% of the strategies used to break down source information will utilize this information that is being created. From device machines and applications [4]. The IoT development relies upon certain things to oversee and keep up with our prosperity and improving advancements. Constant information assortment from different sources, for this situation, a limitless number of patients. Throughout a far reaching timeframe, utilizing the capacities of IoT should turn out to be uncommonly straightforward and speedy [5]. It ought to be especially basic and fast to utilize the capacities of IoT. The force of IoT health and clinical benefits are constrained by shrewd sensors that precisely measure, screen and examine wellbeing status Indicators. These markers embrace fundamental essential wellbeing manifestations, for example, beat rate and pulse, oxygen and glucose levels in blood and pulse. Brilliant sensors are regularly coordinated into medication and tablet bottles, which are associated with the organization. The patient might foster cautions concerning whether they are taking an endorsed prescription [6].

A lot of movement and basic changes are occurring in the field of IoT human administrations. The technique for connecting and speaking with individuals and various contraptions is changing and giving indications of progress bit by bit. Suitable organization of clinical benefits brings about a lessening in human administrations costs, enabled by consistently creating data furthermore, comparing strategies. Clinical benefits associations are getting unparalleled and less limited by social affair, recording, examining and sharing current information viably continuously [7]. Also, as the world is getting a handle on this routinely making a advancement of IoT, different wasteful perspectives in human administrations will be reduced. For instance, different therapeutic gadgets like wellbeing social occasions, thriving watching constructions, and medication limits will have talented sensors implanted in them that collect raw information, store it, look at it, and direct tests that enable specialists to make a suitable move [8].

1.1.1 REMOTE MEDICAL MONITORING SYSTEM BASED ON PARAMETER WITH WIRELESS NETWORK

The idea is to collect and monitor physiological parameters, and then load the data with minimal effort [6]. The parameter monitor is large in size and expensive, which is not conducive to remote monitoring. Combining built-in and mobile communication technology, a substitute for a medical multi-physiological parameters of monitored and it was golden hospital server. In this methodology, all the health parameters of patients can be taken and may be sent to the health monitoring system [9]. This type of monitoring system consists of an ARM-based embedded system this microcontroller is used to give proper suggestions based on the health parameters. This ARM controller connected with server really Martin system and was well programmed, depending on previous patients data effect and analysis. This system is an Internet of Medical Things-based monitoring system and human to machine interaction happened here, so as to issue an alarm when a dangerous situation occurs. The system can record and display heart rate, vital signs, blood oxygen saturation, blood heat and many other physiological parameters in real time [10].

1.1.2 PDAB-BASED WIRELESS PHYSIOLOGICAL MONITORING SYSTEM FOR PATIENT

PDAB system gives idea of mobile monitoring system for patience and functioning with jointly working of WLAN and PDAB technology. This patient monitoring system is one of advanced digital monitoring system for patient and combinedly working with local area network. A WSN-based personal digital assistant health monitoring system if continuously monitoring and record patient health parameter like pulse rate, temperature, oxygen, level 3-channel ECG via SpO2. Using WLAN, recorded patient data transmitted through wireless sensor network and doctors can view their previous medical files. Propose the necessary operations from your desktop, use the wireless network as an access point, and obtain all user data from the hospital management and doctors' handheld computers [11].

1.1.3 HETEROGENEOUS-BASED REMOTE HEALTH OBSERVING SYSTEM USING WIFI

This idea aims to collect data about patients' biosignals and send it to healthcare providers. A patient connection monitor that uses heterogeneous wireless transceivers collects biosignal data from sensors and transmits the data to e-healthcare providers via a radio access network (RAN). Since different biosignal data may have different quality of service (QoS) require-ments, devices connected to the patient use traffic planning to determine whether and what to transmit over an available wireless connection [12].

1.2   EXISTING HEALTH MONITORING SYSTEM

Health monitoring is done in most higher-end hospitals who have enough financial access to all the medical equipment and are updated to with the current technology and their where abouts. The current system provides health monitoring to patients who are admitted in hospitals and who have difficulties in mobility. There are systems which are used to monitor patients in a large indoor area where they are provided with a wearable sensor.

There is also a system which has in indoor localization algorithms which communicates through Bluetooth to respond to any emergency. Different nodes to collect various parameters such as the skin temperature, respiratory rate, heart rate is obtained in the terminal and is connected to Bluetooth and the results are displayed in the android device connected to it. All of the obtained data from the sensor is used only for a particular patient for continuous monitoring. Online doctor consulting services are available where the patient gets a live interaction with the doctor only during allocated time and not during emergency time.

There are also real-time heart monitoring machines available to monitor the patient continuously through wearable sensor and sends an alarm when absorbs any abnormalities. This system does not follow any wireless protocols/procedures.

1.3   IOMT-BASED TELEMEDICINE MONITORING MACHINE

With this pandemic situation going doctors may not be available all the time to check on regular local patients. The proposed system aims to provide access to all the wearable sensors to the general public who can't afford the cost of buying one. The proposed system measures multiple parameters to detect the type of fever or disease. It is a simple user interac-tive module which provides the different symptoms from which the user can select and narrow down their illness. The user can get an immediate diagnosis of their illness with no live doctor present. With the predefined instruction and cases provided uploaded to the system can easily narrow down to the user's illness.

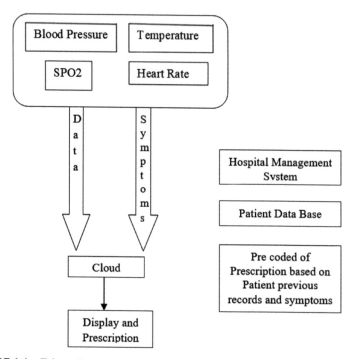

FIGURE 1.1   Telemedicine monitoring machine.

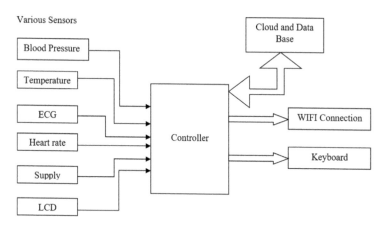

FIGURE 1.2   Mobile unit of telemedicine monitoring machine.

The module provides an immediate display of all the recorded parameters and prints the necessary medication that has to be taken by the user. All the recorded parameters of the patient are updated to the cloud and is stored in the hospital's database. The recorded parameters are used for future reference when the patients visit the hospital in person.

Each module is connected to a nearby by hospital, where the patient has to register themselves beforehand. The user will be provided with a separate login id and password. The input parameters such as the blood pressure, heart rate, SpO2 level and the temperature are collected using different sensors which are connected to the Arduino. From the recorded parameters, the system displays certain choices of symptoms to narrow down the problem. A predefined set of instruction is updated to the system with which the module accesses to provide the required medicine of the patient needs that is printed on the bill. The measured inputs are recorded and it is sent to the cloud. Going through the recorded parameters and the patient's record with the hospital, the frequent drug used by them is suggested. The medicines are printed on the prescription accordingly. This connection between the module, cloud and hospital is done with a help of a Wi-Fi module. All the recorded parameters are updated and stored in the hospital database and are used for future reference.

The proposed telemonitoring system advantages are discussed in Figure 1.3. This system is mainly used for continuous monitoring and controlled medicine system for covid patients and effective medicines are prescribed by doctors using this concept. It is cost-effective and safest tele-monitoring system, because patients do not need to visit hospital and meet doctors directly but they got the same benefit and impact from this system. It is one of the latest advanced treatment, patients got opportunity to discuss with international doctors and possibility to get very quality medicine. All the proposed concepts and ideas have been implemented in digital internet, so it is easy to reach all countries people with low cost. The mentioned system is very suitable and gives better solution for the pandemic situation.

The proposed IoT-based monitoring system very useful for pandemic situation and preferred for yielded people, physically handicapped people. Other than pandemic situation, IoT-based telemonitoring is suitable for people those who were continuously monitor and need treatment such that heart problems, blood pressure, pregnant women extra. This type of concept can implement in various places to connect all the people; for example, the village people facing the problem of meet the doctor get hospital facilities in 24*7 due to many reasons. All The villages are not getting their quality Hospital facilities and doctors, village people not meet the doctor due to long distance between village and cities. All above mention problem can be overcome to implement the IoT-based monitoring system. Some yielded people are really needed continuous monitoring and health checkup due to age condition. Yielded people is unable to visit the hospital physically and meet doctor. To apply the proposed concept so people can monitored by doctors and they can get treatment. They can also follow the doctor's advice, when its requirement people can visit to the hospital in easy way like vehicle can arrange in advance and the doctor appointment also booked early. So the people got lot of advantages compared with conventional one.

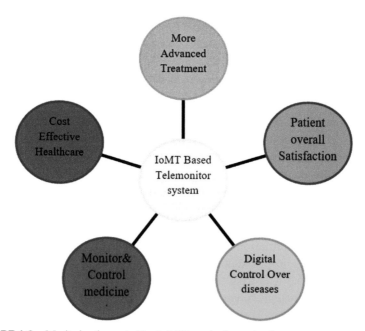

FIGURE 1.3   Merits implemented by IoMT-based telemonitoring system.

IoMT-based health monitoring system is also preferred for children's medical checkups and monitor. Cchildren's growth is very crucial for the age of 0 to 4 years, because in this age children unable to convey their health condition to parents and also need to follow various vaccines and medicine based upon their ages. So our proposed system is very useful for health checkup and monitoring, and also give awareness to the parents regarding vaccine, health conditions, and taking medicines. So does not need to visit the hospital unnecessarily and meet doctors. Parents get very relaxation and do not worry about child growth. The proposed IoMT-based health monitoring system is give the multi-application purpose. IoMT-based proposed system is also utilized to physical challenge people for health monitoring and checkup. Because challenged people unable to come to the hospital directly to meet doctor, they need someone help always. So using the proposed idea, they are monitoring by IoT device and they will get from guidance from doctors. They can avoid to come hospital directly to meet the doctors.

1.4 CONCLUSION

With the help of this module, we can perform contactless parameter check of the patient. This module helps to keep the record of the patient's drug usage. This module provide solutions for local patients who cannot find local available doctors during this pandemic. This module provide immediate diagnosis of patients with the help of AI and the parameters recorded. This system can be placed in large apartments where the people count is more, and they can get their weekly health check up with minimal travel and effort. The system can be interfaced with a camera and provide facial recognition for easy login. The system can also be modified to store all the frequently used medicines and provide it to the user immediately. The module can be connected with several other advanced health sensors for future use.

KEYWORDS

- **health monitoring**
- **health parameters**
- **medications**
- **pandemic**
- **self-medication**

REFERENCES

1. Yamuna, A., Kesavan, T., & Sivashankari, V., (2015). Harmonic compensation in residential distribution system with MPPT. *International Journal of Applied Engineering Research, 10*(20), 15737–15741.
2. Lakshmi, K., Kesavan, T., Kavin, R., Senthilkumar, M., & Gomathy, V., (2021). Quick search optimization algorithm-based implementation of virtual power plant for distribution network. *Advances in Intelligent Systems and Computing, 1163*, 261–272.
3. Subhashini, N., Gnanamalar, S., Geethamani, R., Gomathy, V., & Kesavan, T., (2018). Effectiveness of pitch control scheme in load balance of WECS. *Journal of Advanced Research in Dynamical and Control Systems, 10*(11), 542–545.
4. Kesavan, T., Sheebarani, G. S., Sivaranjani, S., Radhakrishnan, G., & Sitharthan, R., (2020). SVM-based reduction of input current harmonics in three phase rectifier. *IOP Conference Series: Materials Science and Engineering, 937*(1), 012058.
5. Kesavan, T. A., Sheebarani, S., Gomathy, V., Kavin, R., & Sivaranjani, S. (2020). Renewable Energy Based on Energy Conservation and Crossover System. *2020 6th International Conference on Advanced Computing and Communication Systems (ICACCS)*, 155–157.
6. Kavin, R., Kesavan, T. A., Sheebarani Gnanamalar, S., & Rameshkumar, K. (2019). Optimal Charging and Discharging Planning for Electric vehicles in Energy saving system. *2019 5th International Conference on Advanced Computing & Communication Systems (ICACCS)*, 976–978.
7. Ruman, M. R., Barua, A., Rahman, W., Jahan, K. R., Jamil, R. M., & Rahman, M. F., (2020). IoT-based emergency health monitoring system. *International Conference on Industry 4.0 Technology.*
8. Kesavan, T., & Lakshmi, K. (2022). Optimization of a Renewable Energy Source-Based Virtual Power Plant for Electrical Energy Management in an Unbalanced Distribution Network. *Sustainability, 14*(18), 11129. MDPI AG. Retrieved from http://dx.doi.org/10.3390/su141811129.
9. Yuan-Hsiang, L., I-Chien, J., Ko, P. C. I., Yen-Yu, C., Jau-Min, W., & Gwo-Jen, J., (2014). A wireless PDA-based physiological monitoring system for patient transport. *IEEE Transactions on Information Technology in Biomedicine, 8*(4), 439–447.
10. Ding, S., & Wang, X., (2020). Medical remote monitoring of multiple physiological parameters based on wireless embedded internet. *IEEE Access, 8*, 78279–78292.
11. Tirkey, A., & Jesudoss, A., (2020). A non-invasive health monitoring system for diabetic patients. *International Conference on Communication and Signal Processing.*
12. Liau, J. C., & Ho, C. Y., (2019). Intelligence IoT (internal of things) telemedicine healthcare space system for the elderly living alone. *IEEE Eurasia Conference on Biomedical Engineering, Healthcare and Sustainability.*
13. Amin, P., Anikireddypally, N. R., Khurana, S., Vadakkemadathil, S., & Wu, W., (2019). Personalized health monitoring using predictive analytics. *IEEE Fifth International Conference on Big Data Computing Service and Applications.* doi: 10.1109/bigdataservice.2019.00048.

CHAPTER 2

COVID-19 Detection Using Convolutional Neural Networks from Chest X-Ray Images

MANDIPALLI SAI PREETHI,[1] BANALA RAJITHA,[1]
KUSA SUSHMI REDDY,[1] BANTU KOVELA,[1] and
SANTHOSH KUMAR VEERAMALLA[2]

[1]*Student, Department of ECE, BVRIT Hyderabad College of Engineering for Women, Hyderabad, Telangana, India*

[2]*Associate Professor, Department of ECE, BVRIT Hyderabad College of Engineering for Women, Hyderabad, Telangana, India*

ABSTRACT

Across the globe, as of 22 May 2021, more than 16 crores people have been infected by Coronavirus disease 2019 or COVID-19. World Health Organization has declared it a global pandemic. More than 34 lakhs people have lost their lives. One of the main reasons for people's death is the lack of fast testing mechanism. In many places, the current existing covid test takes around 48 hours to get the results. And also, some underdeveloped countries are not in a situation to purchase laboratory kits for testing. This is one of the main reasons for the rapid increase in the cases which lead to a dreadful situation. A new rapid testing method would benefit both patients and doctors. So we propose a method that gives us the results instantly by taking the chest x-ray images as input.

Internet of Medical Things in Smart Healthcare: Post-COVID-19 Pandemic Scenario.
Saravanan Krishnan, PhD and Aboobucker Ilmudeen, PhD (Eds.)
© 2024 Apple Academic Press, Inc. Co-published with CRC Press (Taylor & Francis)

2.1 INTRODUCTION

COVID-19 is a highly contagious and infectious disease that has spread to over 200 nations in the last year. In the meanwhile, COVID-19 has become an important global health issue causing breathing issues, heart infections, and even death. Due to extensive travel between nations, this virus, which was first detected in a human person in December 2019 in Wuhan, China, quickly spread throughout the continent. The effect on the international economy of COVID-19 was bad, too [1, 2]. According to research, the COVID-19 virus has a negative impact on the lungs and quickly mutates before the patient gets any diagnosis-based treatment. When the symptoms are similar to those of the common flu, as in the instances in Southeast Asia and Central Asia, the situation becomes more serious. COVID-19 virus incubation time is around 1 week, according to experts. This is critical because the infected patient functions as a viral carrier and unwittingly spreads the virus during this time. It spreads more quicker than it is detected due to its highly infectious nature. In healthcare applications, machine learning algorithms are increasingly popular. Varied methods of detecting a COVID-19 virus are utilized in patients, such as Reverse Transcription Polymerase Chain Reaction (RT-PCR) [3], X-ray imaging [4, 5], CT scanning, fast antigen testing, serologic testing, etc.

The RT PCR is the most successful method for detecting COVID-19 by far. This approach takes a lot of time (even days), and calls for particular kits that may have geological, social, and economic obstacles that may not be accessible in isolated areas. The fast antigen test instead investigates the presence of the nasal swab viral antigens, but has a greater probability of false negatives. The serology test examines the immune system's antibodies to the virus from the patient's blood sample. It does not aid early viral identification; however, it only examines the antibodies IgM/IgG during or after recovery. CT and X-ray scans are employed by both of them to identify any kind of irregularity in the invisible electromagnetic spectrum, employed for preliminary detection and of high clinical significance.

During our investigation, we discovered that chest X-ray exams are reasonably priced, and the findings are simple to interpret. Chest X-ray tests, mobile versions, and a reduced radiation risk are readily offered. CT scans, however, entail a significant radiation risk, are costly, need clinical knowledge, and are non-portable. As a result, X-ray scans are more convenient to use than CT scans [6].

Artificial intelligence (AI) models have been shown to be effective in processing data in a medical environment. New machines with AI models that do the same with specialists in specialized assessment tasks have already been created. In addition, the use of AI systems for extracting information from medical imaging is an appropriate application with a view to producing instruments for reducing mistakes in diagnosis, increasing efficiency, and reducing expenses. To assist imaging experts, these tools are frequently incorporated into image-based decision-support systems. Medical imaging is best used for assessing the level of danger, for finding out what is wrong, for predicting how the patient will respond to treatments, and for decoding multi-omics diseases. Computing power does not need more infrastructure and supplies, nor does it need the employment of healthcare workers. Medical image analysis, since it also has the potential to be used in the detection of COVID-19, may assist with the diagnosis of COVID-19 [7].

To do clinical analysis and help with the detection of COVID-19 in patients, AI-based models that use radiological medical images as input provide an alternative to utilizing automated technologies for this purpose. Due to the imaging equipment required, consolidation of exams has made an enormous contribution to accelerating data gathering using specialist equipment (e.g., Chest X-ray (CXR) image). Additionally, since CXR is a standardized examination, it is easy to generate and validate models based on previously accessible data. The advantage of being this way is that it eliminates the discomfort of making patients uncomfortable in order to get fresh information [8, 9].

One of the most often used [10] techniques for detecting pneumonia is the use of chest X-rays. Although not often employed in therapeutic settings, it is also very quick, inexpensive, and widely used as a research method [11–14]. The chest X-ray has been shown to result in a lower dosage of radiation than other diagnostic imaging methods, such as CT and MRI scans. To be able to successfully recognize the right diagnosis, one must possess the required level of expertise in the field of x-ray imaging. Chest X-rays are considerably more difficult to diagnose than other imaging modalities, such as CT or MRI.

It is only through the use of a chest X-ray that COVID-19 can be identified and diagnosed by a specialist. The number of diagnosis specialists is less than the number of normal physicians. Even in non-emergency situations, there aren't enough physicians per person to go around. Greece ranks top, with 607 physicians per 100,000 people, according to 2017 statistics. This number is much lower in other countries. We'll inevitably face a situation where we are unable to provide adequate healthcare since the hospital beds and health staff are inadequate in the event of a major pandemic like COVID-19. Accordingly, with regard to being contagious, COVID-19 is a highly contagious disease, and medical workers and care providers are the most vulnerable. Prevention is just as important as early diagnosis in order to limit the development of the epidemic and assist in the healing process.

Computer-aided diagnosis (CAD) makes the process of diagnosing pneumonia on a chest X-ray much faster and more accurate [11]. Due to the AI's ability to process datasets beyond human potential, there is increasing use of AI methods [15, 16]. Radiologists who integrate CAD methods into their diagnostic systems will see their workload significantly reduced while also boosting quantitative analysis. The popularity of CAD systems based on deep learning and medical imaging is growing.

Despite earlier AI-based models developing CT and/or CXR image-specific COVID-19 identification, several of them have significant draw-backs, such as:

- misuse of personal data results in findings that cannot be reproduced.
- The database set was comprised of a small number of data sets, which may not be varied enough to discover relevant symptoms in the co-occurrence of COVID-19 and other disorders.
- even when superior photos of higher dimensions could be made available, they may not be utilized since the enterprise is unable to fully exploit them, for instance, because it lacks flexibility.

With that in mind, we encourage this discussion to move beyond our focused concern with providing AI models with data and into the more general discussion on how valuable it is to implement and utilize an AI model using datasets as well as applying data augmentation (DA) for classes with small amounts of data (images related to COVID-19, in this work). As such, we predict that the model will be free of bias while testing datasets owing to the unique characteristics of each data source as well as when using the current accessible photos from COVID-19 instances, which are all that remain. The CNN models that we constructed were exclusive to our experiment and were specifically intended to differentiate healthy and sick individuals [17].

2.2 RELATED WORKS

Technological advances in artificial intelligence (AI) are being used in diverse areas such as the early identification of many types of brain tumors, as well as the detection of breast cancer [18–21]. Deep learning methods may reveal visual characteristics that were not visible in the original photos, allowing them to be discovered. Convolutional Neural Network (CNN) has shown to be very adept at identifying and learning things, making it an important component of scientific study [22]. CNN was used to high-speed video endoscopy pictures in order to better comprehend the quality of low-light images acquired from a high-speed endoscopy, as well as to discover the definition of the concept of an aspiratory knob. In this case, CT images helped differentiate the idea of pediatric pneumonia. Additionally, while recording colonoscopies, robotized markings of polyps were used to identify cryptoscopic picture detection. The application of machine learning algorithms on chest X-rays is on the rise due to the accessibility of low-cost imaging technologies and the huge quantity of accessible training data. Using ImageNet models [24] and their ensembles, the authors [23] were able to detect pneumonia using pre-trained models. In Ref. [25], the authors utilized a modified VGG16 model for lung area identification and characterization of different types of pneumonia, and the results were promising. Using a large dataset, in Ref. [26], they have shown indications of improvement results, whereas in Ref. [27], the authors demonstrated signs of improvement results using a small arrangement of images, using image augmentation in conjunction with CNN. On the other hand, in Ref. [28], they reported the use of an ensemble of various networks to detect 14 unique diseases, including pneumonia, on chest X-rays using a 121-layer CNN. In Ref. [29], the accurate diagnosis of 14 thoracic illnesses was achieved via the use of a pre-trained DenseNet-121 and feature extraction methods. AlexNet and GoogLeNet were employed together with picture augmentation to achieve an Area Under the Curve (AUC) of 0.95 in pneumonia detection, according to [30].

Convolutional Neural Networks (CNNs) have been used by many researchers in the field of image categorization, most of whom implement unique neural network designs. Convolutional neural networks are a strong class of deep learning models, and they have proven useful in a wide variety of machine learning applications. CNNs can perform four distinct functions, which include training the weights from scratch, fine-tuning the weights of an existing pre-trained CNN, training CNNs before putting inputs into them, and initializing unsupervised pre-trained CNNs. CNN networks LeNet-5 is credited with creating the first "architectural template" or framework of CNNs. Since then, several designs used this approach, adding additional convolution and pooling layers until the system became a fully-connected or convolutional system. According to its predecessor CNN, AlexNet [31] was enhanced with three more convolutional layers, making it the deepest neural network available at the time of its creation. ReLUs was the first CNN activation function that was used in AlexNet, and it was the first CNN structure to use it. Although researchers wanted to test many more designs, they opted to stack several layers on top of one another to increase the number of hidden layers, and VGG-16 [32] was created. ReLU activations were retained from AlexNet, with 13 convolutional layers and 3 fully connected layers. The VGG-19 network, which was created as a successor to the preceding network, merely added additional layers.

There have already been a number of research investigations conducted on COVID-19 detection. Chest radiography pictures are mostly processed using deep learning methods with the goal of detecting infected individuals and the findings have proven quite accurate. An advanced deep convolutional neural network is described in Ref. [17] that can successfully identify coronavirus disease from chest X-ray (CXR) pictures. In order to achieve a high level of prediction accuracy from a limited number of pictures, the CNN is built on learned transfer models, such as ResNet50, InceptionV3, and Inception-ResNetV2. The pictures are divided into two categories: regular photographs and COVID-19 images. The ImageNet dataset is also used to use a transfer learning method in order to overcome the lack of data and training time in this study. The findings demonstrated that the ResNet50 model outperformed the other models in terms of accuracy throughout both the training and testing stages. When it comes to image classification, Abbas et al. [34] proposed a new CNN architecture that relied on transfer learning and class decomposition to enhance the performance of pre-trained models on X-ray pictures. The planned architecture is referred to as DeTraC, and it is divided into three stages.

Local feature extraction is performed using an ImageNet pre-trained CNN during the first step. After the training process, a stochastic gradient descent technique is used to find the best solutions for training, and then the class composition layer is used to identify the class assignments for classification. ImageNet networks such as the ResNet18 pre-trained ImageNet network were utilized in this study, and the findings revealed that the accuracy on CXR pictures was 95.12%. According to [35], a novel deep anomaly detection model for quick and accurate screening of COVID-19 using CXR images has been developed. An anomaly detection head is one of the three components of the proposed model. The other two components are a backbone network and a classification head. Classification and anomaly detection are done on pictures sent into the backbone network. In order to classify images, the classification head employs an updated classification convolutional layer that includes a hidden layer of 100 neurons, a one-neuron output layer and the "sigmoid" activation function, among other things. This head has the same architecture as the classification head, but it produces scalar anomaly scores, which are then used to identify anomaly pictures in the classification results (COVID-19 cases). This model has succeeded in reducing the number of false positives. The COVID-Net convolutional neural network is described in Ref. [36] that is capable of recognizing COVID-19 instances from chest radiographs. This network design is built on two stages: a human-machine collaborative design approach and a machine-driven design exploration stage. As an additional step in the validation of choices, an explainability-driven audit is conducted. For COVID-19 instances, the findings revealed a high sensitivity (87.1%) and an accuracy of 96.4%. One more chapter [37] describes a CNN architecture for COVID-19 identification in additional pneumonia patients. In order to speed up training and decrease training time, a pre-trained ResNet-50 architecture is applied using a three-step process called COVID-ResNet.

A system consisting of seven deep learning image classifiers, dubbed COVIDX-Net, was introduced by Hemdan et al. [38], with the goal of identifying COVID-19 illness from CXR pictures using the framework. The authors examined how Monte-Carlo Dropweights Bayesian convolutional neural networks may enhance the decision accuracy of human-machine systems by providing more information about the expected uncertainty in deep learning algorithms in Ref. [39]. A pre-trained ResNet50V2 model is used to assess model uncertainty using X-ray images from COVID-19. Estimation uncertainty and classification accuracy showed a significant connection, indicating that predictions may be found to be incorrect.

The aforementioned study, conducted by [40], examined the capabilities of five pre-trained CNNs on the ability to identify COVID-19 from a chest X-ray. The findings indicated that VGG19 and MobileNetv2 had the highest accuracy, with 93.48% and 92.85%, respectively, achieving the highest accuracy. Following a review of the literature, it becomes clear that the majority of the work has been done using CT or X-Ray imaging. In addition, the models were trained using limited datasets. This encourages us to expand on our narrow interest in providing AI models with data by advancing to a discussion about the relative significance of utilizing datasets in conjunction with AI models and implementing data augmentation (DA) for classes with a limited quantity of data. Because of the unique features of each data source, we anticipate that the model will be free of bias when testing datasets, as well as when utilizing the currently available pictures from COVID-19 instances, which are the only ones that are still available. We only used CNN models to compare healthy and ill people in our experiment, and these models were designed for that purpose alone.

COVID-19 is classified as binary or multiple in studies that use chest X-rays to diagnose it. Raw data is used in certain research, whereas feature extraction is used in others. The amount of data points utilized in research varies as well. Convolutional neural networks have been shown to be the most popular technique in research.

2.3   MATERIALS AND METHODS

It is known as deep learning because it is a discipline of machine learning that is motivated by the structure of the brain. Since they have been more frequently utilized, deep learning methods have demonstrated remarkable achievements in the area of medical image processing. Clinically relevant findings are extracted by using deep learning on medical data. Much success has been achieved in utilizing deep learning models for many applications, such as classification, segmentation, and lesion detection in medical data. MRI, CT, and X-ray imaging techniques were utilized to collect imaging and signal data for use in analysis [41–46].

AI now has two main branches of Machine Learning: Supervised Learning and Unsupervised Learning. AI is a kind of machine learning that allows a computer to replicate human behavior. Machine learning is a methodology for getting the benefits of AI by training algorithms using data. Machines can now predict a huge amount of the information and details that human lives revolve on. To adapt from non-useful environments, new machines need to do tasks that are as basic as using computer facial recognition and as sophisticated as automobile autonomy. While Machine Learning is become ever-more prominent as a critical component of technological advancement, there is a significant reason to assume that even more data will make it an even more essential ingredient. Figure 2.1 shows the classification of machine learning.

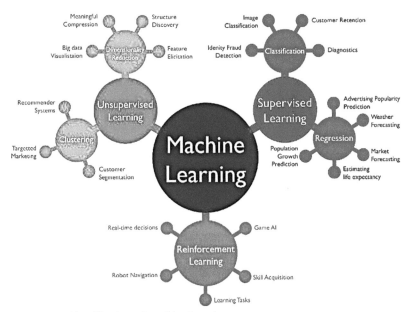

FIGURE 2.1   Classification of machine learning.

Like any other approach, there are a number of approaches to train machine learning algorithms, some of which have benefits and some of which have downsides. In order to grasp the benefits and shortcomings of any machine learning model, we must first look at what sort of data they can process. While machine learning makes use of both labeled and unlabeled data, it may use only one kind of data.

It is both possible and necessary to read the machine-readable pattern for input and output parameters from the unaltered labeled data, but human work is required to label the data in the first place. Unlabeled data is in a machine-readable form only if at least one of the parameters is labeled. If a machine is to be used instead of humans, this reduces the necessity for human labor, but it also necessitates more complicated solutions. At the moment, three broad approaches dominate the field of machine learning: supervised learning, unsupervised learning, and reinforcement learning.

1. Supervised Learning: Supervised learning is one of the most important kinds of machine learning. The method for machine learning in this situation is based on labeled data. Supervised learning may be highly successful when applied under ideal circumstances. The ML method comes with a small training data set for the purpose of performing supervised learning. This data collection is a part of the broader dataset and allows the algorithm to comprehend the problem rudimentarily, solution, and data points. The training data set is very comparable to the final dataset in terms of characteristics and provides the algorithm with the labeled parameters to solve the problem.

To complete the process, the parameters found are placed in a cause and effect relationship with one another, and the algorithm determines which parameters lead to which results. After training, the algorithm understands how the data works and has an understanding of the link between the input and output. This technique, in combination with the additional training dataset, results in the solution being put into production and the algorithm was then trained using the final dataset. Even after the supervised machine learning algorithms have been deployed and are in use, their development is certain. The algorithms will discover new patterns and relationships, resulting in an improvement in their overall performance over time.

2. Unsupervised Learning: Supervised machine learning provides the capacity to work with unlabeled data. Thus, making the dataset machine-readable does not need human work, which allows you to deal with datasets much bigger than you otherwise could. It enables the algorithm to discover exactly how every relationship between two data points connects to each other. An unsupervised learning method is entirely label-free, thus artificial structures are produced that are not visible to the user. When building relationships between data points, the algorithm processes the data in an abstract fashion, with no human input necessary.

It is only via the development of these invisible structures that unsupervised learning algorithms are able to adapt to changes. While unsupervised learning algorithms may adapt to the input by continually updating underlying structures instead of a predefined and fixed problem statement, the algorithms may go as far as incorporating randomness or disregarding data if they are given faulty info. This enables for better post-deployment system growth, as compared to the supervised learning methodologies.

3. Reinforcement Learning: The underlying theory of reinforcement learning derives its cues from the way humans really learn from their experiences in life. It incorporates a trial-and-error mechanism that iterates and improves over time as it learns from various settings. A good consequence is celebrated or "reinforced," whereas a negative consequence is dealt with by suppressing or "punishing." Reinforcement learning follows a psychology notion known as conditioning. By rewarding the algorithm and placing it in a work environment with an interpreter, the system helps the algorithm learn. The algorithm goes through many iterations, and each time it generates a result that is then given to the interpreter. The interpreter then analyzes whether or not the results are useful.

The interpreter benefits the algorithm if the program finds the right answer. The algorithm must keep repeating the process until a better favorable conclusion is achieved, even if it means many attempts at a failed end result. When a majority of the results are positive, the incentive system will be directly proportional to the efficacy of the outcome. When you're using reinforcement learning in a normal context such as finding the shortest route between two points on a map, the result is not an absolute value. A more accurate way to state this is that it determines the effectiveness of the product or procedure as a percentage. The higher this percentage figure is, the greater the incentive given to the algorithm to improve its performance. To arrive at the best possible response while also increasing the quantity of reward, a training algorithm was applied.

2.3.1 DATASET

We acquired pictures from many free sources for our work [33, 47]. CXR pictures of COVID-19-positive patients and healthy people may be found in these open-source public databases. This collection of data includes CXR images of many individuals, only the frontal images of which are taken into consideration, and the lateral images of which are discarded.

This is due to the fact that we are primarily concerned with the lungs, which can be examined more completely from the front than from the side. However, for the sake of this analysis, we have split the images into two major groups: COVID-19 POSITIVE (class 0) and COVID-19 NEGA-TIVE (class 1). The gathered Chest X-ray pictures dataset includes 2295 X-ray images, which are split into 1449 photos for training and 484 images for testing. Figures 2.2 and 2.3 show two instances of covid positive and negative pictures, respectively.

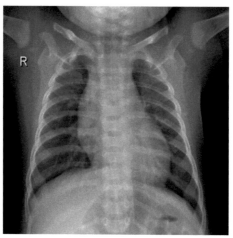

FIGURE 2.2   COVID-19 negative X-ray image.

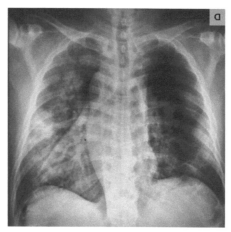

FIGURE 2.3   COVID-19 positive X-ray image.

2.3.2 THE PROPOSED CNN MODEL

CNNs are kinds of deep neural networks, optimized for image recognition issues. Since the incoming images to CNN must be computer-identifiable, the images must be converted into a format that the computer can process before broadcasting can begin. As a result, pictures are transformed to matrix format before processing. The system makes determinations based on differences in pictures and thus matrices to identify which image corresponds to which label. It learns the difference in the label's visual properties during training, and then uses the information to predict new pictures. Convolutional neural networks have three layers: a convolutional layer, a pooling layer, and a fully connected layer. Feature extraction occurs in both the convolutional and pooling layers of the algorithm. Classification, on the other hand, takes place at a fully connected layer.

There are many design patterns and designs used by CNNs, it varies depending on the nature of the problem they are attempting to address. The proposed model is comprised of three convolutional layers, with a max pooling layer after each of those layers after each of those layers. The final layer is a multilayer perceptron that is fully connected. Ultimately, at the conclusion of the calculations, ReLu activation is applied to the convolutional and fully connected layers. Using the input picture as a starting point, the first convolutional layer conducts an averaging operation over 32 kernels of size 3x3. There are 64 kernels in a 4x4 size for the second convolutional layer, which is given after maximum pooling. An additional layer with 512 neurons follows the convolutional layer, which has 128 1x1 kernels at the conclusion of the convolutional layer. The four output classes are given a probability distribution using the softmax function. The Adaptive Moment Estimation (Adam) method is used to train a model to estimate moments. A model is trained with a batch size of 100 and for 1000 epochs to estimate moments.

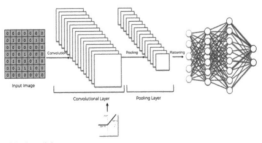

FIGURE 2.4 CNN algorithm steps.

Source: Reprinted from https://www.andreaperlato.com/aipost/cnn-and-softmax/

As shown in Figure 2.4, there are four stages in the CNN algorithm.

1. **Convolution:** Convolution is a mathematical term that refers to the joining of two mathematical functions in order to produce a third function. A combination of two snippets of information is used. In the case of a CNN, convolution is performed on the input data using a filter or kernel to construct a feature map from the data. Convolutional neural networks (CNNs) are constructed using a convolutional layer as its foundation layer. Once the features of the pattern are established, the process may begin. This layer takes in the image as input and processes it via the use of a filter. The feature map is made up of the values that were acquired as a result of the filtering process. In this layer, a collection of kernels is applied to the pattern, and they glide over the pattern in order to extract low- and high-level characteristics from the pattern. When combined with the input pattern matrix, the kernel produces a 3X3 or 5X5-shaped matrix, which is then transformed to create the output pattern matrix. The stride parameter specifies the number of steps that should be taken to account for shifting across the input matrix. As shown in Figure 2.5, the three components that contribute to the action of convolution are the input picture, the feature detector, and the feature map.

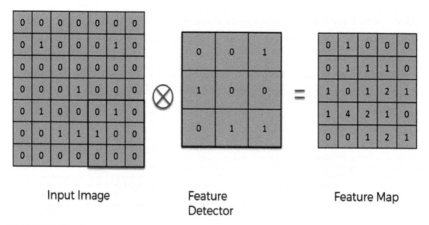

Input Image   Feature   Feature Map
                           Detector

FIGURE 2.5   CNN's convolution.

Source: Reprinted from https://www.andreaperlato.com/aipost/cnn-and-softmax/

2. **Max pooling:** Max pooling, as illustrated in Figure 2.6, is a sample-based discretization technique. To have enough dimensions to rely on assumptions, the binned sub-regions must be reduced in number of dimensions. Following the convolutional layer, the pooling layer is the next layer. We utilize feature maps on average since most of the time we use a pooling layer as well to minimize the number of feature maps and network parameters that we need. In this study, maximum pooling and global average pooling were used. To determine the output for the max-pooling technique, the matrix size is applied in each feature map, resulting in a less number of output neurons. Before the data is pooled into a single dimension, another layer processes it, reducing the number of dimensions that the data is handled with. It is linked to the fully connected layer after the global average pooling layer. We also use a dropout layer to act as a bridge between the two layers. Most of this layer's work involves improving the ability of the system to escape overfitting and divergent patterns.

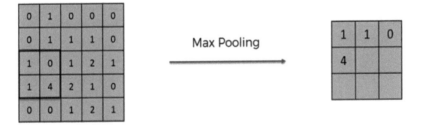

Feature Map   Pooled Feature Map

FIGURE 2.6 Max pooling in CNN.

Source: Reprinted from https://www.andreaperlato.com/aipost/cnn-and-softmax/

3. **Flattening:** As illustrated in Figure 2.7, flattening is the process of converting all the 2D arrays that result from different operations into a single continuous linear vector.

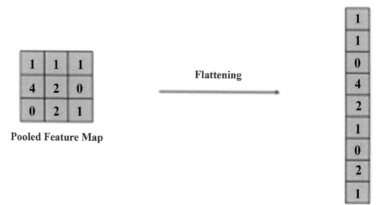

FIGURE 2.7   CNN's flattening.

Source: Reprinted from https://www.andreaperlato.com/aipost/cnn-and-softmax/

4. **Full Connection:** The most important CNN layer is the fully linked layer. This layer and the multilayer perceptron are both based on the same concept. Softmax activation is often employed for training the last layer of a fully connected layer, while ReLU activation is frequently used on completely connected layers. At the end of a CNN, the output of the last Pooling Layer is fed into the so-called Fully Connected Layer. These layers may include a single layer or a combination of many layers, totally connected indicates that every node in the first layer is linked to every node in the second layer. Figure 2.8 is a visual representation of the connection phases' three levels: input layer, completely connected layer, and output layer.

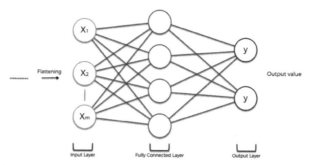

FIGURE 2.8   CNN's full connection.

Source: Reprinted from http://kienthuclaptrinhweb.blogspot.com/2020/10/convolution-and-pooling-trong-cnn-tuan.html?m=1

2.4   IMPLEMENTATION OF PROPOSED APPROACH

The methodology that is created uses an x-ray image as input and employs a convolutional neural network to try to identify if the uploaded image is either covid positive or negative. We have divided our work into three parts, i.e., model training, model testing, and prediction.

2.4.1   INITIALIZATION

- Add first layer (Convolution 2D): We use 64 output filters in the convolution 3*3 filter matrix that will multiply to input RGB size image 64*64 and use activation = relu.
- Apply (MaxPooling2D), Processing, Hidden Layer 1 (2*2 matrix rotates, tilts) to all the images. Steps 1 and 2 are repeated twice.
- Adding Flattening: converts the matrix in a single array.
- Adding full connection (128 final layer of outputs, activation= relu &Dense layer, activation= sigmoid).
- This complete process is given in Figures 2.9 and 2.10.

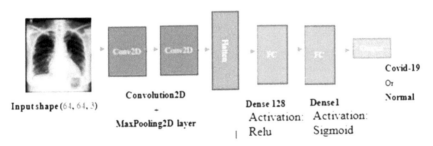

FIGURE 2.9   The layer of CNN architecture.

2.4.2   FIT THE CNN MODEL

In the field of deep learning, a popular Adam algorithm is used because it delivers good results quickly, and it is an optimization algorithm to update iterative network weights based on training data instead of the classic random gradient descent procedure, as given in Figure 2.11.

```
Model: "sequential_1"
```

Layer (type)	Output Shape	Param #
conv2d_2 (Conv2D)	(None, 21, 21, 64)	1792
max_pooling2d_2 (MaxPooling2	(None, 10, 10, 64)	0
conv2d_3 (Conv2D)	(None, 3, 3, 64)	36928
max_pooling2d_3 (MaxPooling2	(None, 1, 1, 64)	0
flatten_1 (Flatten)	(None, 64)	0
dense_2 (Dense)	(None, 128)	8320
dense_3 (Dense)	(None, 1)	129

```
Total params: 47,169
Trainable params: 47,169
Non-trainable params: 0
```

FIGURE 2.10   CNN model summary.

```
Epoch 1/10
14/14 [==============================] - 10s 719ms/step - loss: 0.3289 - accuracy: 0.8430 -
Epoch 2/10
14/14 [==============================] - 10s 709ms/step - loss: 0.3099 - accuracy: 0.8610 -
Epoch 3/10
14/14 [==============================] - 10s 702ms/step - loss: 0.3538 - accuracy: 0.8453 -
Epoch 4/10
14/14 [==============================] - 10s 701ms/step - loss: 0.3111 - accuracy: 0.8632 -
Epoch 5/10
14/14 [==============================] - 9s 675ms/step - loss: 0.3072 - accuracy: 0.8498 - ·
Epoch 6/10
14/14 [==============================] - 10s 699ms/step - loss: 0.2645 - accuracy: 0.8969 -
Epoch 7/10
14/14 [==============================] - 10s 694ms/step - loss: 0.2979 - accuracy: 0.8744 -
Epoch 8/10
14/14 [==============================] - 10s 704ms/step - loss: 0.3345 - accuracy: 0.8274 -
Epoch 9/10
14/14 [==============================] - 10s 685ms/step - loss: 0.2591 - accuracy: 0.9013 -
Epoch 10/10
14/14 [==============================] - 10s 697ms/step - loss: 0.2477 - accuracy: 0.8969
<tensorflow.python.keras.callbacks.History at 0x7f1d8ce09240>
```

FIGURE 2.11   Result of model training in 10 epochs.

Adam, the optimizing method, which is primarily known as an efficient form of gradient descent, in reality, is a kind of gradient descent that typically does not need hand-tuning of the learning rate. To increase the overall training performance, the optimizer works with the gradients of the loss to attempt to reduce the error ("optimize") of the model output by changing the parameters. Kingma et al. (2014) note that is computationally efficient, consumes little memory, is insensitive to diagonal gradient scaling, and is ideally suited for problems with large amounts of data or parameters.

Apply fitting to the training set (steps_per_epoch:100, no. epoch: 10, Validation data: test-set, nb.val.samples (60), callbacks= [early_stop]). shows the results of model training in10 Epochs.

2.4.3 MODEL EVALUATION AND TESTING

On the basis of two-loss criteria (binary cross entropy and mean square error), the CNN model is assessed. An important aspect of neural networks is its loss function, sometimes called a neural net predictive error. For the sake of this explanation, we may characterize how a Neural Net is trained as follows: In order to make an adjustment to the weighting of the Neural Net, we must utilize the Loss first, and then, the Loss is utilized to compute the gradients.

In the binary classification tasks, while Binary Cross Entropy (BCE) loss is used. For categorizing data into two classes, we apply the BCE loss function only when we require an output node, and hence the output value should be sent via Sigmoid activation and output range should be provided (0 – 1). As can be seen in, the Cross-Entropy (CE) loss may be stated as stated by. In order to test our model, certain samples of cells are provided in order to identify the covid-19. The images have been imported and transformed to an array, so the model can predict if the picture is 19-point or normal. Figure 2.12 depict a hypothetical model for scanning fresh X-ray pictures.

FIGURE 2.12 New prediction model.

2.5 RESULT AND DISCUSSION

In the first experiment, a dataset consisting of 2,295 chest X-ray pictures was utilized for training and testing, whereas a dataset of 1449 pictures was utilized for training and a subset of 484 pictures was utilized for testing. The model was trained using 1449 X-rays of persons with Covid-19 and normal and a test set of 484 chest x-rays split between those with Covid-19 and non-infection. To optimize the learning process, the whole data set must pass many times to the same neural network.

Experience has shown the ability of certain models to accurately identify COVID-19 in human samples by enhancing the training sample, enabling patients to be identified. Figure 2.13 represents while training the model, and we are totally doing 30 epochs. These graphs are epochs (x-axis) vs. accuracy (y-axis). The first graph represents training and validation accuracy at each point. An epoch is one complete pass of the training dataset through the algorithm. Figure 2.14 is the model prediction code, and Figure 2.15 is the code black. We can see that when an image is uploaded, it gives an output (last line of the image).

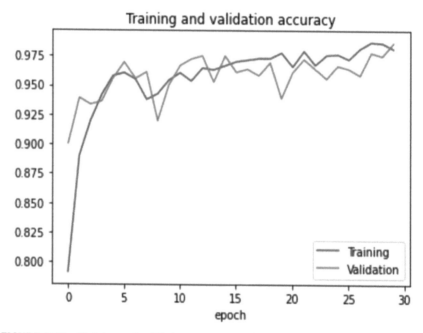

FIGURE 2.13   Training and validation accuracy graph.

We proposed a new technique in this article that allowed CNN to completely automate the screening of COVID-19. An X-ray of the chest has been used to predict whether individuals would test positive for COVID-19. The model was trained using COVID-19, normal, and viral pneumonia chest X-ray pictures that were not utilized in the training phase. With a classification accuracy of more than 96%, we have achieved the best performance.

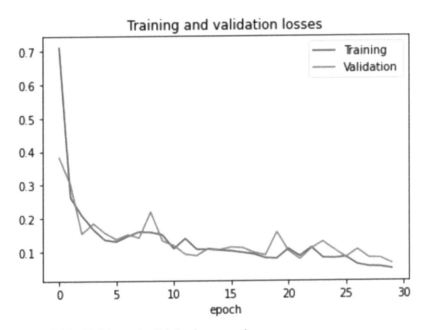

FIGURE 2.14   Training and validation losses graph.

Prediction

```
from google.colab import files
from keras.preprocessing import image
uploaded = files.upload()
for filename in uploaded.keys():
  img_path = '/content/' +filename
  img = image.load_img(img_path,target_size=(150,150))
  images = image.img_to_array(img)
  images= np.expand_dims(images,axis=0)
  prediction = model.predict(images)
  print(filename)
  if prediction == 0:
    print("covid postive")
  else:
    print("covid negative")
```

```
Choose files  No file chosen        Upload widget is only available when the cell has been executed in the current browser session. Please rerun this cell to enable.
Saving covid1.jpg to covid1.jpg
covid1.jpg
covid postive
```

FIGURE 2.15   The result showing the given x-ray image is positive or negative.

AI-based systems are commonplace in COVID-19 surveillance, particularly in regard to their ability to differentiate COVID-19 cases from others. In the literature, there is a lot of research on this topic. COVID-19 positive and COVID-19 negative are often distinguished in binary classification. Furthermore, it is critical to differentiate between COVID-19-positive individuals and those who have viral or bacterial pneumonia, which are two different kinds of lung illnesses that may occur simultaneously. Very few studies that use several classes are found in the literature.

The automated identification and follow-up of patients with suspected COVID-19 is suggested using a high-accuracy decision support system. Looking at the pandemic in a global context, there is an increase in the workload of radiologists. The fatigue of the expert during these manual diagnoses and judgments may cause the mistake rate to rise. Clearly, this will need decision support systems to get rid of the issue. In other words, a more thorough diagnostic may be performed.

The advantages of the proposed model are it decreases the diagnostic time, it reduces the financial costs, this provides valuable assistance to doctors who are diagnosing COVID-19, not painful, whereas the existing methods are a bit painful. There are some limitations, i.e., the suggested model is meant as a tool to help develop, maintain, and evaluate models. Thus, a more comprehensive review of the medical evidence requires a collection of individual pieces of evidence, so as to get to a final medical diagnosis. To compound the problem, even though there are around 10,000 photographs that have been intentionally created to have the appearance of having been taken with DA, the total number of original photographs for COVID-19 instances is very limited (i.e., 573). A higher quantity of images would be preferred and would serve to illustrate various COVID-19 aspects more clearly. Training and assessing photographs is far more time-consuming than just processing photos. Telling a computer to look at a single picture to be analyzed in less than a second only takes a fraction of a second, even on a high-powered computer. To do this, training the suggested models requires considerable computing power, which took around 5 to 6 hours to complete using a GPU on high-resolution images. This conclusion follows from the above facts. If the suggested approach can't be applied to low-end computers, training new models based on this technique is impossible. Limitations in the amount of data available prevent this research from being completed. Enabling the development of more reliable systems is made easier by increasing the data, running it through the data in many different locations, and testing it thoroughly. Future research will use image processing techniques on X-ray and CT images to extract the characteristics. Features that best separate classes will be discovered from these extracted features, and classification performance values will be evaluated using various methods. The research will also use deep learning models in order to ensure accuracy. In addition, data from many other centers will be examined on the outcomes of the research.

2.6 CONCLUSION

In conclusion, the results of this unique research show a potential role of a very accurate AI algorithm to quickly identify patients, which could be useful and effective in combating the current outbreak of Covid-19. We are almost certain that it is possible for the proposed CNN model, which shows the equivalent of the highest score for the accuracy of a specialized chest radiologist, to represent a very effective examination tool for the rapid diagnosis of many infectious diseases such as the COVID-19 epidemic that do not require the introduction of a radiologist or physical examinations.

In future studies, we recommend addressing other topics, such as outbreak escalates, as well as trying to explore different approaches to convolutional neural networks, including deep learning models and improved interpretation of CNN models. This helps the doctors as well as patients to take measures and treatments as required so that the patient can be cured.

FINANCIAL DISCLOSURE

The authors state no funding is involved.

CONFLICT OF INTEREST

The authors declare no potential conflict of interest.

ETHICAL APPROVAL

The conducted research is not related to either human or animal use.

KEYWORDS

- **classification**
- **CNN**
- **COVID-19**
- **X-ray**

REFERENCES

1. Di, W., Tiantian, W., Qun, L., Zhicong, Y., (2020). The SARS-CoV-2 outbreak: What we know, *International Journal of Infectious Diseases, 94*, 44–48, ISSN 1201-9712, https://doi.org/10.1016/j.ijid.2020.03.004.

2. Roosa, K., Lee, Y., Luo, R., Kirpich, A., Rothenberg, R., Hyman, J. M., Yan, P., & Chowell, G., (2020). Real-time forecasts of the COVID-19 epidemic in China. *Infect. Dis. Model., 5*, 256–263.

3. Bustin, S. A., (2000). Absolute quantification of mRNA using real-time reverse transcription polymerase chain reaction assays. *J. Mol. Endocrinol., 25*(2), 169–193.

4. Mangal, A., Kalia, S., Rajgopal, H., Rangarajan, K., Namboodiri, V., Banerjee, S., & Arora, C., (2020). *CovidAID: COVID-19 Detection Using Chest X-Ray.* arXiv:2004.09803.

5. Ke, Q., Zhang, J. S., Wei, W., Połap, D., Woźniak, M., Kośmider, L., & Damaševičius, R., (2019). A neuro-heuristic approach for recognition of lung diseases from x-ray images. *Expert Syst. Appl., 126*, 218–232.

6. Xu, X. W., Jiang, X. G., Ma, C. L., Du, P., Li, X. K., Lv, S. Z., Yu, L., et al., (2020). *Deep Learning System to Screen Coronavirus Disease 2019 Pneumonia.* arXiv preprint arXiv: 2002.09334, 2020.

7. Singh, D., Kumar, V., Vaishali, & Kaur, M., (2020). Classification of COVID-19 patients from chest CT images using multi-objective differential evolution-based convolutional neural networks. *Eur. J. Clin. Microbiol. Infect. Dis., 39*, 1379–1389.

8. Apostolopoulos, I. D., & Bessiana, T., (2020). COVID-19: Automatic detection from x-ray images utilizing transfer learning with convolutional neural networks. *Phys. Eng. Sci. Med.,* 1–6.

9. Ilyas, M., Rehman, H., & Nat-Ali, A., (2020). *Detection of COVID-19 from Chest X-Ray Images Using Artificial Intelligence: An Early Review.* arXiv:2004.05436.

10. Jaiswal, A. K., Tiwari, P., Kumar, S., Gupta, D., Khanna, A., & Rodrigues, J. J., (2019). Identifying pneumonia in chest X-rays: A deep learning approach. *Measurement, 145*, 511–518.

11. Antin, B., Kravitz, J., & Martayan, E., (2017). *Detecting Pneumonia in Chest X-Rays with Supervised Learning.* http://cs229.stanford.edu/proj2017/final-reports/5231221. pdf (accessed on 11 January 2022).

12. Narayan, D. N., Kumar, N., Kaur, M., Kumar, V., & Singh, D., (2020). Automated deep transfer learning-based approach for detection of COVID-19 infection in chest x-rays. *IRBM.* https://doi.org/10.1016/j.irbm.2020.07.001.

13. Ayan, E., & Ünver, H. M., (2019). Diagnosis of pneumonia from chest x-ray images using deep learning. In: *Scientific Meeting on Electrical-Electronics and Biomedical Engineering and Computer Science (EBBT)* (pp. 1–5). Istanbul, Turkey. https://doi.org/10.1109/EBBT.2019.8741582.

14. Gaál, G., Maga, B., & Lukács, A., (2020). *Attention U-Net Based Adversarial Architectures for Chest X-Ray Lung Segmentation.* arXiv:2003.10304.

15. Liang, G., & Zheng, L., (2020). A transfer learning method with deep residual network for pediatric pneumonia diagnosis. *Comput. Methods Programs Biomed., 187*, 104964.

16. Jaiswal, A., Gianchandani, N., Singh, D., Kumar, V., & Kaur, M., (2020). Classification of the COVID-19 infected patients using DenseNet201-based deep transfer learning. *J. Biomol. Struct. Dyn.* https://doi.org/10.1080/07391102.2020.1788642.

17. Narin, A., Kaya, C., & Pamuk, Z., (2020). *Automatic Detection of Coronavirus Disease (COVID-19) Using X-Ray Images and Deep Convolutional Neural Networks.* arXiv preprint arXiv: 2003.10849.

18. Tahir, A. M., et al. (2020). A systematic approach to the design and characterization of a smart insole for detecting vertical ground reaction force (vGRF) in gait analysis. *Sensors (Basel Switzerland), 20*(4), 957.

19. Chowdhury, M. E. H., et al., (2019). Wearable real-time heart attack detection and warning system to reduce road accidents. *Sensors (Basel Switzerland), 19*(12), 2780.

20. Chowdhury, M. E. H., et al., (2019). Real-time smart-digital stethoscope system for heart diseases monitoring. *Sensors (Basel Switzerland), 19*(12), 2781.

21. Kallianos, K., et al., (2019). How far have we come? Artificial intelligence for chest radiograph interpretation. *Clinical Radiology, 74*(5), 338–345.

22. Krizhevsky, A., Sutskever, I., & Hinton, G. E., (2012). ImageNet classification with deep convolutional neural networks. *Presented at the Proceedings of the 25th International Conference on Neural Information Processing Systems, 1.*

23. Chouhan, V., et al., (2020). A novel transfer learning-based approach for pneumonia detection in chest x-ray images. *Applied Sciences, 10*(2), 559.

24. Gershgorn, B. D., (2017). *The Data that Transformed AI Research—and Possibly the World. Quartz, 26*(2013-2017), 52.

25. Gu, X., Pan, L., Liang, H. Y., & Yang, R., (2018). *Classification of Bacterial and Viral Childhood Pneumonia Using Deep Learning in Chest Radiography*, 88–93.

26. Wang, X., Peng, Y., Lu, L., Lu, Z., Bagheri, M., & Summers, R., (2017). . "Chestx-ray8: Hospital-scale chest x-ray database and benchmarks on weakly-supervised classification and localization of common thorax diseases." In *Proceedings of the IEEE conference on computer vision and pattern recognition*, pp. 2097–2106.

27. Ronneberger, O., Fischer, P., & Brox, T., (2015). U-net: Convolutional networks for biomedical image segmentation. *Medical Image Computing and Computer-Assisted Intervention – MICCAI 2015*, 234–241.
28. Rajpurkar, P., et al., (2018). Deep learning for chest radiograph diagnosis: A retrospective comparison of the CheXNeXt algorithm to practicing radiologists. *PLOS Medicine, 15*(11), e1002686.
29. Ho, T. K. K., & Gwak, J., (2019). *Multiple Feature Integration for Classification of Thoracic Disease in Chest Radiography, 9*(19), 4130.
30. Lakhani, P., & Sundaram, B., (2017). Deep learning at chest radiography: Automated classification of pulmonary tuberculosis by using convolutional neural networks. *Radiology, 284*(2), 574–582.
31. Krizhevsky, A., Sutskever, I., & Hinton, G. E., (2017). ImageNet classification with deep convolutional neural networks. *Commun. ACM, 60*(6), 84–90 [Online]. Available: https://doi.org/10.1145/3065386.
32. Simonyan, K., & Zisserman, A., (2015). *Very Deep Convolutional Networks for Large-Scale Image Recognition.* CoRR, abs/1409.1556.
33. Wang, L., Wong, A., Lin, Z. Q., Lee, J., McInnis, P., Chung, A., Ross, M., et al., (2020). *Figure 1 COVID-19 Chest X-Ray Dataset Initiative.* https://github.com/agchung/Figure1-COVID-chestxray-dataset (accessed on 11 January 2022).
34. Abbas, A., Abdelsamea, M. M., & Gaber, M. M., (2020). *Classification of COVID-19 in Chest X-Ray Images Using DeTraC Deep Convolutional Neural Network.* arXiv preprint arXiv:2003.13815.
35. Zhang, J., Xie, Y., Li, Y., Shen, C., & Xia, Y., (2020). *COVID-19 Screening on Chest X-Ray Images Using Deep Learning Based Anomaly Detection.* arXiv preprint arXiv:2003.12338.
36. Wang, L., & Wong, A., (2020). *Covid-net: A Tailored Deep Convolutional Neural Network Design for Detection of COVID-19 Cases from Chest Radiography Images.* arXiv preprint arXiv:2003.09871.
37. Farooq, M., & Hafeez, A., (2020). *COVID-ResNet: A Deep Learning Framework for Screening of COVID-19 from Radiographs.* arXiv preprint arXiv:2003.14395.
38. Hemdan, E. E. D., Shouman, M. A., & Karar, M. E., (2020). *COVIDX-Net: A Framework of Deep Learning Classifiers to Diagnose COVID-19 in X-Ray Images.* arXiv preprint arXiv:2003.11055, Google Scholar.
39. Ghoshal, B., & Tucker, A., (2020). *Estimating Uncertainty and Interpretability in Deep Learning for Coronavirus (COVID-19) Detection.* arXiv preprint arXiv:2003.10769.
40. Apostolopoulos, I. D., & Mpesiana, T. A., (2020). COVID-19: Automatic detection from x-ray images utilizing transfer learning with convolutional neural networks. *Physical and Engineering Sciences in Medicine, 1.*
41. Yildirim, O., Talo, M., Ay, B., Baloglu, U. B., Aydin, G., & Acharya, U. R., (2019). Automated detection of diabetic subject using pre-trained 2D-CNN models with frequency spectrum images extracted from heart rate signals. *Comput. Biol. Med., 113*, 103387.
42. Saba, T., Mohamed, A. S., El-Affendi, M., Amin, J., & Sharif, M., (2020). Brain tumor detection using fusion of hand-crafted and deep learning features. *Cogn. Syst. Res., 59*, 221–230.

43. Kassani, S. H., & Kassani, P. H., (2019). A comparative study of deep learning architectures on melanoma detection. *Tissue Cell, 58*, 76–83.

44. Ribli, D., Horváth, A., Unger, Z., Pollner, P., & Csabai, I., (2018). Detecting and classifying lesions in mammograms with deep learning. *Sci. Rep., 8*, 4165.

45. Celik, Y., Talo, M., Yildirim, O., Karabatak, M., & Acharya, U. R., (2020). Automated invasive ductal carcinoma detection based using deep transfer learning with whole-slide images. *Pattern Recogn. Lett., 133*, 232–239.

46. Yu, X., Kang, C., Guttery, D. S., Kadry, S., Chen, Y., & Zhang, Y. D., (2020). ResNet-SCDA-50 for breast abnormality classification. In: *IEEE/ACM Transactions on Computational Biology and Bioinformatics* (pp. 1–8). https://doi.org/10.1109/TCBB.2020.2986544.

47. Irvin, J., Rajpurkar, P., Ko, M., Yu, Y., Ciurea-Ilcus, S., Chute, C., Marklund, H., et al., (2019). CheXpert: A large chest radiograph dataset with uncertainty labels and expert comparison. AAAI Press. ISBN: 9781577358091.

CHAPTER 3

An AI-Powered IoMT Model for Continuous Remote Patient Monitoring using COVID Early Warning Score (CoEWS)

SAKTHI JAYA SUNDAR RAJASEKAR,[1] SWARNALINGAM THANGAVELU,[1] and VARALAKSHMI PERUMAL[2]

[1]*Melmaruvathur Adhiparasakthi Institute of Medical Sciences and Research, Melmaruvathur, Tamil Nadu, India*

[2]*Madras Institute of Technology, Anna University, Chennai, Tamil Nadu, India*

ABSTRACT

The COVID-19 pandemic has brought the world to a standstill. The countries have imposed lockdowns to curb the transmission of the disease and augment the public health facilities for fighting against the pandemic. The healthcare workers have been at the forefront of the fight against the pandemic. The issue of lack of sufficient bed facilities has haunted the governments of almost all nations. This work proposes a novel AI-powered IoMT model for Continuous Remote Patient Monitoring using COVID Early Warning Score (CoEWS). Various sensors like temperature sensors, BP sensors, and breath rate sensor record the patients' vital parameters who undergo home quarantine and these are communicated to a dedicated application. This data is then transmitted to the cloud server where further

Internet of Medical Things in Smart Healthcare: Post-COVID-19 Pandemic Scenario.
Saravanan Krishnan, PhD and Aboobucker Ilmudeen, PhD (Eds.)

processing takes place. The concerned physician will be able to track the patient's health status round the clock. The proposed COVID Early Warning Score (CoEWS) will be computed automatically using various AI regression models, and the CoEWS would be predicted. The proposed model is used to remotely monitor the health status of the patient continuously, which helps the physician and healthcare workers take necessary migratory activities whenever needed, like immediate shifting of the patient to the better healthcare institutions.

3.1   INTRODUCTION

A mysterious pneumonia outbreak took place in the Chinese city of Wuhan in December, 2019. It was probably not known at that time that this outbreak would turn out to be one of the worst disaster that mankind has ever faced. The virus which caused this outbreak was initially termed as the novel Coronavirus (nCoV). However, this virus was officially designated as the Severe Acute Respiratory Syndrome Coronavirus 2 (SARS-CoV-2). The disease caused by this virus is termed as the Corona Virus Disease 2019 (COVID-19). This disease was labeled as a pandemic by the World Health Organization in the month of March 2019. The deadly COVID-19 pandemic has spread to almost all corners of the globe infecting over 170 million people and leaving over 3.5 million dead as of 1st June 2021 [1]. The first wave of COVID-19 has caused a significant dent in the public health infrastructure of the world. This pandemic has shed light on the insufficient doctor-to-patient ratio, insufficient beds in healthcare facilities, and an insufficient number of life-saving medical equipment like ventilators. From experiences of earlier pandemics, such as the 1918 Influenza pandemic, we could predict that the subsequent waves would be of a much higher intensity when compared with the first one. Reports from several Middle East countries state that the fourth wave of the COVID-19 pandemic has already begun to set in. In India, the number of cases reported even during the peaks of the first wave are much lower than what is being reported right in the beginning of the second wave. Also, we anticipate the third wave too. Experts have suggested that the third wave could start by the month of August in India, which would peak by October [21]. From this, we could smell the fact that there is a high possibility that there would be an acute shortage of bed facilities for the patients.

Insufficient beds could impair the healthcare delivery system during the pandemic. We cannot afford this situation as it would lead to increased mortality rates. These scenarios have been experienced in countries like the United States of America right in the first wave itself. Patients could not get admitted in hospitals due to the rapid surge in cases which built an enormous burden on the healthcare system. In order to combat this deficit, countries need to work rapidly on augmenting their resources in terms of hospital beds, doctors, paramedical staff and other healthcare facilities like ventilators and Personal Protective Equipments (PPE). Various strategies have been utilized by various countries. Some of them include the make-shift hospitals in southern Laos [22] and conversion of railway coaches into isolation centers and temporary hospitals [23]. Currently, the patients experiencing mild symptoms are advised to undertake home quarantine. This practice is undertaken to ensure bed facilities for the more severe patients in hospitals. They are required to constantly monitor their health status and report to the concerned doctors. However, there are certain challenges in bringing this practice into operation. These include fear and inability to adapt to usage of smart medical equipment, lack of adherence to regular recording practice of the vitals and unfamiliarity with medical terminologies and the procedure to record the vitals from the medical devices. These challenges need to be overcome so that we could convert the home-based setup into a mini ICU setup when the demand for the bed facilities sky rockets. This proposed work puts forth an novel solution to mitigate this challenge. This involves the utilization of various sensors and recording of the patients' vitals, which is then transmitted to the concerned physicians and the authorities for their real-time monitoring. Also, the real time surveillance of the patient vitals could be used to monitor as well as predict the patients' health status in the near future, which also includes evaluating the need for hospitalization. Sensing of the need for hospitalization much before the need arises, could provide the physicians scope to assess and utilize the limited resources much more effectively. This innovative model could be very handy in times of the peak of the future waves of the pandemic. The Internet of Things (IoT) and Artificial Intelligence (AI) technologies have been a boon for medical professionals during the COVID-19 pandemic. These techniques have been used in combatting the pandemic as in scanning of the general population for rise in temperature, contact tracing, hand sanitization, diagnosis of COVID-19 infection from imaging modalities like X-ray, computed tomography, ultrasound images, evaluating the significance of various biomarkers in assessing the prognosis of the COVID-19 infection and utilization of AI techniques in eliciting novel drug targets and for drug repurposing for COVID-19. Contact tracing has been one of the mainstays for effective control of COVID-19 in the earlier phases of the pandemic. Though this was done manually when the cases were sporadic and low, the need to automate this process arise through the course of the pandemic. Several countries around the globe have brought in various practices to automate this process. These include the introduction of apps like Arogya Setu by the Government of India. An innovative model for contact tracing using deployment of Radio Frequency Identification tags and IoT technology was proposed in Ref. [24]. This could drastically improve the efficacy of the contact tracing process. However, there were some concerns revolving around the privacy of the users using the contact tracing apps. A survey of the various security and privacy concerns of the contact tracing applications have been described. The various approaches and mechanisms of these applications have also been briefed. To summarize, the various research gaps and the proposed solutions have been dealt with [25].

Diagnosis of COVID-19 infection from Chest X-ray images of patients have been one of the hot research topic during the pandemic. Researchers all over the globe have been devising new algorithms and AI models for the automated detection of COVID-19 infection. A novel approach of using Transfer Learning in the detection of COVID-19 using various imaging modalities like chest X-ray images and computed tomography Images have yielded excellent results. The work classifies the test dataset into community-acquired, bacterial, viral, and COVID-19 pneumonia. These advanced AI models could aid radiologists by making the diagnosis rapid and more accurate [26]. Hybrid learning techniques have been employed to diagnose COVID-19 infections from Chest Computed Tomography images. This proposed work has achieved better performance metrics with an accuracy of 96.69%, specificity of 98%, and sensitivity of 96% [27]. A more comprehensive scoring protocol, known as the COVID Criticality Score, has been proposed. The key hallmark of this proposed scoring system is that it takes an inclusive approach of weighing various parameters like laboratory parameters, clinical features, and features extracted from computed tomography images. These parameters are processed using hybrid regression models and the COVID Criticality Score (CC Score) is calculated. This work has been able to successfully to distinguish between the Early and the Critical stages of COVID-19 [28]. A transfer learning model for COVID-19 diagnosis using ultrasound images have been proposed and this model achieved an impressive accuracy of 89% [29].

The proposed model is used to compute the CoEWS based on the various aggregated vitals of patients from the various sensors deployed with patients remotely in order to handle the lack of medical facilities during this pandemic with the help of the emerging Internet of Medical Things (IoMT), Artificial Intelligence (AI), and Cloud Computing technologies to serve the mankind.

3.2   RELATED WORKS

The applications of Internet of Things Technology in the Healthcare sector are briefed. Artificial intelligence, when combined with the Healthcare Internet of Things, could improve the quality of service to the patient to a much larger extent. Moreover, technologies like Blockchain Technology and Software Defined Networking transform the functioning of H-IoT systems [3] to a greater height. The novel Open Body Sensor Networks, their applications and research challenges are discussed. The Open BSN could improvise the aspects like system scalability, energy efficiency, and privacy support [4]. A Body Sensor Network framework is developed for healthcare monitoring platforms which are capable for the applications like better posture recognition [5]. A Continuous patient monitoring system is proposed using an End to End architecture which is powered by blockchain technology. Blockchain technology guarantees the security of the data being transmitted from sensors of the Body Area Network (BAN) [2].

A remote patient monitoring system is proposed. The system aggregates various body vitals from sensors. This data is being transmitted to an Android device from which it gets deposited in the server. The system also tracks the subjects using the Global Positioning System (GPS), enabling the emergency healthcare teams to reach the patient at the earliest in case of any healthcare emergency [6]. The Remote Patient Monitoring system discussed here aggregates three vital parameters such as temperature, blood pressure, and heart rate, through the respective sensors, which are interfaced through Arduino. The data of vital parameters aggregated are sent to the Fuzzy Inference System which aids in decision-making depending upon the data aggregated from the sensors. This would help physicians in making better-informed decisions [7]. A remote healthcare monitoring system based on technologies like Global System for Mobile Communications (GSM) and Global Positioning System (GPS) is discussed. In case of an emergency, the system sends a SMS to the doctor containing the vital parameters, which would enable the physician to learn about the patient's health status [8]. The various wireless technologies in patient monitoring system in the context of Wireless Sensor Network (WSN) are compared. Parameters like delay and energy consumption are analyzed and the best wireless technology is evaluated. The pros and cons of the various technologies are weighed in Ref. [9]. iHeart, a smart wearable-based ECG monitoring system is described. The algorithm to detect abnormalities of the heart functioning, as in arrythmias is implemented in the ECG sensor to minimize power consumption. This novel system alerts the patients and caregivers about the abnormal condition. The implementation and working of this system are detailed in Ref. [10].

The chapter aimed to estimate the usage of Modified Early Warning Score (MEWS) as a triage instrument to predict the requirement of hospital admission and estimating the risk of in-hospital death [11]. The clinical judgment was compared with the accuracy of prediction of the Modified Early Warning Score. A retrospective observational study over a two-month period was undertaken. It was concluded that the detection has improved after the inclusion of the MEWS [12]. A new adjusted MEWS is proposed which significantly proves better in predicting healthcare outcomes in COVID-19 patients [13]. A diagnostic model was constructed using the multivariate logistic regression analysis. Various new parameters added to the COVID-19 Early warning score was found to warn patients more accurately [14]. An Early Warning Scoring model is proposed following the common symptoms analyzed from literature survey. This model could help physicians detect patients who are highly suspected for acquiring the COVID-19 infection. This could help them to protect themselves from getting exposed to unnecessary infection during the perioperative period [15].

Data of 68 patients were analyzed using the National Early Warning Score 2 (NEWS2). As a corollary of the findings, the NEWS2 has predicted the necessity of an ICU admission accurately [16]. The study aimed at identifying Early Warning System which is the most accurate for determining health outcome of COVID-19 patients admitted to the Emergency Department (ED). From the results of the study, it was found that NEWS and Rapid Emergency Medicine Score (REMS) evaluated during the arrival of the patient to the ED were the most precise determinants of a 7-day Intensive Care Unit admission or death [17]. The study aimed to explore the rapid scoring systems in COVID-19 patients who are critically ill. The REMS is found to be highly effective due to its high negative prediction value for screening patients [18]. The study proposes a novel quantitative tool for estimating the mortality risk in COVID-19-infected patients much earlier. The ANDC score may be of great help to the physicians to manage patient stratification [19]. A novel Early Warning System called the "Deep Early Warning System (DEWS)" was proposed. The proposed system was validated with the vitals of patients admitted to Oxford University Hospitals. This proposed system was superior in terms of performance and performed better compared to the National Early Warning Score (NEWS) [30].

The importance of data-driven smart models in clinical deployment of personalized healthcare was emphasized. A new Early Warning System titled the Christiana Care Early Warning System (CEWS) was proposed. This system was trained with a dataset of Electronic Health Records of 6000 patients, which were analyzed retrospectively [31]. A smart alerting system based on the Qatar Early Warning System was developed. This system revolves principally around two data variables (i) Oxygen Saturation, and (ii) Heart Rate. Both these vitals are recorded from the pulse oximeter. These vitals are recorded and analyzed according to the Qatar Early Warning System. Furthermore, in case of any abnormality, a SMS is sent to the hospital with the recordings of these vitals. This SMS would consist of GPS co-ordinates of the patient. The patient is then contacted. If he/she doesn't respond, an ambulance is dispatched [32]. A model for the early prediction of Sepsis is proposed. This model weighs in a lot of parameters like Heart Rate, Systolic Blood Pressure, Temperature, Respiratory rate and a range of hematological parameters like White Blood Cells and Platelets and biochemical parameters like glucose and creatinine. These are scored using various scoring methods like Sequential Organ Failure Assessment which is shortly known as the SOFA score and Prehospital Early Sepsis detection (PRESEP). The KNN classifier was used to train this dataset. This proposed system achieved an impressive accuracy of 97% [33]. Another model for early prediction of Sepsis was proposed.

This model was built using Convolutional Neural Network and Random Forest. The dataset used in this work was from PhysioNet. The data consisted of vitals of patients admitted to the ICU for the past 24 hours. The proposed model achieved an utility score of 0.266 with the test data [34]. The electronic Early Warning Score was proposed. This is presented in such a way that the healthcare professionals could be well aware of the patients' health status. The pros and cons of the proposed Electronic Early Warning System is weighed against the paper-based Early Warning System [35].

An novel scoring system comprised of 12 lead Electrocardiogram data, Heart Rate Variability (HRV), and vital signs was proposed. This scoring system was proposed to aid clinicians to identify the patients who might develop cardiac complications [36]. A machine learning powered Early Warning Scoring system is developed. This is built upon the dataset of patient details from 6 hospitals in Brazil. Various models were utilized for testing in the multicenter trial [37]. The nature of cardiac arrest and the usage of Cardio Pulmonary resuscitation techniques is briefed. The Early detection system for the detection of Cardiac arrest events was built using machine learning techniques. The dataset used in this work is from the Electronic Health Records of adult patients aged more than or equal to 20 years who had visited the Emergency Department of the National Taiwan University Hospital (NTUH). These models could be used to aid the physicians in the Emergency Department with effective medical resource allocation which could further improve the quality of the medical care provided to the hospitals [38]. The need for an effective health monitoring for patients has been emphasized. Also, the possible changes in the patients' vitals 24 hours prior to an adverse event have been briefed. The wearable-based healthcare monitoring system which could operate remotely has been proposed [39]. There is a dire need to develop systems that could diagnose and, if possible, quantify or grade the depression. One such approach is put forth in this paper. The social diary of the individual is scanned. This would generate a score. If the generated score is above the threshold, the individual as well as his/her friends would be notified. This could thereby serve as Early Warning System for patients affected with depression [40].

The routine procedure of collection of the patients' vitals like electrocardiogram, electroencephalogram, SpO_2, temperature, blood pressure, etc., by the healthcare professionals (HCPs), often the nurses has been detailed. Furthermore, parameters which are subjective in nature, like level of alertness, level of pain, extent of awareness and various other behavioral responses have also been recorded. This was traditionally done on a paper-based setup. Later, this was transformed on a PC-based setup. Here, the HCP is only required to enter the inputs. The scoring is automatically done through the intelligent computer software. This chapter proposes a handy alternate to this method. The authors propose a mobile phone-based intelligent scoring system that could be handheld and hence, provided greater flexibility in the workstyle. Moreover, there would be less chances of error since the HCP feeds the data as soon as it is collected right at the patient's bedside. A major pros of this work is that these could be used by even people with less medical knowledge and civilians too. This would be a boon in triaging patients in times of natural calamities where the availability of a proper HCP is not guaranteed at all times [41]. A smart scoring device which scores based on the Modified Early Warning Score (MEWS) has been proposed. This could enable the physicians to regularly monitor the patient and analyze their health in a quantitative fashion [42].

Based on the literature survey, the CoEWS is proposed to remotely monitor the patients during this COVID-19 pandemic period to mitigate the lack of medical facilities in healthcare centers. The patients are brought to the healthcare centers from home quarantine or home isolation only if necessary so that the healthcare facilities will be effectively utilized for the required critical patients.

3.3 MATERIALS AND METHODS

The proposed model aims at developing an AI-powered IoMT Model which enables Continuous Remote Patient Monitoring even from their homes thereby, eliminating the need for less severe patients to frequently visit the healthcare facilities. The model also proposes a novel COVID Early Warning Score (CoEWS) which could assist in monitoring the real time health status of the patient. The architecture of the proposed model is shown in Figure 3.1. The proposed model would lessen the burden of the high bed occupancy in spite of an increasing number of COVID-19 cases. This could help the physicians focus more on the more severe patients who are more likely to be patients with co-morbid conditions; cancer patients who have undergone transplantation surgeries and are on immunosuppressive drugs where chances of complications are significantly high. This could aid in better management of the patients who undeniably require admission. With the continuous monitoring and predictive analytic models, the home quarantined patients could be moved to the higher healthcare facilities whenever the need arises.

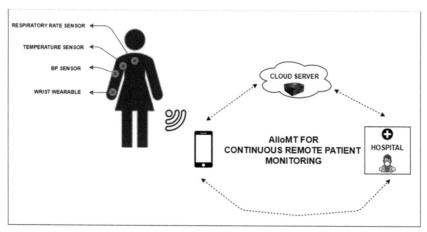

FIGURE 3.1   Architecture of the proposed model.

The proposed IoMT Model would have two parts: Mobile app and a Sensor Module. The app would have a login page for both doctors and patients. Both the doctors and physicians would need to register themselves by giving their basic details and contact information. This would be validated by a One Time Password (OTP) mechanism. The patients undergoing home quarantine would need to register themselves by entering their Basic Details such as Name, Age, Sex, Occupation, Address, Blood Group, Contact Details like Mobile Number and E-mail address and medical history including the COVID-19 related history. The COVID-19 related history records the date of onset of symptoms, the date on which the patient visited the doctor, RT-PCR Test Results, if any and Rapid Anti-body Test Results, if any. The patient would also have an option to store the prescriptions and other test results like biochemical tests in a local repository. The physician would also need to register him selves/her selves with Basic Details similar to the patients, the Registration Number and specialty. This would also be validated by an OTP mechanism. The patient needs to place a request to add the concerned physician with his mobile number. This request would be considered by the concerned physician and be approved if the particular patient is consulted by him/her.

The Sensor Module would consist of a temperature sensor which would record temperature, a Wrist wearable which records SpO2 and Heart Rate, a Blood Pressure sensor which records the Systolic Blood Pressure and breath rate sensor which records the respiratory rate. The above-mentioned vitals and the units in which they are measured are listed in Table 3.1. These sensors are connected with the patient and the patient would be advised to carry out his routine work. These sensors would transmit the recording of the vitals along with a timestamp on a regular interval to the Smartphone of the patient through Bluetooth Technology. Thus, the mobile app would display the vitals' recordings along with the timestamp. These data would be transmitted and stored in a cloud server ensuring the highest degree of security. The concerned physician would also be able to track the patient's health status remotely. This allows real time Health monitoring of the patient.

The vitals stored in the cloud server would be processed further using the Artificial Intelligence Techniques. The COVID Early Warning Score (CoEWS) is proposed to indicate the severity of the progression of the disease. This scoring system is proposed following slight modifications to the National Early Warning Score (NEWS). The scoring pattern for the parameters of CoEWS is shown in Figure 3.2. The proposed CoEWS is computed as given in Eq (1).

$$CoEWS = 1/5 \sum_{i=1}^{5} wipi \qquad (1)$$

Where wi represents the weights assigned based on the importance of the parameters to know the health status of the patients, p1 represents the temperature, p2 represents the SpO_2 value, p3 represents the heart rate, p4 represents the blood pressure and p5 represents the respiratory rate. All these parameter values are normalized using min-max normalization method. The stages of severity according to the proposed CoEWS score are listed in Table 3.2.

The Artificial Intelligence Techniques analyzes dataset of the patient's vitals. The AI regression models like decision tree, Support Vector Machine (SVM), and Artificial Neural Network (ANN) are employed to predict the CoEWS score. SVM regression models provide a better regression score compared to other models. This predicted score would be used to evaluate the health status of the patient and estimate his/her need for hospitalization. Whenever the score turns abnormal, the AI model would alert the physician and the caregivers about the need for immediate hospitalization. This approach would not only solve the issue of unavailability of bed facilities but also predicts the health outcome of the patient in time. This early prediction would lead to better planning and decision making by the physicians.

TABLE 3.1   Body Vitals with Their Respective Units

Physiological Parameters	Units
Temperature	Degree Celsius (°C)
SpO_2	Percentage (%)
Heart Rate	Beats per minute (Bpm)
Systolic Blood Pressure	Millimeter of Mercury (mm. Hg)
Respiratory Rate	Breaths per minute (Bpm)

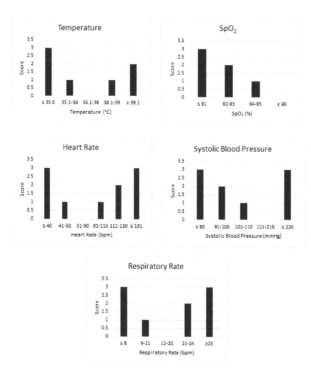

FIGURE 3.2   CoEWS scoring pattern (data from Ref. [20]).

TABLE 3.2   Severity Stages depending upon CoEWS

Score Range	Stage	Recommended Action
0–1	Low	Immediately report to the concerned physician and follow the advice.
2–4	Medium	Shift to hospital. Might require a hospital ward admission.
≥ 5	High.	Life threatening situation. Might need ICU admission

3.4   RESULTS AND DISCUSSION

The proposed model tries to emulate the continuous monitoring of an ICU setup right in the patient's home. The scoring system includes parameters like Temperature, SpO_2, Heart Rate, Systolic Blood Pressure and Respiratory Rate which are physiologically very significant. The other two parameters omitted from the National Early Warning Score (NEWS) are the presence of supplementary oxygen and the level of conscious-ness. Since the parameter, level of consciousness is a very subjective one and is generally elicited by the Healthcare Professional, the nurse or the physician, rather than being measured with a medical device, is omitted from the proposed CoEWS scoring system. The reason of omittance of the presence of supplementary oxygen parameter is that the supplementary oxygen therapy is provided to the patients in the hospital. The proposed CoEWS is specifically designed keeping in mind the needs of the patients who are quarantined or isolated in home or isolation center rather than a hospital. Hence, to cater to this specific purpose, this parameter is omitted. The scoring pattern is being proposed and would need significant research studies and trials to be validated and brought into operational use. The authors would like to highlight that this proposed scoring system should not be used in clinical practice unless approved by the competent medical authority of the respective jurisdictions. The pros of this model are isola-tion of patients exhibiting no symptoms or those with mild symptoms in home rather than hospital, relaxes the burden on the healthcare facilities over shortage of bed facilities and early prediction of need of hospitaliza-tion of patients, thereby helping the physicians and the emergency teams plan better. This model would be very-smart in managing the healthcare scenario by further extending the break-point of the healthcare infrastruc-ture of the nation even in the worst phases of the pandemic. The cons of this model include the higher costs associated with the setting up of this model, i.e., the costs associated with sensors and smartphone. This model would help to lessen the burden on the healthcare facilities to house the increased number of COVID-19 patients, even if subsequent waves hit the world. This would ensure that adequate beds in healthcare facilities are also be maintained. This would reduce the anxiety among physicians as well as the general public, even amidst the peak of the pandemic. On the whole, this model would serve as a "Game-Changer" on the eve of managing the COVID-19 pandemic.

KEYWORDS

- **artificial intelligence**
- **continuous remote patient monitoring**
- **COVID early warning score**
- **COVID-19**
- **IoMT**

REFERENCES

1. World Health Organization (WHO). Who coronavirus disease (covid-19) dashboard. https://www.who.int/ (accessed on 1st June 2021).
2. Uddin, M. A., Stranieri, A., Gondal, I., & Balasubramanian, V., (2018). Continuous patient monitoring with a patient centric agent: A block architecture. *IEEE Access, 6,* 32700–32726.
3. Qadri, Y. A., Nauman, A., Zikria, Y. B., Vasilakos, A. V., & Kim, S. W., (2020). The future of healthcare internet of things: A survey of emerging technologies. *IEEE Communications Surveys Tutorials, 22*(2), 1121–1167.
4. Yang, N., Wang, Z., Gravina, R., & Fortino, G., (2017). A survey of open body sensor networks: Applications and challenges. In: *2017 14th IEEE Annual Consumer Communications Networking Conference (CCNC)* (pp. 65–70).
5. Sameer, I., Filippo, T. B., Raffaele, G., Antonio, G., Giancarlo, F., & Sangiovanni-Vincentelli, A., (2010). A framework for creating healthcare monitoring applications using wireless body sensor networks. *ICST, 5.*
6. Mohammed, B. K., & Loay, G., (2013). Remote patient tracking and monitoring system. *IAENG International Journal of Computer Science and Mobile Computing, 2*(12), 88–94.
7. Aqeel, H., & Alaa, K., (2017). Online real-time fuzzy inference system based human health monitoring and medical decision making. *International Journal of Computer Science and Information Security, 15,* 197–204.

8. Saed, T., Kahtan, A., Shadi, A., & Salah, H. I., (2016). Smart Real-Time Healthcare Monitoring and Tracking System using GSM/GPS Technologies. *International Journal of Computer Applications 142*(14), 19–26.

9. Zatout, Y., (2012). Using wireless technologies for healthcare monitoring at home: A survey. In: *2012 IEEE 14th International Conference on e-Health Networking, Applications and Services (Healthcom)* (pp. 383–386).

10. Hyuma, W., Masatoshi, K., Akira, S., & Kentaro, Y., (2013). Wearable ECG monitoring and alerting system associated with smartphone: IHeart. *International Journal of E-Health and Medical Communications (IJEHMC), 4*(4), 1–15.

11. Burch, V. C., Tarr, G., & Morroni, C., (2008). Modified early warning score predicts the need for hospital admission and in hospital mortality. *Emergency Medicine Journal, 25*(10), 674–678.

12. James, N. F., Charlotte, L. P., Natalie, E. S., Samantha, J. B., & Gavin, D. P., (2012). Is the modified early warning score (mews) superior to clinician judgement in detecting critical illness in the pre-hospital environment? *Resuscitation, 83*(5), 557–562.

13. Linda, S., Lano, O., Sandra, M. A., Stefanie De, G. T., & Mark, G. J. De. B., (2020). *Evaluation of a Modified Early Warning Score (MEWS) Adjusted for COVID-19 Patients (CEWS) to Identify Risk of ICU Admission or Death.* medRxiv.

14. Cong-Ying, S., Jia, X., Jian-Qin, H., & Yuan-Qiang, L., (2020). *COVID-19 Early Warning Score: A Multi-Parameter Screening Tool to Identify Highly Suspected Patients.* medRxiv.

15. Zulfiqar, A., Umesh, G., Pradeep, D., Rakesh, G., Sudheesh, K., Harsoor, S., & Bhaskar, S., (2020). Development of a preoperative early warning scoring system to identify highly suspect COVID-19 patients. *Journal of Anaesthesiology Clinical Pharmacology, 36*(5).

16. Anna, G., Giuseppe, V. De. S., Samuele, S., & Daniela, F., (2020). Predictive value of national early warning score 2 (news2) for intensive care unit admission in patients with SARS-CoV-2 infection. *Infectious Diseases, 52*(10), 698–704.

17. Marcello, C., Claudio, S., Michele, S., Luca, S., Benedetta, S., Maria, G. B., Veronica, O., Marcello, C., Massimo, A., Antonio, G., et al., (2020). Predicting intensive care unit admission and death for COVID-19 patients in the emergency department using early warning scores. *Resuscitation, 156*, 84–91.

18. Hai, H., Ni, Y., & Yanru, Q., (2020). Comparing rapid scoring systems in mortality prediction of critically ill patients with novel coronavirus disease. *Academic Emergency Medicine, 27*(6), 461–468.

19. Zhihong, W., Qiaosen, C., Sumeng, L., Huadong, L., Qian, Z., Sihong, L., Li, W., Leiqun, X., Bobin, M., Di, L., et al., (2020). ANDC: an early warning score to predict mortality risk for patients with Coronavirus Disease 2019. *Journal of Translational Medicine, 18*(1), 1–10.

20. Michelle, H. V. V., Felicia, A., Dimitris, V., Glenn, W., David, B., & Attila, K., (2019). ChroniSense national early warning score study (chess): A wearable wrist device to measure vital signs in hospitalized patients—protocol and study design. *BMJ Open, 9*(9). https://doi.org/10.1136/bmjopen-2018-028219.

21. https://thelogicalindian.com/trending/covid-19-third-wave-kerala-prediction-covid-peak-30042 (accessed on 11 January 2022).

22. http://www.china.org.cn/world/Off_the_Wire/2021-07/30/content_77662839.htm (accessed on 11 January 2022).

23. https://indianexpress.com/article/india/rail-coaches-covid-hospitals-6392436/ (accessed on 11 January 2022).

24. Rajasekar, S. J. S., (2021). An enhanced IoT based tracing and tracking model for COVID-19 cases. *SN Comput. Sci., 2,* 42. https://doi.org/10.1007/s42979-020-00400-y.

25. Sowmiya, B., Abhijith, V., Sudersan, S., et al., (2021). A survey on security and privacy issues in contact tracing application of COVID-19. *SN Comput. Sci., 2,* 136. https://doi.org/10.1007/s42979-021-00520-z.

26. Perumal, V., Narayanan, V., & Rajasekar, S. J. S., (2021). Detection of COVID-19 using CXR and CT images using transfer learning and Haralick features. *Appl. Intell., 51,* 341–358. https://doi.org/10.1007/s10489-020-01831-z.

27. Varalakshmi, P., Vasumathi, N., & Sakthi, J. S. R., (2021). Prediction of COVID-19 with computed tomography images using hybrid learning techniques. *Disease Markers, 2021,* 15. Article ID 5522729. https://doi.org/10.1155/2021/5522729.

28. Varalakshmi, P., Vasumathi, N., & Sakthi, J. S. R., (2021). Prediction of COVID criticality score with laboratory, clinical and CT images using hybrid regression models. *Computer Methods and Programs in Biomedicine, 209,* 106336, ISSN 0169-2607. https://doi.org/10.1016/j.cmpb.2021.106336.

29. Perumal, V., & Theivanithy, K., (2021). A transfer learning model for COVID-19 detection with computed tomography and sonogram images. In: *2021 Sixth International Conference on Wireless Communications, Signal Processing and Networking (WiSPNET)* (pp. 80–83). doi: 10.1109/WiSPNET51692.2021.9419419.

30. Shamout, F. E., Zhu, T., Sharma, P., Watkinson, P. J., & Clifton, D. A., (2020). Deep interpretable early warning system for the detection of clinical deterioration. In: *IEEE Journal of Biomedical and Health Informatics* (Vol. 24, No. 2, pp. 437–446). doi: 10.1109/JBHI.2019.2937803.

31. Li, B., Zhang, S., Hoover, S., Arnold, R., & Capan, M., (2019). Microsimulation model using Christiana care early warning system (CEWS) to evaluate physiological deterioration. In: *IEEE Journal of Biomedical and Health Informatics* (Vol. 23, No. 5, pp. 2189–2195). doi: 10.1109/JBHI.2018.2874185.

32. Alshorman, S., Jaber, F. T., & Bensaali, F., (2015). A wireless oxygen saturation and heart rate monitoring and alarming system based on the Qatar early warning scoring system. 2015 *International Conference on Computational Science and Computational Intelligence (CSCI), 787*–790. doi: 10.1109/CSCI.2015.75.

33. Biglarbeigi, P., et al., (2019). Early prediction of sepsis considering early warning scoring systems. In: *2019 Computing in Cardiology (CinC)* (pp. 1, 4). doi: 10.23919/CinC49843.2019.9005630.

34. Pou-Prom, C., Yang, Z., Sidhaye, M., & Dai, D., (2019). Development of an early warning system for sepsis. In: *2019 Computing in Cardiology (CinC)* (pp. 1, 4). doi: 10.23919/CinC49843.2019.9005923.

35. Zarabzadeh, A., et al., (2012). Features of electronic early warning systems which impact clinical decision making. In: *2012 25th IEEE International Symposium on Computer-Based Medical Systems (CBMS)* (pp. 1–4). doi: 10.1109/CBMS.2012.6266394.

36. Liu, N., et al., (2014). Risk scoring for prediction of acute cardiac complications from imbalanced clinical data. In: *IEEE Journal of Biomedical and Health Informatics* (Vol. 18, No. 6, pp. 1894–1902). doi: 10.1109/JBHI.2014.2303481.

37. Kobylarz, R. J., et al., (2020). A machine learning early warning system: Multicenter validation in Brazilian hospitals. In: *2020 IEEE 33rd International Symposium on Computer-Based Medical Systems (CBMS)* (pp. 321–326). doi: 10.1109/CBMS49503.2020.00067.

38. Liu, J., Chang, H., Wu, C., Lim, W. S., Wang, H., & Jang, J. R., (2019). Machine learning based early detection system of cardiac arrest. In: *2019 International Conference on Technologies and Applications of Artificial Intelligence* (TAAI) (pp. 1–6). doi: 10.1109/TAAI48200.2019.8959922.

39. Anzanpour, A., et al., (2017). Self-awareness in remote health monitoring systems using wearable electronics. *Design, Automation & Test in Europe Conference & Exhibition (Date), 2017,* 1056–1061. doi: 10.23919/DATE.2017.7927146.

40. Fang, Y., Tai, C., Chang, Y., & Fan, C., (2014). A mental disorder early warning approach by observing depression symptom in social diary. In: *2014 IEEE International Conference on Systems, Man, and Cybernetics (SMC)* (pp. 2060–2065). doi: 10.1109/SMC.2014.6974225.

41. Fahim, S., Qiang, F., & Irena, C., (2008). A mobile phone based intelligent scoring approach for assessment of critical illness. In: *2008 International Conference on Information Technology and Applications in Biomedicine* (pp. 290–293). doi: 10.1109/ITAB.2008.4570633.

42. De Jager, D., Mazomenos, E. B., Banerjee, A. K., Maharatna, K., & Reeve, J. S., (2010). A low-power simplified-MEWS scoring device for patient monitoring. In: *2010 4th International Conference on Pervasive Computing Technologies for Healthcare* (pp. 1–4). doi: 10.4108/ICST.PERVASIVEHEALTH2010.8870.

CHAPTER 4

Automatic Intravenous Fluid and Health Monitoring using an IoT System

S. SABENA,[1] K. SELVAKUMAR,[2] and L. SAI RAMESH[3]

[1]Anna University Regional Centre, Tirunelveli, Tamil Nadu, India

[2]National Institute of Technology, Trichy, Tamil Nadu, India

[3]CEG Campus, Anna University, Chennai, Tamil Nadu, India

ABSTRACT

In day-to-day life, every hospital plays a major role in securing the patient's life. In all hospitals, nurses and the attenders are responsible for monitoring the intravenous fluid level and the health of the patients. Most of the times, the observer may not watch the level of the saline bottle frequently. This may cause backflow of blood from patients veins to IV tubes. If the bottle gets empty, air enters the tube and in turn into the veins, which may affect the patient. So automatic intravenous fluid and health monitoring system is designed. In this system, IR sensors and blood pressure sensor are used.IR sensors are used to predict the level of the intravenous fluid bottle. If the fluid bottle comes to an end, it is sensed by the Arduino UNO energized with the sensors setup. At first the message notification is sent to the nurse's phone number. And then, after some time, the automatic emergency call is generated, and the call alert will be sent to the control room with indicating the room number. Then at the critical stage, the buzzer sound is alarmed continuously. Blood pressure sensor is used to check the

Internet of Medical Things in Smart Healthcare: Post-COVID-19 Pandemic Scenario.
Saravanan Krishnan, PhD and Aboobucker Ilmudeen, PhD (Eds.)
© 2024 Apple Academic Press, Inc. Co-published with CRC Press (Taylor & Francis)

systolic, diastolic pressure and the pulse rate of the patient. The proposed system can also be monitored remotely by using IoT platform.

4.1 INTRODUCTION

An IoT (Internet of Things) is a technology that enables communication between devices over the Internet. In simple terms, an IoT can be defined as the collection of devices such as laptops, vehicles and home appliances which are embedded with software, sensors, and actuators. Interaction among those devices is possible through the connectivity between them. IoT is a widely used technology because it provides machine-to-machine communication which reduces human entrance during the communications between devices. So the proposed work uses IoT technology in order to provide the status of the intravenous fluid bottle. Most of the research performed on developing intravenous fluid monitoring and indication system usually focus only on monitoring the saline bottle and gives an alerting sound. It would be better if there is a nurse who will monitor the intravenous fluid bottle and change the bottle when the fluid level comes to end, which is not possible in such situation at all time in every hospital. So, instead of allocating such a guide, the proposed system contains automatic monitoring system which will monitor the fluid level in the bottle through the sensors fixed in it. The monitoring process is done from anywhere at any time through a mobile application which is based on IoT technology. The proposed system also has an indication system, which indicates the nurse about the saline level in appropriate time when it needs to change. The major setback of traditional fluid level Indication system is through the Bluetooth. Hence, the information generated by the sensors is conveyed up to a limited distance. So in many hospitals, the information that is conveyed is not feasible. The low cost solution to such problem is to introduce the Wi-Fi technology. The Wi-Fi technology-based system is used to cover a large distance and the information transmission is feasible.

The proposed work presents an IoT-based system that contains a monitoring system and indication facility. When any of the fixed IR sensors on the saline bottle senses the fluid level, the system will provide an indication in the mobile at the nurse station. The information about the level of the intravenous fluid will be sent to the nurse station with a notification message, automatic emergency call and an alerting buzzer sound. The notification message which is first sent to the nurse mobile number provides the information that the bottle is quarter level consumed. The automatic emergency call which is sent after the notification message to the nurse mobile number is used to show that the saline bottle is going to be empty. The alerting sound which is connected with a buzzer is used for the alerting purpose to indicate that the intravenous fluid level is very low and it reaches the critical point in the saline bottle. This information is corresponding to the IR sensors which are detecting the intravenous fluid level in the saline bottle. A blood pressure sensor is used to monitor the systolic and diastolic pressure. Systolic means relaxation of heart muscle, diastolic means contraction of cardiac muscles and heartbeat. This sensor is also used to measure the pulse rate of the patient. By using the information from this monitoring and indication system, nurses can easily handle and monitor the patients' health in all rooms in the hospitals. The main advantage of the proposed system is, the system provides the monitoring method using the IoT-based technology and three ways of indication of the intravenous fluid and health condition of the patient. Traditional fluid detection and alert system provides only a buzzer sound. In the proposed work, the level of fluid is monitored and indicated, and then it is updated to the nurse station for the safety of patient's health, and it is used to take further evacuation processes in the hospitals.

The objectives of the proposed system are:

- To develop a system to monitor and indicate the intravenous fluid level in the glucose bottle.
- To alert the nurse using alert notification, automatic emergency call and buzzer sound.
- To monitor the fluid level, blood pressure and heart beat using Internet of Things(IoT).

4.2   LITERATURE REVIEW

Navya and Murthy [1] provide the health monitoring system for needed people using Zigbee node. The node provides the signal to the monitoring system where the signals are processed to analyze the human body temperature and heart rate. This is the initial level work in health monitoring system from which the other mechanisms are evolved.

Prabha et al. [2] provides the IoT-based system for monitoring the human health data through the sensors which are connected via the application in android system. Continuous monitoring process helps to view the data related to human health and suggest the precautionary measures based on the observed data if it needs. Sangeetha et al. [3] suggest the smart intravenous fluid monitoring system which works on the threshold value-based system. Automatic indication is available with this system to monitor the patient even during night times which reduce the human error in the monitoring process. If any air bubbles create in the patient's blood stream is identified and indicated through the mobile application.

Another work of Ray et al. [4] proposed a system with IoT which is also semi-automatic and real time monitoring of fluid level. The intimation sends to the hospital staff when there is level reduction in the fluid level of the saline bottle. Rao et al. [5] proposed the intravenous infusion system using IoT. This system investigates the drop count of the liquid level and track the status and informed it to the nursing station. Velmurugan et al. [6] suggested the automatic health monitoring services to monitor the intravenous therapy which identifies the blood related flow activities in the human body. The system reduces the stress factor among medical people by continuously monitoring saline flow and change it automatically without any human efforts.

Arabelli et al. [7] is another system used for intravenous monitoring system using IoT which identifies the reverse flow of the fluid in the saline bottle which is not mentioned in existent monitoring systems. Sensors are directly interacting with the medical equipment's to detect the problems which is aid in the instrument with the patient's. Rosdi et al. [8] gives the fluid administration environment which monitors pump system for IV drips. This system monitors the flow rate of the fluid in the human body with infusion-interruption problems via the mobile applications connected through the sensors. But this is not verified in real time hospital management environment.

Saranya et al. [9] provides the intelligent medical system for storing and retrieving the medical data in a secure way which involves machine learning approaches for efficient execution. Ambika et al. [10] provides the system to get the decision based on the data received from the IoT devices. The data received from the sensors or from any other perspectives are analyzed using the intelligent approaches to decide the diagnosis for hypertension.

Yusro [11] developed the system which monitors the droplets through the web and android applications simultaneously. This one helps to observe the infusion volume and its level to detect the absence of intravenous fluid. Deraemaeker et al. [12] detects the damages in measured equipment by applying Eigen properties and Fourier transform. This work identifies the damages or any deviations in measurements because of any environmental changes.

Banerjee and Madhumathy [13] suggested the IoT-based advanced monitoring system which observes the heart rate and provides intelligent decision based on the observed values. The data observed from the sensors are fused and send to the microcontroller where the information stored in the database. The real time data of heart beat and saline fluid level will support medical staff to provide proper medication to the patients. Reddy et al. [14] provides the smart saline monitoring system with the alert mechanism. Another system developed by Sardana et al. [15] for drip monitoring device which connected via the internet to receive the data without any delay. SaiRamesh et al. [16] discusses the system to locate the sensor devices or IoT enabled devices where it is lost. For patient monitoring, this mechanism is helpful to locate the people with the wearable IoT devices. Oros et al. [17] designed a intravenous fluid system to monitor the fluid level and also regulate the fluid flow by closing the infusion flow when it is not needed or it is reached the level.

After researching many papers, it is found that many of the system presented above has some considerable issues. Some of the work does not have any proper alerting system. In some paper, there is no indication and alerting of observer, only monitoring process carried out. In some other paper, load sensor is used to measure the weight of the bottle. For that purpose, S type load cell is used (cost: Rs. 4,200). This weight hanger is manufacture separately. So, it is not a cost efficient. In other paper, LED display is used for monitoring purpose. The display should be easily understandable but, the cost of LED is very high (cost: Rs. 4,700). In some other paper, RF-based automatic alerting and indication device is used. According to the survey the RF radiation can be harmful, it causes heating of biological tissue. In other paper, Bluetooth module is employed, Bluetooth module can cover only a limited distance and it is a relatively slow process.

4.3   PROPOSED SYSTEM FOR FLUID MANAGEMENT SYSTEM

4.3.1   *CIRCUIT OVERVIEW*

The working principle of the proposed work describes the interdependent functionality of the components and their output. The overview of the fluid management model is represented in Figure 4.1. In the proposed system, all the components are initialized by supplying the required power of +12v which is mainly for the GSM module. All other components in the system needs 5v for their working. The power supply is given by using adapter. There is an IR sensor used in the prototype to detect the intravenous fluid level. When the fluid level is detected these detection values are passed as the input to the Arduino UNO. There is another sensor called Blood Pressure sensor which is used to sense the pulse rate and the blood pressure of the patient. Sensor is connected to Arduino UNO board for monitoring the level of the intravenous fluid. GSM module is connected to the Arduino Uno board for the indication purpose. The GSM module sends an alert message and generates an automatic emergency call. Arduino UNO is responsible for updating the current information of the intravenous fluid monitoring system to the IoT server using Wi-Fi module. In the proposed work, Thinkspeak.com is used as an IoT server. It generates read and write key for the fields generated in a channel. Write key is used to update the current value generated by the sensor in the server. The read key is used for reading this information from the server to the webpage which will be displayed and refreshed always at the mobile phone in the nurse station.

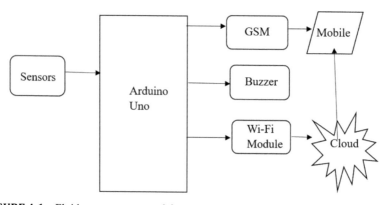

FIGURE 4.1   Fluid management model.

4.3.2   IR SENSOR

The infrared sensor (IR sensor) is used here to identify the level of the saline in the bottle once it is provided to the patient's and provide the indication to the base station. Infrared radiation thus has wavelength λ between (780 nm) and 1mm, which corresponds to a frequency range from 300GHz to 400THz. IR sensors work on infrared waves and receiver treats it as a signal.

4.3.3   BLOOD PRESSURE SENSOR

The blood pressure is used in this work for measuring the systolic pressure. And it also determines the pulse rate and pass on that information to the ADC and the readings are displayed on the monitor.

4.3.4   BUZZER

Buzzer is an output device, which is used to provide an audible identification or alert that can be heard by the users. It is also called beeper. It is a signaling device used to alert the people. In the proposed system buzzer provides an alarm sound to alert the people when the fire sensors sense the fire in the building. By using the alarm sound, users will get prior knowledge about the fire occurrence.

4.3.5   WI-FI MODULE

The ESP8266 is a low cost Wi-Fi module. ESP8266 uses serial transceiver (TR/RX) to send and receive data and serial command to query and change the configuration of Wi-Fi. It only requires two wires (TR,RX) for communication between microcontroller and Wi-Fi module. In the proposed system it transmits the location co-ordinates to the fire station through the cloud server when the fire sensor detects fire. At the fire station, this location information is provided with a notification sound.

4.3.6   GSM (GLOBAL SYSTEM FOR MOBILE)

GSM is used to provide the communication between the sensor connected Arduino and the information received through sensors. It also creates a path between the base station and mobile devices which helps to get the information as quickly as possible in healthcare systems.

4.4 SYSTEM OVERVIEW

From research on related works, it is found that most of the present systems on intravenous fluid level detection and health monitoring have few considerable issues. In some systems there is no proper information is provided to the nurse station. In some work load sensor and RF-based transceiver is used to detect the intravenous fluid level. In another system, proper alert facility is not provided. On considering these issues, the proposed work has an IR sensor which is used to detect the intravenous fluid level in the bottle and system architecture is shown in Figure 4.2. The sensor detects whether the bottle is full or going to be empty. The detected values are sent to the Arduino Uno as an input. The GSM module is connected to the Arduino Uno board. After receiving the input values from the IR sensor, the GSM first sends an alert message (Going to be empty) to the nurse's mobile phone. Then after 10 minutes the GSM automatically sends an emergency call to the nurse's mobile phone which indicates that the intravenous fluid level is low and it is going to be empty. After the emergency call, the nurse comes to the patient room and ready to change the saline bottle. If there is no response from the nurse, it waits for some minutes and when the intravenous fluid level reaches at the critical point it automatically generates the buzzer sound and it alarmed continuously at the patient room. The proposed system also has a blood pressure sensor which is used to measure the systolic pressure and the diastolic pressure. It is also used to measure the pulse rate of the patient. The other major advantage of the proposed work is IoT. Using this IoT, the whole process can be monitored by anyone from anywhere.

4.4.1 INDICATION OF MESSAGE TO NURSE ROOM

4.4.1.1 CONNECTION WITH ARDUINO CONTROLLER

The IR sensors are connected with the Arduino Controller. Here, the microcontroller used is ATmega328. The ATmega328 is a single chip microcontroller which includes the RISC processor with the storage size 8 bits. Data transfer between the IR sensor and Arduino is done by serial communication.

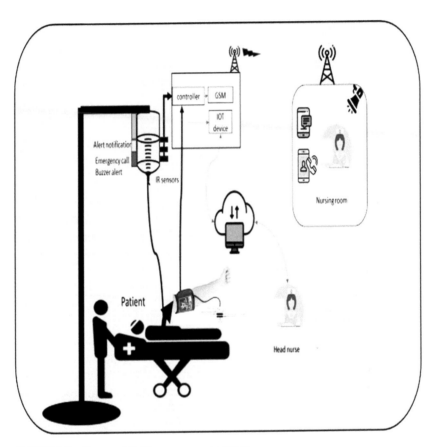

FIGURE 4.2   Proposed fluid management system.

4.4.1.2   CONNECTING ARDUINO WITH GSM

The GSM connection was done separately with 12 V adapter, and the transceiver and receiver are connected with the Arduino microcontroller. Data transfer between GSM and Arduino microcontroller is done by serial communication.

4.4.1.3   GSM WORKING PRINCIPLE

In GSM module, we insert the Sim Card to establish a connection between the stations and make them connected through the mobile devices. The BTS was connected with the Base Station Controller (BSC). BSC is connected with the Mobile Station Controller. The Mobile Station makes a connection with the Circuit Switched, and connected with the Base Transceiver Station and thus makes a connection with them. Then the message was sent to the nurse's mobile number in the nurse room.

4.4.2   INDICATION OF CALL TO NURSE ROOM

4.4.2.1   CONNECTION WITH ARDUINO CONTROLLER

As discussed above, the IR sensors are connected with the Arduino Controller. Here, the microcontroller used is ATmega328. The ATmega328 is a single chip microcontroller which includes the RISC processor with the storage size 8 bits. Data transfer between IR sensor and Arduino is done by serial communication.

4.4.2.2   CONNECTING ARDUINO WITH GSM

As discussed above, the GSM connection was done separately with 12 V adapter, and the transceiver and receiver are connected with the Arduino microcontroller. Data transfer between GSM and Arduino microcontroller is done by serial communication.

4.4.2.3   GSM WORKING PRINCIPLE

As discussed above, in GSM module, we insert the Sim Card to establish a connection between the mobile and the Base Transceiver Station. The Base Transceiver Station was connected with the Base Station Controller. BSC is connected with the Mobile Station Controller. The Mobile Station Makes a connection with the Circuit Switched, and connected with the Base Transceiver Station and thus makes a connection with them. Then the Call was generated and sent to the nurse mobile number in the nurse room.

4.4.3   INDICATION OF BUZZER ALARMING SOUND

4.4.3.1   BUZZER CONNECTION WITH ARDUINO UNO

The buzzer is connected with 7th pin of Arduino board and GND (ground pin) of the Buzzer is connected with the Arduino in the space of ground pin. Data transfer between the Buzzer and Arduino is done by serial communication.

4.4.3.2   WORKING OF BUZZER

In this work, Buzzer which is connected with Arduino UNO will receive the input values from the Arduino Uno controller. The Buzzer automatically generates the alerting sound in the patient room when the intravenous fluid level in the bottle reaches the critical level.

4.4.4   VIEWING AN APPLICATION USING IOT

4.4.4.1   LOGIN

Nurses/attenders can view the level of the Glucose bottle using an application. The application is named as Glucose Meter. The user can only access the application with the username and the password in the login page. This process is carried out for the authentication purposes. All the information and the data are stored in the database. When the authentication is succeeded, then the user can login into the application and access it.

4.4.4.2   VIEWING THE GLUCOSE LEVEL

After completing the login process, the next *Screen* will be displayed. It shows the list of Patients Room Number. All the Patients room number in the hospital is displayed here. The nurse can easily check the level of the glucose bottle for the required patient room number just by clicking it. This can be done by using IoT technology.

In this glucose bottle, we can set four types of different colors: (i) If the level of the glucose bottle in the patient room is full, it shows green color in the bottle. (ii) If the level of the glucose bottle in the patient's room is half consumed, it shows yellow color in the bottle. (iii) If the level of the glucose bottle in the patient's room is quarter level consumed, it shows orange color in the bottle. (iv) If the level of the glucose bottle in the patient room is at the critical stage, it shows red color in the bottle.

4.4.4.3   VIEWING THE BLOOD PRESSURE AND PULSE RATE

The nurse can easily check the blood pressure and the pulse rate of the patient within the level of the glucose bottle using this IoT-based application. Diastolic pressure metrics was considered for measuring the pressure level and as in the same way heart beat basic parameters was considered for measuring pulse rate.

4.4.5   OVERALL INTERFACING WITH ARDUINO

In this proposed intravenous fluid monitoring and indication system IR sensor is connected to the Arduino board. When this IR sensor detects the intravenous fluid level, the signal will pass to the controller. On receiving this signal from IR sensor, buzzer which is connected to the Arduino UNO gets turn on and provides alarm sound in the patient room to indicates that the bottle is going to be empty. Digital output pin of the IR sensor is connected to the Arduino in the space of input for digital. In this prototype, the digital pin of the IR sensor was connected to the digital pin of 4th digital pins of the Arduino UNO board respectively. GND (ground pin) of the IR sensor is connected with the ground pin of the Arduino. Similarly, 5v pin of IR sensor is connected with 5v of the Arduino. The buzzer is connected with the 7th pin of Arduino board and 5V is provided to the buzzer by connecting to the Arduino 5V. Data transfer between IR Sensor and Arduino is done by serial communication.

In this work, blood pressure sensor which is connected to the Arduino UNO will receive the input values from the controller. When this sensor detects the pulse rate and blood pressure, the signal will pass to the controller. On receiving the signal from the blood pressure sensor, the controller sends to the cloud. All the information is stored in the cloud. We can view the patients details through an application using IOT. In this prototype, the T_x of the blood pressure sensor is connected to the 6th pin of the controller which is taken as R_x. GND (ground pin) of the blood pressure sensor is connected with the Arduino in the space of ground pin. Similarly, 5v pin of the blood pressure sensor is connected with 5v of the Arduino.

In this work, the GSM receiver which is connected with Arduino UNO will receive the input values from the controller. The GSM automatically generates the message and call to the nurse's mobile number. At first, the GSM transmit the data to the Base Station. Next, the Base Station sends an Acknowledgement to the Mobile Station. Then the Mobile Station dispatches the request to the Base Station, and then the Base Station sends the message to the nurse mobile number as an Alert notification and then the Automatic Call is generated. The transmitter pin (TX) of the GSM is connected to the receiver pin (RX) of the Arduino board. The receiver pin (RX) of the GSM is connected to the transmitter pin(TX) of the Arduino board. Power supply is enabled in GSM by connecting 5V and the GND to Arduino Board (5V, GND). Data transfer between GSM and Arduino is done by serial communication.

In this work, Wi-Fi module which is connected with Arduino UNO is used to monitor the Intravenous Fluid level in the bottle using the Internet of Things. All the information is stored in the cloud according to the output from IR Sensor during the installation of the system. The transmitter pin (TX) of the Wi-Fi Module is connected to the 2nd pin as the receiver pin (RX) of the Arduino board. The receiver pin (RX) of the Wi-Fi Module is connected to the 3rd pin as the transmitter pin(TX) of the Arduino board. Power supply is enabled in the Wi-Fi module by connecting 5V and the GND to Arduino Board (5V, GND). Data transfer between Wi-Fi module and Arduino is done by serial communication.

In this work, Buzzer which is connected with Arduino UNO will receive the input values from the Arduino Uno controller. The Buzzer automatically generates the alerting sound in the patient room when the intravenous fluid level in the bottle reaches the critical level. The buzzer is connected with 7th pin of Arduino board and GND (ground pin) of the Buzzer is connected with the ground pin of the Arduino. Data transfer between the Buzzer and Arduino is done by serial communication.

4.5   EXPERIMENTAL RESULT

Table 4.1 shows that the intravenous fluid level has detected during observation, then the call and alert message is send and also buzzer turned on upon the low level detection of Intravenous Fluid. Otherwise, the buzzer, call and the message will not provide any alerts. This prototype has three IR sensors and so there are four possible results can be obtained.

TABLE 4.1   Experimental Results

Ex: No	IR Sensor			Message54	Call	Buzzer	Decision
	1	2	3				
1	ND	ND	ND	OFF	OFF	OFF	High Level
2	D	ND	ND	ON	OFF	OFF	Quarter Level Consumed
3	ND	D	ND	OFF	ON	OFF	Half Level Consumed
4	ND	ND	D	OFF	OFF	ON	Going to be empty

D – Fluid Level Detected

ND – Fluid Level Not Detected

Result of experiment 1 shows that when all the IR sensors are not detect the intravenous fluid level, the message, call and the buzzer will be turn OFF. That takes the decision that the intravenous fluid level is High and the bottle is FULL. Result of experiments 2 shows that when the 1st IR sensor detects the intravenous fluid level, the message will get turn on and the automatic alert notification is send to the nurse mobile number. Result of experiment 3 shows that when the 2nd IR sensor detects the intravenous fluid level, the call will be turned on and the automatic emergency call will be generated and sent to the nurse's mobile number. Result of experiment 4 shows that when the 3rd IR sensor detects the intravenous fluid level, the Buzzer will be turned ON and the sound is alarmed continuously.

After the detection of intravenous fluid level by the system, the detection information will be updated on the cloud server. Then the bottle level of the intravenous fluid and the patient room number will be displayed on the mobile application at the Nurse Station.

4.5.1 RESULTS OBTAINED

An alert message is sent to the nurse mobile number.

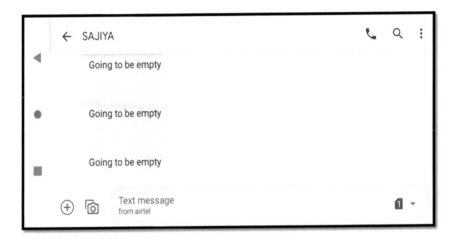

FIGURE 4.3   Message notification.

Figure 4.3 shows that the alert message is sent to the nurse's mobile number. The message shows that the bottle is going to be empty. Using this message notification, the nurse can easily identify that the bottle is half consumed and it is going to be empty.

Automatic Emergency Call is generated to the nurse Mobile Number based on emergency. The call is generated when the level of the bottle comes to be low. Using this automatic Emergency call, the nurse can easily identify that the bottle is Quarter level consumed and it is going to be empty. The Glucose bottle can also be Monitored by using the IoT-based Android Application.

The name of the Android Application is Glucose Meter. It contains two options at the login page, such as Username and Password. By giving the username and password the nurse can login into the application. Figure 4.4 shows the list of Patients Room Number. All the Patients room number in the hospital is displayed here. The nurse can easily check the level of the glucose bottle for the required patient room number just by clicking it. This can be done by using IoT technology.

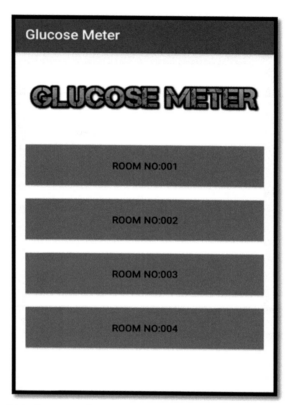

FIGURE 4.4   List of room number.

If the level of the glucose bottle in the patient room is full, it shows green color in the bottle in that IoT-based android application. If the level of the glucose bottle in the patient's room is half consumed, it shows yellow color in the bottle in that IoT-based Android application. If the level of the glucose bottle in the patient's room is quarter level consumed, it shows orange color in the bottle in that IoT-based Android application. If the level of the glucose bottle in the patient room is at the critical stage, it shows red color in the bottle in that IoT-based Android application.

4.6   CONCLUSION AND FUTURE SCOPE

To reduce the uncertainty and backflow of blood during dripping intravenous fluid into the patient body, this automatic intravenous fluid and health monitoring system based on IoT is designed. With the proper implementation and integration of current technologies, the proposed automatic intravenous fluid and health monitoring system will help in case of the busy schedule of the nurse. This advanced system would provide an alert message, automatic call and the buzzer sound for the patient protection from the patient room to the nurse station in the hospital to prevent the loss of blood from the patient body. Alert message, call and the buzzer sound which will be given as the immediate response after the detection of intravenous fluid level from the saline bottle will avoid the backflow of blood from patients veins to IV tubes. Immediate detection and response of the proposed system avoids the air which enters into the tube and in turns into the veins that causes a huge damage in the patient body which in turn leads to death. As soon as the bottle gets empty, the nurse comes to the patient room and change the saline bottle. This system also checks and provide the pulse rate, diastolic and systolic pressure of the patient. The details of the patient can be viewed at any time and from anywhere.

The main intention of the submitted work is to make the life of patients in the hospitals to be safe during the dripping of intravenous fluid into their body by providing information for nurses from the patient room by sensing the intravenous fluid level in the saline bottle using the automatic indication and health monitoring system. The nurses in the hospitals will be provided with the information about the level of the intravenous fluid in the saline bottle. They can also monitor the fluid level, pulse rate and blood pressure by using the mobile application through the IoT technology from their nurse station itself. So the system effectively makes the life of the patient safer. The presented automatic intravenous fluid monitoring and indication system is realized as a small, compact and advanced technology in the medical field. It also has an appreciable advantage such as small size, affordable cost, high accuracy, easy handling and completely automated. This development will be an essential unit in the patient health monitoring system.

4.6.1 FUTURE SCOPE

In future, the system can be improved by providing a way for finding the accurate level of the intravenous fluid in the saline bottle with a single sensor. So that, it will be very compact and small in size. The system can also be improved by providing the entire details of the patient health who are admitted in the hospital by using the mobile application based on the IoT technology, which will be more helpful for the observer and the doctors in the hospitals and also for their family members.

KEYWORDS

- **Arduino controller**
- **GSM module**
- **health monitoring**
- **intravenous fluid**
- **IoT**

REFERENCES

1. Navya, K., & Murthy, M. B. R., (2013). A ZigBee based patient health monitoring system. *Int. Journal of Engineering Research and Applications, 3*(5), 483–486.
2. Prabha, S. C., Ganishka, G., Anto, M. S. S., & Gayathri, S., (2021). IoT based automatic monitoring and control system. In: *Journal of Physics: Conference Series* (Vol. 1916, No. 1, p. 012087). IOP Publishing.
3. Sangeetha, K., Vishnuraja, P., & Vijaya, K., (2021). Smart intravenous fluid monitoring system. *Annals of the Romanian Society for Cell Biology*, 199–209.
4. Ray, P. P., Nishant, T., Dinesh, D., & Debashis, D., (2019). Novel implementation of IoT based non-invasive sensor system for real-time monitoring of intravenous fluid level for assistive e-healthcare. *Circuit World*.
5. Rao, K. R., & Koluthuri, E. S., (2020). Design and development of IoT based intravenous infusion system. In: *Emerging Trends in Electrical, Communications, and Information Technologies* (pp. 487–499). Springer, Singapore.
6. Velmurugan, S., Shanthi, G., Raja, L., & Nirmala, S., (2021). Fully automated single window saline fluid flow control and automatic container changing system. In: *2021 7th International Conference on Advanced Computing and Communication Systems (ICACCS)* (Vol. 1, pp. 1259–1263). IEEE.
7. Arabelli, R., Rajababu, D., Anuradha, P., & Bernatin, T., (2021). Smart intravenous infusion monitoring and controlling system using the internet of things. *Materials Today: Proceedings*.
8. Rosdi, M. R., & Audrey, H., (2021). A smart infusion pump system for remote management and monitoring of intravenous (IV) drips. In: *2021 IEEE 11th IEEE Symposium on Computer Applications & Industrial Electronics (ISCAIE)* (pp. 285–288). IEEE.

9. Saranya, M. S., Selvi, M., Ganapathy, S., Muthurajkumar, S., Sai Ramesh, L., & Kannan, A., (2017). Intelligent medical data storage system using machine learning approach. In: *2016 Eighth International Conference on Advanced Computing (ICoAC)* (pp. 191–195). IEEE.

10. Ambika, M., Raghuraman, G., SaiRamesh, L., & Ayyasamy, A., (2020). Intelligence–based decision support system for diagnosing the incidence of hypertensive type. *Journal of Intelligent & Fuzzy Systems, 38*(2), 1811–1825.

11. Yusro, M., (2018). Development of smart infusion control and monitoring system (SICoMS) based web and android application. In: *IOP Conference Series: Materials Science and Engineering* (Vol. 434, No. 1, p. 012201). IOP Publishing.

12. Deraemaeker, A., Edwin, R., Guido De, R., & Jyrki, K., (2008). Vibration-based structural health monitoring using output-only measurements under changing environment. *Mechanical Systems and Signal Processing, 22*(1), 34–56.

13. Banerjee, I., & Madhumathy, P., (2019). IoT-based fluid and heartbeat monitoring for advanced healthcare. In: *Classification Techniques for Medical Image Analysis and Computer Aided Diagnosis* (pp. 179–197). Academic Press.

14. Reddy, D. R., Srishti, P., Andukuri, D., Sravan, K., & Prakash, K., (2020). Smart saline monitoring system for automatic control flow detection and alertness using IoT application. In: *Congress on Intelligent Systems* (pp. 745–757). Springer, Singapore.

15. Sardana, P., Mohit, K., & Amit, S., (2019). Design, fabrication, and testing of an internet connected intravenous drip monitoring device. *Journal of Sensor and Actuator Networks, 8*(1), 2.

16. Sai, R. L., Shyam, S. S., Selvakumar, K., & Sabena, S., (2021). Tracking of wearable IoT devices through WAP using intelligent rule-based location aware approach. *Journal of Information & Knowledge Management, 20*(supp01), 2140005.

17. Oros, D., Penčić, M., Šulc, J., Čavić, M., Stankovski, S., Ostojić, G., & Ivanov, O., (2021). Smart intravenous infusion dosing system. *Applied Sciences, 11*(2), 513. https://doi.org/10.3390/app11020513.

CHAPTER 5

Hygieia: Multipurpose Healthcare Assistance Using the Internet of Things

JOSE ANAND[1] and R. DHANALAKSHMI[2]

[1]Department of ECE, KCG College of Technology, Karapakkam, Chennai, Tamil Nadu, India

[2]School of Computer Science and Engineering, Vellore Institute of Technology (VIT), Chennai, India

ABSTRACT

Chatbots is a software program executed on a computer that pretends an ordinary human chat discussion. Consumers are interconnected with a chatbot using the chat text interface or by the audio message, similar to that of people talking normally. Chatbots construe and progression with respect to consumers comments in the form of words or phrases and replies with a predefined set of answers. Natural Language Processing (NLP), is the involuntary operation of natural language, such as speech and text, by a program. In the healthcare domain, chatbots have a potential market of about 1 billion. The main goal of Hygieia is not to be like a chatbot but it is a system where the users can book appointments using Internet of Things (IoT), schedule their daily healthcare needs, and acts as a voice assistant to give users a hassle-free experience. Overall, the Hygieia application is an informative, conversational, and prescriptive chatbot.

Internet of Medical Things in Smart Healthcare: Post-COVID-19 Pandemic Scenario.
Saravanan Krishnan, PhD and Aboobucker Ilmudeen, PhD (Eds.)
© 2024 Apple Academic Press, Inc. Co-published with CRC Press (Taylor & Francis)

5.1   INTRODUCTION

Hygieia is a system where it can act as a chatbot as well as a voice assistant. It can also book appointments using IoT and schedule the daily healthcare requirements for the users. Chatbots in healthcare are extremely critical for the advancement of efficient and accurate patient care. Chatbots can extract affected person records by the usage of easy questions such as name, address, symptoms, contemporary doctor, and coverage details. Chatbots then shop these records in the scientific facility device to facilitate affected person admission, symptom tracking, doctor-affected person communication, and scientific document keeping [1]. A Chabot is programmed to do things in their own way from a human operator. It can solve questions formulated to it in NLP and reply like an actual man or woman. It gives responses totally on an aggregate of predefined scripts and system gaining knowledge of applications [2]. NLP facilitates chatbots to understand, examine and prioritize the questions in line with the complexity and this allows bots to reply to client queries quicker than a human being. Faster responses assist in constructing client to agree with and subsequently to get extra business. Artificial Intelligence (AI) powered NLP allows chatbots to imitate human conversation. They can become aware of the underlying motive at the back of the textual content like an actual man or woman types, then supply a reaction that fits that motive. Hygieia is an informative, conversational and prescriptive chatbot that provides instant conversational responses and makes connecting users in a simple way [3]. Hygieia can play a wonderful role in supporting these users and guide them with authentic and reliable information using IoT. It will also support the user's need of creating an affordable and sustainable healthcare environment [4].

The main objective of the personal healthcare application is to monitor our health continuously using IoT. Due to the current pandemic, users are moving to remote consultation rather than direct consultations. So the appointments are scheduled seamlessly and longer queues are avoided. The doctors cannot reach the rural areas at the point of emergency. So, at that instant, the healthcare applications will make sure that people affected in rural areas will be treated through remote consultation [5]. This will make sure that there will be an effective consultation throughout the day and there will be better health management. Currently, the market size is growing enormous in the field of healthcare because of these healthcare applications [6]. So, the productivity will increase and the cost will be decreased. With the digitization of healthcare and the growing influence of AI, researchers acknowledged chatbots' potential to improve patients accessibility to medicine, strengthen physician-patient communication, and help in managing the unceasing demands of various related services. Chatbots can be actively employed in health education and coaching, often coupled with other functions such as symptom checker, online triage, interactive live feedback and so on using the IoT [7].

Nevertheless, there remains limited research on the acceptability of chatbots and that truly motivates individuals to use them. As such, researchers administered a semi-structured interview and a 24-item online survey via social networking. Responses are then documented, transliterated, and systematically analyzed. Three comprehensive themes; "Understanding of Chatbots," "AI Hesitancy," and "Motivations for Health Chatbots" are drafted to outline issues regarding accurateness, cyber security, and the capability of AI-led facilities to empathize. As the world becomes unpredictable (like covid-19 pandemic) absolutely everyone needs to be geared up with their backup healthcare support [8]. On a positive note, users said they are willing to use chatbot for minor health concerns or to replace the traditional medical hotline, to seek rapid guidance or when they struggle to get through the phone line when in need. Surely, the study is the first of its kind and did not incorporate a large pool of participants, including those who are using or had benefited from chatbot services. However, it does provide some preliminary thoughts on how people think of new technologies, which is probably what designers and developers will like to know at the moment [9]. As the researchers themselves suggested, chatbots will need to adhere to users' needs in order to succeed. The role of the doctor is essential in any healthcare process and hygieia helps users to achieve it. Improper healthcare routines like inaccessible areas, missing an appointment, long queues, forgetting to take pills, etc., are unjustifiable. The designed application using IoT will be user friendly and the simplicity in the application makes the user more comfortable and conversational. Hygieia has a variety of options like Chatbot with voice assistant, booking appointments and schedule for daily healthcare [10].

This chapter is systematized as follows: Section 5.2 involves of the related work to the healthcare domain and chatbots. Section 5.3 entails of the proposed solution and system implementation with various algorithms. Section 5.4 consists of software requirement specifications, the features of the software used in the system, the use case diagrams, the software architecture diagram, and the diagrams for the modules used in the proposed solution. Section 5.5 describes the outcomes and discussions of the proposed system and the modules in the user's perspective. Section 5.6 is the system testing that contains various testing cases for different segments. Section 5.7 contains the conclusion of the work with its future scope.

5.2   RELATED WORKS

The chapter contributed in the direction of integrating chatbots into tele-medicine. The answer "Aapka Chikitsak" consists of a multilingual voice utility primarily based on NLP to offer number one healthcare training and recommendation to continual sufferers and ladies wanting antenatal care. Using AI, it converts the person speech to textual content that is processed and understood by the usage of NLP and output is generated that is then transformed again to speech and back to the person [11]. The software program covers the maximum commonplace sicknesses in rural India with a unique emphasis on ladies' healthcare. One of the main demanding situations that India as a rustic face is to cater to precise exceptional and low-cost healthcare to its developing populace. The global healthcare file is issued through World Health Organization (WHO) has ranked India's healthcare devices at 112 out of one hundred ninety countries [12]. The green methods to offer well-timed scientific care, get admission to, and exceptional remedy to the affected person, the position of telemedicine comes into play which connects sufferers with healthcare vendors and healthcare facts. Due to the current "COVID-19" pandemic, social distancing will live in India for a protracted time, specifically for sufferers with continual sicknesses, thereby enforcing a limitation for the populace to get admission to healthcare facilities [13]. By the usage of conversational synthetic intelligence, healthcare vendors can diagnose and deal with sufferers without the want for a private visit, at the same time as selling social distancing and decreasing the danger of COVID-19 trans-mission. In the contemporary developing age of digitalization, AI-powered chatbots are gambling a main position through exemplifying the feature of a digital assistant that would control a communique through speech or textual methods. It uses voice queries to get solutions, and carry out movements and guidelines in step with person's wishes. They are adaptable to the person's character language usages, searches, and desire with persevering with the use [14]. A conversational bot with a voice and/or chat interface can play a foremost position through overcoming the contemporary obstacles in the direction of making number one healthcare low-cost, on-hand and doubtlessly sustainable in the new virtual economy through advanced communication technology [15]. The main capability customers in healthcare voice assistants are sufferers and physicians, who use those packages to get admission and report the affected persons facts. At the affected persons quit it's far a less expensive opportunity. It's a 24 x 7 offerings, human beings tormented by continual sicknesses, disabled sufferers and sufferers residing in rural and farther regions could gain maximum from such effective digital assistant's tools. The device has many blessings like decreased time at a part of physicians, stepped forward safety of affected person facts, on-call for healthcare facts. Thus making healthcare on hand and low-cost for all with an intuitive interface [16]. A conversational structure is used to have interaction with vintage age populations to acquire facts, non-stop tracking of fitness conditions, specifically after discharge from the hospital. A pharma bot is introduced, a pediatric well-known medicinal drug representative chatbot designed to prescribe and render beneficial facts on well-known drugs for kids. Telehealth is the distribution of fitness-associated offerings through digital and telecommunication technologies. It allows lengthy distance sufferers to get care, recommendation, reminders, training, tracking and faraway admissions from clinicians [17]. India being a rustic with a various populace talking exclusive languages, get admission to healthcare at gift has a couple of barrier consists of in it. Telehealth is poised to tailor the fitness carrier to customers wishes to enhance their fitness carrier to customers wishes to enhance their fitness circumstance through imparting treasured consultations and facts to sufferers on the consolation in their domestic. Now let's have a glance on structure of conversational bots. It's a server much less structure. In current years, server much less architectures are gaining traction as an opportunity manner of presenting backend offerings without requiring a devoted infrastructure [18]. For our utility, Firebase cloud features and Google cloud platform as our backend infrastructure is furnished. The process of content-based image analysis is explained and used for medical applications [19, 20]. A system is embedded with NLP and Natural Language Understanding (NLU) to recognize the customers question and go back to respective responses. The first degree of processing in our structure offers with audio input and output. When a person makes a question, the person question is transformed from audio to textual content and that is known as speech-to-textual content. In the second one degree of processing, the extracted textual content is used as a foundation for appearing NLU at the generated textual content to decode the semantic which means of the person enter and apprehend morphemes. It is then mapped to the respective purpose on conversation waft. Once the purpose mapping is finished, an HTTP POST request is dispatched through conversation waft for achievement to internet hook to reply to the person [21]. For the bot, cloud features are used for firebase to create an internet hook. The reaction message includes reaction that ought to in the end be dispatched to the person. Further, in case of voice interface the textual content reaction is once more transformed to speech and back to the person. For conversational utility, the hybrid version is used to appoint a partially rule-based and device mastering approach. By default, dialog waft tries each of those algorithms and chooses the pleasant end result [22]. The hybrid version tries to shape in step with rule-based total grammar. If a shape isn't made, it switches to ML matching. This mode is taken into consideration to be the pleasant and an optimized answer for maximum use instances, thinking about that it really works as it should be with an enough wide variety of schooling phrase. The communique of the bot has been framed and designed in a manner to imitate human conduct to increase a person-pleasant chat device that lets in them to sense at ease, overcoming the unfairness of device interplay [23]. Entities in conversation waft are significant sequences of characters or lexemes. It is used to extract unique key phrases in customer's questions. For the use case, conversational device waft of discussion has been meant to address the subsequent use instances. Providing facts approximately the bulk of commonplace sicknesses in India together with their voice primarily-based totally tele-fitness bots [24]. The interplay procedure designed in the back of the voice bot makes it extraordinarily easy and smooth to talk with customers. Now let's examine the layout of voice person interface. A usual Voice User Interface (VUI) makes viable human chat with computer systems through speech popularity to recognize spoken phrases and solution questions, and specially makes use of textual content to speech to create a reply. Speech Synthesis Markup Language (SSML) is used to make the voice revel in greater interactive and robust [25]. Conversational person interfaces of the messaging apps permit us to invoke a textual content chat through an easy button click. Designing approach carried out in the conversational person interface aren't much like the traditional Graphical User Interface (GUI) pattern. This is certainly considered as a type of customized healthcare bot that is touchy to the wishes and information of the Indian rural populace presents well-known healthcare facts together with preventive measures for commonplace sicknesses [26]. It has extra functions inclusive of domestic remedies, region primarily based on weight-reduction plan recommendation, age and gender-unique fitness checkup recommendation, emergency helpline numbers and may be related with actual time messaging utility like WhatsApp. The purpose of this utility isn't simply to save the malicious infectious sicknesses in the grappling populace however to assist acquire universal wellness. The system bringing expert healthcare in the direction of the customers through presenting stay connectivity with docs and inclusive of functions like appointments through a tap [27].

There are quite a few current chatbots for the healthcare area serving exclusive functionalities. (Example: Endurance, Casper, Medwhat, etc.). The trouble with those chatbots is they simply offer monotonous solutions to customers' questions. They aren't able to organize a clever communique with the person simply as a health practitioner does [28]. To make a traditional chatbots feature like digital friends, strategies of NLU, NLG and ML require to be integrated into the device. These strategies make the device greater communicative in the herbal language. An evaluation at the chat interface unit is the front quit of the device. It will acquire the person queries from the person which might be the enter to the device. Entire communique takes region here. It is a mediator among person and device [29]. The question that person fires at the chat interface is exceeded directly to the chatting backend which acts as a message handing over device among chat interface and device mastering layer. The form of interface relies upon the necessities of the person which are to be glad through the device. An evaluation at the NLU engine is a subpart of NLP which allows the device to recognize the herbal language spoken through customers. Thus obtained from the person is in unstructured textual content layout which the device can't recognize [30]. The unstructured textual content content obtained from the person is transformed to an established layout through extracting critical phrases and styles from the person's textual content through the usage of the NLU strategies. The preliminary assignment is the segmentation of sentences into character phrases. Word segmentation procedure is used for solving phrase segmentation, a technique on calculating all individual areas are used and end result changed into regarding mathematical calculations as a result proves to be slower than the others [31]. Another way is to describe the identical trouble to put into effect phrase segmentation. This uses Natural Language Tool Kit (NLTK) package deal which includes in-built tokenizer. The end result changed into easy to put into effect as does now no longer require any coding. Faster and greater correct. For identical trouble to put into effect phrase segmentation, a Conditional Random Fields (CRF) algorithm is used [32]. This set of rules trains the device for areas among the characters. This set of rules proves to be greater correct and much less complicated than the primary however much less green compared to NLTK. To recognize the phrase, the device wishes to recognize the grammar of the sentence. This may be finished through understanding the Parts of Speech (PoS) of every phrase in that sentence. A trouble of imposing PoS tagging is discussed for a latent analogy set of rules. It calls for schooling of big quantities of facts. Hence includes complexity. Also there is identical trouble of imposing PoS tagging. This uses a neural community set of rules [33]. As the set of rules works in layers, it presents excessive accuracy, however, isn't time green. Another approach to put into effect the PoS tagger is following the conventional approach, i.e., keeping a dictionary of tags for the given language [34]. The NLTK technique presents above accuracy at minimal complexity. After understanding the grammatical weightage of every phrase, they are parsed to recognize the dependency amongst them. This is the maximum critical step in which the phrase with the best dependency is extracted, from which the purpose of the device may be known. Trouble to create a dependency parser is used with the technique of dependency tree to recognize the dependencies. The conventional technique which accuracy relies upon at the schooling of the facts [35]. An identical trouble is to create a dependency parse uses a technique of graph facts shape for the implementation of the parser. An improvised model of the above-referred-to set of rules presents better visibility, and understandability and improves accuracy. It isn't viable that the information base could incorporate the precise sentence that the person has dispatched. It may incorporate a sentence with an identical purpose, however with exclusive phrases utilized in it. To in shape those forms of synonymic sentence, synonym willpower and sentence matching are required. A trouble of synonym detection and extraction uses dictionary technique. It is a conventional technique which calls for to preserve a dictionary of synonyms global wise [36]. Provides much less accuracy than self-schooling models. Another identical trouble of synonym detection and extraction uses the function choice technique through calculating function polarity which presents excessive accuracy and much less complexity compared to the dictionary technique. A trouble on imposing sickness predictions with eager choice tree technique is used. The dynamic nature of the tree makes it greater green [37]. Provides excessive charge of accuracy because of the updating mechanism found in it. An identical trouble on imposing the sickness predictions using fuzzy approach technique used here. It presents excessive accuracy, however isn't green to put into effect because it includes the scanning of the whole database for every iteration [38]. Though the quantity of the facts decreases on every iteration, however but to start with the facts is pretty big to be scanned. By the usage of that technique, can capable of make a chatbot device as clever. It presents an important evaluation of the duties worried in NLU and Machine Learning (ML) for inclusion in chatbot structures to cause them to be clever. It is observed that there are a huge variety of algorithms for implementation of all of the duties worried in NLU and ML [39]. The choice of the ideal set of rules relies upon the functionalities to be furnished through the chatbot and additionally the area wherein the offerings are to be furnished. Also, the facts layout performs an important position for the choice of a set of rules [40].

5.3 PROPOSED SOLUTION AND IMPLEMENTATION

In the existing system, the chatbot is a conversational bot which does self-diagnosis for chronic diseases. The proposed system is a conversational, prescription chatbot that helps the users with a self-diagnosis of all types of diseases. It can interact with the users and is useful for blind people who cannot view the responses generated by the user. Uses dialog flow for the user interface in the chatbot while the proposed work uses Django for the website and Hygieia's interface. The proposed system also has a website for the users to visit and the chatbot is integrated in the website as well using IoT. The mobile application is developed for the users to have a seamless experience and have a sustainable environment. Figure 5.1 shows the structure of the proposed system.

5.3.1 CHATBOT

Software program that conducts a communique with customers thru auditory or textual methods. Hygieia chatbot allows the process of a healthcare company and facilitates enhance their overall performance via way of means of interacting with customers in a human-like way. Hygieia chatbots provide a customized technique to each user, in methods that may be greater convenient, and green that surpass human capabilities.

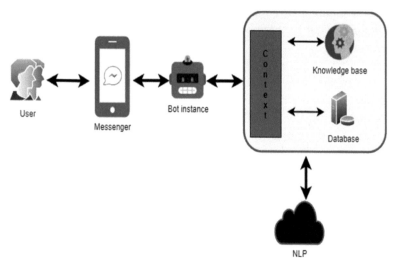

FIGURE 5.1   System architecture.

5.3.2 VOICE ASSISTANT

Audio support integration has voice recognition, speech synthesis, and NLP. The response is created on rule-based discourse or ML algorithm with key element as voice. The voice assistant will provide self-care instructions for diseases and other situations providing quick hands-free answers.

5.3.3 BOOKING APPOINTMENTS

Provides way to schedule appointments without getting overwhelmed with calls using a date time module to schedule the appointments. The chatbot makes it utterly convenient to manage the requests and confirm them accordingly for a hassle-free appointment scheduling environment using IoT.

5.3.4   SCHEDULE FOR DAILY HEALTHCARE

Provide daily health tips for the users and guidance for nutrition and life-style. Offers a medicine reminder facility for users to feed their input to the chatbot and then Hygieia will notify the users to ensure that they take their medicine on time. This feature is implemented by using notify2, schedule and Espeak modules using IoT.

5.3.5   CHATBOT IMPLEMENTATION

Chabot is a Python library designed to make it smooth to create software program which could interact in verbal exchange. An untrained example of Chatbot begins off evolved off and not using a know-how of the way to communicate. Each time a consumer enters an announcement, the library saves the textual content that they entered and the textual content that the announcement changed into in reaction to. As Chatbot gets greater enter the variety of responses that it could respond and the accuracy of every reaction on the subject of the enter announcement increase. The software selects the nearest matching reaction through attempting to find the nearest matching recognized announcement that suits the enter, it then chooses a reaction from the choice of recognized responses to that announcement. Chatbot is a personal computer software that stimulates verbal exchange with human beings both with textual content or voice. Chatbot makes it simpler to broaden chatbots that could interact in conversations. It begins off evolved through developing an untrained chatterbot that has no earlier revel in or know-how concerning the way to communicate. This makes it smooth to generate automatic responses to a consumers enter. Here, the chatbot gives the basic information regarding healthcare on users' query. For text chatbot the data should be ready in dataset to answer users questions and for voice recognition chatbot URLs of recognized and authorized websites should be included in the program from those websites users can get their answers. If the required information is not available in voice chatbot, they can directly tell the bot to take them to google and they can find it over there by saying 'query' in Google and users can also get the gist of the answers through Wikipedia by saying 'query' in Wikipedia. The text chatbot works with the help of libraries like chatterbot and trainers and voice chatbot works with the help of libraries like pyttsx3, speech recognition, web browser, google, Wikipedia. All these modules and libraries make the chatbot run successfully.

5.3.6 MEDICINE REMINDER IMPLEMENTATION

Django is a Python-based free and open-source web framework that follows the model–template–views architectural pattern. In this module, the calendar application is a medicine reminder. To get the calendar application work, include the URLs details in the Django calendar program. To see the events daily and what time daily events will start, end and what the event is about, we should create the events. The event has a title with less than 200 characters in length, a description field, start time and end time. Then, register it in admin.py thus adding events through the admin interface. To access the admin interface, one needs to create a super user. Calendar class have all of HTML Calendar's attributes and methods. In the html file of the calendar we use the prev_month and next_month's var as request parameters. This means that when we press on the prev/next month button, the corresponding date gets passed to request and we can get it from our views using self.request.GET.get ('month', None). In Django, we can use the handy Model Form which takes all of the Event files and turns them into a form. Django date time fields don't work well with html inputs. To work around that, we can use Added widgets to format the date time fields to make them show on the html form and Specified input_formats to parse HTML5 date time local input to date time fields. The event view can be specified to handle both new events and editing current events. event_id represents the id of the event to update. If it exists, that object is used and if it doesn't one should create a new object. Create a new template for the form. First declare the title of the page, followed by a link back to the calendar, and the form will get displayed while entering the medicine details in the event form. And Finally, Run the migration and start the server to check the calendar layout of the medicine reminder.

5.4   SOFTWARE REQUIREMENTS

The software components required for Hygieia application is given as follows:

Web Application	Django
Chatbot	NLP, Machine Learning
Backend	Python
Database	SQLite
Mobile Application	Kivy
E-mail Notification	SMTP

5.4.1   FEATURES OF CHATTERBOT

Chatterbot is a python library in particular designed to generate chatbots. This set of rules makes use of a choice of device gaining knowledge of algorithms to manufacture various responses to customers as according to their requests. Chatterbot makes it less difficult to expand chatbots which could have interaction in conversations. It begins off evolved through developing an untrained chatterbot that has no earlier revel in or information concerning the way to communicate. As the customers input statements, the library saves the request made through the person as properly because it additionally saves the responses which might be dispatched returned to the customers. As the range of times will increase in chatterbot, the accuracy of the responses made through chatterbot additionally will increase. Chatterbot is skilled to go looking the nearest analogous reaction through locating the nearest analogous request made through customers this is equal to the brand new request made. Then it selects a reaction from the already current responses. The USP of chatterbot is that it permits builders to create their very own datasets and systems at ease.

5.4.2   FEATURES OF DJANGO

Django become designed as a way to make a framework which takes much less time to construct net programs. The task implementation is very time-ingesting however Django creates it rapidly. Django takes safety severely and allows builders to keep away from many not unusual place safety mistakes, consisting of SQL injection, cross-web page scripting, cross-web page request forgery, etc. Its person authentication device presents a steady manner to control personal debts and passwords. Django is scalable in nature and has the capacity to fast and flexibly transfer from small to big scale utility projects. Django consists of numerous assisting venture modules and libraries which may be used to address not unusual place Web improvement tasks. Django looks after person authentication, content material administration, web page maps, RSS feeds, etc. Django is flexible in nature which permits it to construct programs for one-of-a-kind-one-of-a-kind domains. Nowadays, Companies are the usage of Django to construct numerous kinds of programs like: content material control systems, social networks web sites or medical computing structures, etc. Django is an open supply net utility framework. It is publicly to be had without price and is downloaded with supply code from the general public repository. Open supply reduces the full price of the utility improvement. Django is one of the maximum famous net frameworks. It has a broadly supportive network and channels to proportion and connect.

5.4.3 FEATURES OF SQLITE

Transactions are atomic, consistent, isolated, and durable (ACID) even after device crashes and strength failures. Zero – configuration and does now no longer want any setup or administration. Full-featured SQL implementation with superior competencies like partial indexes on expressions, JSON, not unusual place desk expressions, and window functions. A whole database is saved in an unmarried cross-platform disk record. Great to be used as a utility record format. SQLite Supports terabyte-sized databases and gigabyte-sized strings and blobs. It is much less than 600KiB completely configured or a great deal much less with non-obligatory functions omitted. SQLite is a simple, clean to apply API. In a few cases, SQLite is quicker than direct filesystem I/O. It is written in ANSI-C. The TCL bindings are included. Bindings for dozens of different languages to be had separately. It has well-commented supply code with 100% department take a look at coverage. SQLite is to be had as a unmarried ANSI-C supply-code record that is simple to collect and therefore is simple to feature into a bigger task. There aren't any outside dependencies. Android, BSD, iOS, Linux, Mac, Solaris, VxWorks, and Windows (Win32, WinCE,

WinRT) are supported out of the box. Easy to port to different systems. Sources are in the public domain. It may be used for any purpose. Comes with a standalone command-line interface (CLI) patron that may be used to manage SQLite databases.

5.5   OUTCOMES AND DISCUSSIONS

Hygieia will welcome the user through its speech recognition module. Then, the bot will ask for the user's query. Once the user gives the response the bot will recognize and display the text as well. If the user asks anything related to disease, it gets the related information from Google and displays it immediately to the user in the chatbot interface and also through the speech module the bot can speak out to the user what is displayed in the interface. This will also be an advantage to the blind people who cannot view the information.

Hygieia can display a medicine reminder for the users in our system. The medicine reminder layout is like a calendar where once the user gets logged in, their name is displayed and the users can navigate through the calendar. The user should create an event or a reminder to get displayed in the calendar layout. In the title field, the user should enter the name of the medicine which has to be set as a reminder. The description of the medicine is optional. The next two input fields are start time and end time. This should be entered by the user, followed by the day in which the reminder should be kept. The user's medicine reminder event will be reflected in the calendar layout whenever the user submits the details. The event name and the description of the medicine is displayed. The members of this medicine event reminder will be displayed. And the medicine event reminder can be edited afterwards. The user's name and e-mail id will be displayed here because the e-mail id is synced with the calendar of Hygieia.

5.5.1   REGISTRATION

First and foremost, the user should fill all the mandatory details given in the registration form. Once the above step is completed, they will be prompted to enter the website successfully. If they are a registered user, then they can directly enter the website with their login credentials. The user's password is validated in the registration phase. Hygieia will recommend its users to suggest a strong password since the user's details are kept in the database and it should be secured as well.

5.5.2   LOGIN

Here the user can enter his/her login credentials and they will be prompted to the website only if their credentials are matched and verified with the database. This step is mandatory for all the users, since it has important particulars are stored in the database. Every time the user visits the application, the system prompts the user to login. Then, Hygieia will redirect the user to his/her homepage.

5.5.3   BOOKING APPOINTMENTS

This module using IoT helps the user to book appointments and Hygieia will make sure that the user has multiple slots to select and they can have their appointment with the respective doctor based on their comfortable day and time. Once the appointment is confirmed, Hygieia sends a confirmation message to the user stating that the appointment has been confirmed. Overall, this module gives a hassle-free experience to the user.

5.5.4   MEDICINE REMINDER

Here in this module, Hygieia sends a notification to the user's mobile through a calendar by creating an event, and it helps the user to take the medicines on time. This can be repeated daily. At first, when the user sets the medicine reminder, the user needs to fill in all the details like the medicine name, the time of medicine intake, etc. Moreover, this module helps people who are having a busy schedule. This will help the people not only take their medicines on time but also make sure that they will follow everything which can lead them to a healthy life.

5.5.5   VOICE AND TEXT-ENABLED CHATBOT

Hygieia chatbot is integrated with speech and text recognition. In this module, the user enters the query in the form of text, or his/her own voice will be taken as an input and in return, Hygieia will respond back in the form of text or voice. Moreover, the chatbot will also fetch information from Wikipedia as well to give the users detailed information on a particular query. Hygieia will also suggest a diet plan for the user, so that they can maintain a healthy life. Overall this module will respond to the user's query in the form of voice and text.

5.5.6 APPOINTMENT REMINDER

After booking the appointment, the user gets notified about the confirmation through e-mail and message services using IoT. The user will get an automated reply from Hygieia about their confirmation of the appointment as well as a reminder notification on the day of the appointment.

5.6 TEST CASES

The following are the different test cases which were used to verify the system modules, such as Chatbot and the Medicine Reminder as shown in Table 5.1.

TABLE 5.1   Test Cases

Test Case ID	Test Case Description	Expected Output	Actual Output	Test Result
TC001	Ask a question to the chatbot	Provides answer	Answer provided	PASS
TC002	Ask a question with a spelling error to the chatbot	Spell checker have to identify the error and should provide the most relevant answer	Spell checker identifies the error and provides the most relevant answer	PASS
TC003	Ask an invalid sentence to the chatbot	Sentence parser should identify the error	Sentence parser identified the error	PASS
TC004	Audio message to the chatbot	The chatbot converts the audio message to text and should reply with an appropriate answer	The chatbot converts the audio message to text and replies with an appropriate answer	PASS

TABLE 5.1 *(Continued)*

Test Case ID	Test Case Description	Expected Output	Actual Output	Test Result
TC005	Doctor checks patient's medical history	The patient's medical history should be displayed	The patient's medical history is displayed	PASS
TC006	Add Medicine Reminder Activity - Medicine Details	The user enters the medicine details, dosages and specific instructions	The user enters the medicine details, dosages and specific instructions	PASS
TC007	Add Medicine Reminder Activity - Date and Time	The user enters the date and time for intaking the medicines	The user enters the date and time for intaking the medicines	PASS
TC008	Displaying the medicine reminders in Calendar Format	The Calendar should display all the medicine reminders in a calendar format	The Calendar displays all the medicine reminders in a calendar format	PASS
TC009	Edit a particular Medicine Reminder Activity	The updated details of a medicine reminder activity should be reflected in the calendar	The updated details of a medicine reminder activity is reflected in the calendar	PASS
TC010	Medicine Reminder web page	Medicine reminder web page should display all the medicine reminders. Also, the page should have a "Add Medicine Reminder" button, to add a new medicine reminder activity.	Medicine reminder web page displays all the medicine reminders. Also, the page has an "Add Medicine Reminder" button, to add a new medicine reminder activity.	PASS
TC011	Receiving alert alarm for medicine reminder	Alert alarm should be received at the specified time given in the medicine reminder activity	Alert alarm is received at the specified time given in the medicine reminder activity	PASS

TABLE 5.1   *(Continued)*

Test Case ID	Test Case Description	Expected Output	Actual Output	Test Result
TC012	Login	Login successful	Login successful	PASS
TC013	Log out	Log out successful	Log out successful	PASS
TC014	User submits invalid e-mail id and password	System rejects the login	System rejects the login	PASS
TC015	User submits feedback about the chatbot or about Hygieia application	Feedback should be submitted	Feedback is submitted	PASS
TC016	Administrator views the Feedback	System rank and feedback is displayed	System rank and feedback is displayed	PASS

5.7   CONCLUSIONS AND FUTURE WORK

Hygieia application is useful for common people and helps the users to get clarified with the queries regarding their health issues or any general information related to health. Hygieia take the role as a chatbot and act as a voice assistant for the blind people who cannot view their responses but can hear what Hygieia has generated. The system also schedule daily medicine reminders. Moreover, the application sends daily tips to the users to have a balanced diet using IoT. The future implementation of Hygieia is to have a mobile application for users, so that they can have the application handy on their mobile devices. Then an electronic mail service will be implemented using SMTP to send confirmations with respect to the user's upcoming appointment confirmation using IoT. The notifications of the medicine reminder are implemented to notify the users. Hygieia will be upgraded every time with unique features. Overall, Hygieia is not only a system related to healthcare but also acts as a guide to the user to lead a balanced and healthy life.

KEYWORDS

- **chatbot**
- **healthcare**
- **Hygieia**
- **Internet of Things**
- **voice assistant**

REFERENCES

1. Bharti, U., Bajaj, D., Batra, H., Lalit, S., Lalit, S., & Gangwani, A., (2020). Medbot: Conversational artificial intelligence powered chatbot for delivering telehealth after COVID-19. In: *2020 5ᵗʰ International Conference on Communication and Electronics Systems* (pp. 870–875).
2. Anand, J., Raja, P. P. J., & Meganathan, D., (2017). Q-learning-based optimized routing in biomedical wireless sensor networks. *IETE Journal of Research, 63*(1), 89–97.
3. Bennet, P. M. S., Sagari, S., Chailshi, C., & Divya, S., (2019). AI healthcare interactive talking agent using NLP. *International Journal of Innovative Technology and Exploring Engineering, 9*(1), 3470–3473.
4. Jose, A., Gowtham, H., Lingeshwaran, R., Ajin, J., & Karthikeyan, J., (2021). IoT based smart electrolytic bottle monitoring. *Advances in Parallel Computing Technologies and Applications, 40*, 391–399. IOS Press.
5. Niranjana, S., Hareshaa, S. K., Irene, Z. B., & Jose, A., (2020). Smart monitoring system for asthma patients. *International Journal of Electronics and Communication Engineering, 7*(5), 5–9.
6. Anand, J., Dhanalakshmi, M., & Raja, P. P. J., (2019). Smart indication system for spinal cord stress detection. *International Journal of Recent Technology and Engineering, 8*(3), 6164–6168.
7. Aditya, R., R., Ajay, H., Balavanan, M., Lalit, R., & Anand, J., (2017). A novel cardiac arrest alerting system using IoT. *International Journal of Science Technology & Engineering, 3*(10), 78–83.
8. Nivedita, B., Subhash, T., Sayali, R., & Shubham, N., (2019). A literature review on chatbots in healthcare domain. *International Journal of Scientific & Technology Research, 8*(7), 225–231.
9. Gupta, I., et al., (2018). Towards building a virtual assistant health coach. In: *2018 IEEE International Conference on Healthcare Informatics (ICHI)* (pp. 419–421).
10. Bickmore, T. W., Schulman, D., & Sidner, C. L., (2011). A reusable framework for health counseling dialogue systems based on a behavioral medicine ontology. *Journal of Biomedical Informatics, 44*(2), 183–197.

11. Boufaden, N., Lapalme, G., & Bengio, Y., (2001). Topic segmentation: A first stage to dialog-based information extraction. *Natural Language Processing Pacific Rim Symposium NLPRS0l.*

12. Ahmed, F., (2018). *Beyond Patient Monitoring: Conversational Agents Role in Telemedicine and Healthcare Support for Home Living Elderly Individuals.* Computers and Society.

13. Lutze, R., & Waldhör, K., (2017). Personal health assistance for elderly people via smart watch based motion analysis. *IEEE International Conference on Healthcare Informatics (ICHI),* 124–133.

14. Setiaji, B., & Wibowo, F. W., (2016). Chatbot using a knowledge in database: Human-to-machine conversation modeling. In: *2016 7ᵗʰ International Conference on Intelligent Systems, Modelling and Simulation* (pp. 72–77).

15. Monisha, V. A., & Jose, A., (2021). Analysis of dynamic interference constraints in cognitive radio cloud networks. *International Journal of Advanced Research in Science, Communication and Technology, 6*(1), 815–823.

16. Mosa, A. S. M., Yoo, I., & Sheets, L., (2012). A systematic review of healthcare applications for smartphones. *BMC Med. Inform. Decis. Mak., 12,* 67.

17. Araújo, L. V., Letti, B. C., Cantagalli, F. T., Silva, G. S., Ehlert, P. P., & Araújo, L. M. Q., (2015). A health mobile application and architecture to support and automate in-home consultation. In: *2015 IEEE 28ᵗʰ International Symposium on Computer-Based Medical Systems* (pp. 151–156).

18. Lutze, R., & Waldhör, K., (2015). Smartwatches as next generation home emergency call systems. In: *8ᵗʰ German AAL Conference* (pp. 29–30).

19. Anand, J., Arul, F. T. G., & Anu, S. P., (2013). Finger-vein based biometric security system. *International Journal of Research in Engineering and Technology, 2*(12), 197–200.

20. Sibia, E. V., Mareena, G., & Anand, J., (2014). Content based image retrieval technique on texture and shape analysis using wavelet feature and clustering model. *International Journal of Enhanced Research in Science Technology & Engineering, 3*(8), 224–229.

21. Imteaj, A., & Hossain, M. K., (2016). A smartphone based application to improve the health care system of Bangladesh. In: *2016 International Conference on Medical Engineering, Health Informatics and Technology (MediTec)* (pp. 1–6).

22. Emily, W., (2019). *How AI and Voice Assistants Will Change Healthcare.* https://voicebot.ai/2019/03/23/how-ai-and-voice-assistants-will-change-healthcare/ (accessed on 11 January 2022).

23. Wirawan, K. T., Sukarsa, I. M., & Agung, B. I. P., (2019). Balinese historian chatbot using full-text search and artificial intelligence markup language method. *International Journal of Intelligent Systems and Applications, 11*(8), 21–34.

24. Raij, A. B., Johnsen, K., Dickerson, R. F., Lok, B. C., Cohen, M. S., Duerson, M., et al., (2007). Comparing interpersonal interactions with a virtual human to those with a real human. *IEEE Transactions on Visualization and Computer Graphics, 13*(3), 443–457.

25. Amato, F., Marrone, S., Moscato, V., Piantadosi, G., Picariello, A., & Sansone, C., (2017). *Chatbots Meet e-Health: Automatizing Healthcare* (pp. 40–49). WAIAH, AI, IA.

26. Benilda, E. V. C., et al., (2015). Pharmabot: A pediatric generic medicine consultant chatbot. *Journal of Automation and Control Engineering, 3*(2), 137–140.

27. Nivedhitha, P., Sankar, S., & Dhanalakshmi, R., (2019). An efficient hemorrhage detection system using a decision tree classifier. *International Journal of Recent Technology and Engineering, 8*(3), 5728–5732.

28. Dhanalakshmi, R., & Chellappan, C., (2012). Fraud and identity theft issues. In strategic and practical approaches for information security governance: Technologies and applied solutions. *IGI Global*, 245–260.

29. Thanzeem, M. S. S., Venkat, K. J., Vigneshwaran, S., Aida, J., & Jose, A., (2021). Lung cancer detection using VGG NET 16 architecture. *International Conference on Physics and Engineering 2021; Journal of Physics Conference Series*, 2040. IOP Publishing.

30. Weiss, G. M., Timko, J. L., Gallagher, C. M., Yoneda, K., & Schreiber, A. J. (2016). Smartwatch-based activity recognition: A machine learning approach. *IEEE-EMBS International Conference on Biomedical and Health Informatics*, 426–429.

31. Ponmalar, A., Jose, A., Dharshini, S., Aishwariya, K., & Mahalakshmi, S., (2021). Smartphone controlled fingerprint door look system. *Advances in Parallel Computing Technologies and Applications, 40*, 400–407. IOS Press.

32. Jose, A., Raja, P. P. J., & Meganathan, D., (2015). Performance of optimized routing in biomedical wireless sensor networks using evolutionary algorithms. *Comptes Rendus de l'Academie Bulgare des Sciences, 68*(8), 1049–1054.

33. Martins, P. M., Vilaça, J. L., & Dias, N. S., (2021). A study about current digital assistants for healthcare and medical treatment monitoring. *IEEE 9th International Conference on Serious Games and Applications for Health*, 1–7.

34. Inkster, B., Sarda, S., & Subramanian, V., (2018). An empathy-driven conversational artificial intelligence agent for digital mental well-being: Real-world data evaluation mixed-methods study. *JMIR mHealth uHealth, 6*(11), e12106.

35. Moreno, B. E., Pueyo, F. I., Sánchez, S. M., Martin, B. M., & Masip, U. J., (2017). A new artificial intelligence tool for assessing symptoms in patients seeking emergency department care: The Mediktor application. *Emergencias Rev. La Soc. Esp. Med. Emergencias, 29*(6), 391–396.

36. Anand, J., Raja, P. P. J., & Meganathan, D., (2015). Design of GA-based routing in biomedical wireless sensor networks. *International Journal of Applied Engineering Research, 10*(4), 9281–9292.

37. Plumbaum, T., Narr, S., Schwartze, V., Hopfgartner, F., & Albayrak, S., (2013). An intelligent health assistant for migrants. In: *2013 7th International Conference on Pervasive Computing Technologies for Healthcare and Workshops* (pp. 307, 308).

38. Itika, G., Bing, L., & Brian, Z., (2018). Towards building a virtual health assistant health coach. *IEEE International Conference on Health Informatics*.

39. Mary, B., (2019). Health care chatbots are here to help. *IEEE Pulse*.

40. Wei, L., Bonnie, L. M., & Ren, P. L., (2017). Unified fine-grained access control for personal health records in cloud computing. *IEEE Journal of Biomedical and Health Informatics*.

CHAPTER 6

Edge Computing and Artificial Intelligence Systems Adopted in Smart Healthcare: A Comprehensive Survey in Real-Time COVID-19 Pandemic

K. SARAVANAN[1] and G. LAKSHMI PRABHA[2]

[1]*Associate Professor, Department of Computer Science and Engineering, College of Engineering,Guindy, Anna University, Chennai, Tamil Nadu, India*

[2]*PhD Scholar, Department of Computer Science and Engineering, College of Engineering,Guindy, Anna University, Chennai, Tamil Nadu, India*

ABSTRACT

The world has been facing complex crises for more than a year due to the outbreak of the novel coronavirus pandemic (COVID-19). This chapter surveys about the effectiveness of edge computing and artificial intelligence in the Internet of Medical Things (IIoT) to meet all the health service requirements in such an emergency situations. Since critical decision making is an important concern of an IoMT architecture which is responsible for the life of patients, artificial intelligence techniques are employed in such real-time models. Rather than computational speed and decision making in a healthcare server network load and latency can also contribute to the degradation of Quality of Service (QoS) of a healthcare

Internet of Medical Things in Smart Healthcare: Post-COVID-19 Pandemic Scenario.
Saravanan Krishnan, PhD and Aboobucker Ilmudeen, PhD (Eds.)
© 2024 Apple Academic Press, Inc. Co-published with CRC Press (Taylor & Francis)

system. To optimize the latency and network load edge computing is employed thereby improving the availability of the system.

6.1 INTRODUCTION

Remote health monitoring and addressing all the medical needs of patients is an unavoidable option for healthcare providers during the pandemic situation like COVID-19. Throughout this pandemic, technology has played a crucial role in smart healthcare systems to diagnose and prevent Covid-19. Healthcare professionals and patients are the largest group, who are using digital technologies in covid-19 pandemic. Edge computing and AI had delivered the smart healthcare to patients in remote. Dramatic growth in network traffic in such a pandemic situation demanded the need to optimize network services. Integration of edge computing and different AI techniques is reviewed in this chapter. Edge or Internet of Medical Things (IoMT) devices, such as smart medical equipments, wearable sensors, etc., are taking technology nearer to the user and can pre-process the data collected through smart healthcare devices which in-turn reduces the latency, network delay and network traffic and enhances the data security and privacy.

Internet of Things revolutionized smart healthcare in great aspects. Devices including wearable body sensors are the edge devices that collect patient's clinical data and pre-process it at the edge. Delay sensitive monitoring and real-time decision making are crucial needs in a smart healthcare system and therefore IoMT with machine learning techniques deployed in shows high performance. AI also plays a critical role in fighting against the pandemic. Deep learning and deep reinforcement learning have proven their excellence in real-time decision making with applications to e-sporting industry. These can be the promising techniques to acquire knowledge from medical datasets and to model a real-time health monitoring system.

Apart from data processing through deep learning strategies protection of data against vulnerabilities such as data tampering, compromising the privacy of an individual are also critical in real time. So a block chain approach is engineered in the cloud environment to provide security and privacy of the patients in Ref. [54]. Processing overhead and latency in managing clinical data can be reduced while using a distributed ledger technology in IoMT incorporated cloud computing environments. To reduce such processing overhead, high demand of network bandwidth and latency in decision making. Transmitting raw data from IoMT devices directly to the cloud server is replaced by sending such signals to the edge layer which is close to the subject environment. Raw data and medical signals are processed in edge device, and then the results are sent to a cloud repository which is secured by blockchain [65].

Besides from patients monitoring IoMT also have applications in drug and vaccine discovery, contact tracing, delivery of health services and mitigating covid-19 like pandemic. Methodologies that are deployed globally to control and trace the spread of the disease have also been presented in the chapter. The vast chemical space, comprising $>10^{60}$ molecules, fosters the development of a large number of drug molecules, which is a time consuming tack and can be addressed by AI techniques. The applications of AI in the pharmaceutical industry can be found in drug design, poly-pharmacology, chemical re-synthesis, drug repurposing, and drug screening. DL, DTL, and DRL models have shown significant prediction in drug discovery.

Internet of Things for Pharmaceutical Manufacturing (IoTPM) has the power to radically change how pharmaceutical manufacturing plant operates. It gives access to the manufacturing activities to be monitored from any remote location at any given point of time. Optimizing the production costs, waste management, supply chain management, predictive maintenance, and equipment utilization are the major factors that influence the incorporation of IoMT and AI in pharmaceutical manufacturing. However, IoT technologies are in its blossoming stages of development in pharmaceutical industries, but will have a greater impact on global healthcare in the upcoming years. The proposed chapter presents a comprehensive survey of edge computing, AI on IoMT.

6.2   LITERATURE REVIEW

Controlling the spread of viral disease is critical in a high density populated cities and countries; such areas should be monitored and surveillance through modern digital technologies. Floating populated cities may employ technologies such as artificial intelligence, IoMT, blockchain and edge or fog computing. Monitoring a healthcare system in a pandemic situation is a difficult process since the spread of disease is unprecedented and requires continual monitoring. Case studies of healthcare systems that had implemented edge and AI techniques such as Deep Learning (DL), Deep Neural Networks (DNN), Deep Reinforcement Learning (DRL), and Deep Transfer Learning (DTL) are presented in this chapter. Since medical data is crucial to process, and requires decision making in real-time situations an AI-driven edge computing architecture can be implanted in IoMT for diagnosing, surveillance and tracking disease spread. Such healthcare systems allow telemedicine, tele-healthcare, Remote-surgery, etc., to assure patient health monitoring and personalized healthcare at a remote place. A distributed DL neural network framework is proposed in Ref. [37] with DL implemented in both the edge and cloud with two types of DL models Local DL running at the edge and Global DL running at the server.

While AI has its applications on prevention, diagnosis, drug finding and controlling disease, Edge computing (EC) reduces the delay in services through processing nodes nearer to the data generators, such as IoMT devices and Body Area Networks. Sufian et al. [28] proposed a DL and Computer Vision-based surveillance model which employs EC for monitoring ICU and Critical Areas to stop the spread of Covid-19. For remote healthcare, Sodhro et al. [32] proposed a mobile EC framework and a window-based Rate Control Algorithm to optimize the QoS in mobile-based medical applications. Since energy efficiency is an important constraint in low energy edge devices, Abdellatif et al. [31] proposed a data and application specific energy-efficient smart health system that optimizes medical data transmission from edge nodes to the healthcare provider with energy efficiency and quality-of-service and also manages a heterogeneous wireless network through EC to provide fast emergency response.

Authors in Ref. [53] proposed a three layered healthcare framework to fight with the Covid-19 pandemic. The Stakeholder layer consists of the hospitals, signal generating IoMT devices such as heart rate monitor, BP monitors, etc., and other stakeholders who are the actual users of the proposed system. The recent architecture of high-performance computing devices are deployed at the edge level to alleviate the computational latency for local DL processing the signals and data from first layer and the cloud layer which runs the global DL for maintaining integrity of data and is protected by authentication security mechanisms. An energy efficient clustering model is proposed in Ref. [36] which consider distance of cluster head with the server, delay in data transmission and energy remaining in cluster head and number of process requests in the cluster head.

For a real-time learning scenario AI-driven learning models which can learn over time without knowing the complete data is required. Rather than deep learning which requires a complete data set for the training phase, Active learning is suggested by Santhosh [1] where training could be done on the available dataset without waiting for a long time to train the machine. Deployment of edge devices with a computing framework that controls IoMT is proposed in Ref. [54]. Covid-19 symptoms, facial expressions analysis, IoMT devices signal analysis are done using the cutting-edge GPU's deployed in edge devices which are then visualized by using deep learning running at the edge environment in the user side or in the cloud environment. As the edge devices are deployed in user environment, for example the human subject's home, then there will be a less chance for tampering of data so security and privacy of patient's medical record is achieved. Latency is reduced since network traffic is reduced and computing is done at the edge devices.

6.3   ROLE OF ARTIFICIAL INTELLIGENCE IN COVID-19 PANDEMIC

Artificial intelligence (AI) is a promising technology in healthcare where accuracy and real time decision making are the critical factors. AI played a crucial role in tackling the Covid-19 pandemic across the globe such as giving early alerts on the disease outbreak, diagnosis and screening of infection, finding drugs, predicting the sequence of amino acid in the virus, and so on. Machine learning (ML) a subset of AI is deployed in such applications. Apart from these applications listed in this section China employed humanoids in hospitals [37] for entertainment purpose to relieve the stress of corona infected patients and delivering food to them. Conceptual level of many available AI approaches has a limitation that a large dataset is required to diagnosis and real-time decision making. This limitation has a greater effect in tackling fast spreading disease so active learning-based cross-population train/test models that employ multitudinal and multimodal data are required. Active learning strategy provides a better data analysis and decision making when compared to passive learning where a large training data set required. This requirement of large data set for training will require greater time where this is not feasible approach to fight with novel corona virus spread so active learning is a better approach. Algorithms and systems which employs active learning are suitable for tackling pandemic situation where the decision has to be made fast and requires an immediate response.

6.3.1   FORECASTING DISEASE OUTBREAK

Forecasting of infectious areas across the globe can help the individuals to learn about the spread of corona virus and this process requires a machine learning model. Prior to WHO's statement on COVID-19, BlueDot has revealed the emergence of the pandemic [3]. It is an AI-based platform which is used for tracking, forecasting and conceptualizing the spread of corona virus worldwide. A very interactive and informative dashboard is provided by WHO [62]. Covid-19 confirmed cases word wide are presented in this website. Confirmed rate and daily rate were visualized from different areas and the data are updated regularly. Geographical distribution of novel coronavirus cases is presented as visuals and graphs in Ref. [63]. Updated situation of covid cases can be obtained from in across the Europe. Interactive presentation of map dashboard is provided in Ref. [64]. It presents the information about the hospitalization rate, confirmed case, incidence rate, etc.

6.3.2   CONTACT TRACING OF COVID INFECTED PERSONS

Direct exposure of human to human leads to the rapid outbreak of this disease and thereby creating a pandemic situation. Identifying such persons who were in the direct exposure of infectious person is known as contact tracing. To predict the dynamics of pandemic susceptible-infectious removed (SIR) model is proposed where the given population is divided into susceptible, infectious, and removed. SIR model, however, it is the simplest model which assumes the constant parameters and is a deterministic model [7]. Variants of SIR such as susceptible-exposed-infectious-removed (SEIR) model, and susceptible, un-quarantine infected, quarantine infected, confirmed infected (SUQC) model are the other two epidemiological models where the given population and characteristics of the curve are predictively maintained [8]. Bay et al.

[4] proposed a centralized architecture for contact tracing which mainly focused on the privacy preserving of infected patients. Data security and privacy preservation is done by preventing third parties and by accounting all the log information in the system itself. To enhance contact tracing through exposure detection functions Rivest et al. [5] proposed a Private Automated Contact Tracing (PACT) Protocol which traces the contacts through personal digital communication devices. GPS installed in smartphones of human subjects who are infected with covid are backtracked by their GPS location information and their point of contact are gathered to obtain the knowledge of Contact tracing of patients [61].

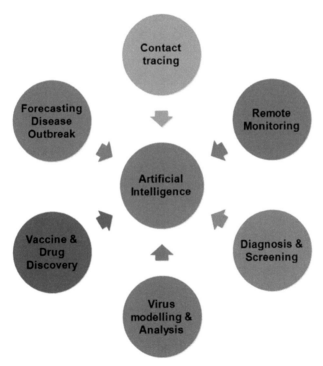

FIGURE 6.1 Applications of AI in smart healthcare.

6.3.3 REMOTE MONITORING THE PATIENTS

Smart healthcare systems and Artificial Intelligence has played a notable role during Covid pandemic in delivering medical services to the doors.

Contactless patient monitoring is an unavoidable option for healthcare providers to break the chain of infection. Remote photoplethysmography (rPPG) is a technique used for non-contact pulse rate estimation by facial data and measurements taken from finger, toe or earlobe. The measurements are highly correlated with the measurements taken from electro-cardiogram (ECG) [15]. Aleksandar et al. [14] proposed an e-health monitoring system through web and mobile applications. They proposed a simple user centric application to collect the required data from patients and send it to doctors and to track the medication given by doctors. Primitive measures on the spread of novel corona viruses are the social distancing between all the persons and quarantining the infected and persons in contact with the infected persons [6]. Such quarantining efforts need the remote health monitoring since direct exposure in any form is a risky one.

6.3.4   DIAGNOSIS OF COVID DISEASE

Early diagnosis of Covid-19 enables the proper medication and quarantine for the infected persons, thereby breaking the chain of disease spread. Wang, et al. [17] proposed Covid-Net, a novel deep neural network model that enables the early diagnosis of disease from CXR images. They used projection-expansion-projection-extension (PEPX) design for reduction of computational complexity and improved representation of observation from CXR images and provides 93.3% accuracy in quantitative analysis of test results. Authors in Ref. [18] proposed a deep learning-based model for diagnosis of Covid-19 through computed tomography (CT) scanned images. The drastically increased population of infected persons causes a high demand for immediate diagnosis and treatment for the disease, but due to the shortage of manual radiologists, there may be a delay and heavy burden for the frontline radiologists. To alleviate this problem, deep learning on high resolution CT images which provides a better accuracy as manual radiologists should be employed. In Ref. [42], the authors have proposed the Truncated Inception Net deep learning model which is based on convolutional neural network. Chest X-ray images from six data sets are included for experimentation of the proposed methodology, which provides a better result in the experiment. The work of authors in Ref. [56] provides 96% of accuracy in diagnosing the Covid-19 with the CT scan images. In Ref. [43], the authors have demonstrated the use of

X-rays images for the mass screening to find the COVID-19 positive cases through the light-weight CNN-based shallow architecture which works with fewer parameters. In Ref. [44], authors have used CT scan images to locate the infected region and infection level of severity in the lungs. They have employed the use of Harmony-Search-Optimization and Otsu thresholding for the image enhancement.

6.3.5 PREDICTING STRUCTURE OF VIRUS

Knowledge about the protein's structure of virus enables researchers about the functionalities of virus. To determine the protein structure from amino acid sequence computational methods are employed [19]. Google's Deep-Mind is making a major contribution in predicting the protein structure and other features of virus. Deepmind's AlphaFold is used three deep-learning-based methods for free modeling (FM) protein structure prediction, without using any template-based modeling (TBM). These methods were based around combinations of three neural networks: (i) to predict the distance between pairs of residues within a protein; (ii) to directly estimate the accuracy of a candidate structure (termed the GDT-net); and (iii) to directly generate protein structures. [20]. Convolutional Neural Network (CNN)-based protein structure prediction is proposed in Ref. [21]. Experimental cryo-electron microscopic maps are used to train the CNN which is referred to here as U-Net. The amino acid sequence is predicted using confusion matrix and protein alignment algorithm which relatively reduces the computational complexity of other traditional methods in predicting the protein structure.

6.3.6 VACCINE AND DRUG DISCOVERY

AI-based drug discovery has revolutionized pharmaceutical industry which enables computational speedup and thereby minimizing the time and cost required for designing a new drug. Pandemic situations need faster discovery of medicine, repurposing the existing drugs and vaccine discovery [25]. Drastically increasing population of infection leads to high demand of corona vaccine and curative drugs in the market. Authors in Ref. [22] proposed a machine learning-based approach to predict and to repurpose the approved drugs for COVID-19. Given dataset is first classified using the Naïve-Bayes approach and then trained with the machine learning model. The drugs predicted by this model are further verified by the docking process.

6.4   EDGE COMPUTING AND IOMT

IoMT that incorporated edge computing has made its remarkable contribution to human wellbeing and healthcare. In this pandemic complete lockdown had lead the working professionals in all sectors to opt work from home there will be a drastically increased data transferred over network every day. Since the latency of data communication increased rapidly due to network overload and computational overhead in server edge computing will definitely be a solution for the such computational delay on the server Figure 6.2 depicts the deployment of edge computing in IoMT. Incorporation of network, computing devices, storage devices, and application core capabilities makes the edge computing technology suitable for alleviating such bottleneck.

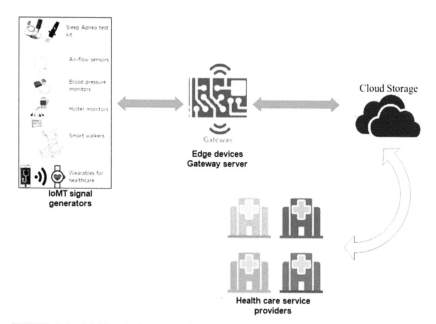

FIGURE 6.2   IoMT and edge computing.

A high demand of network bandwidth while transferring the clinical data and IoMT signals results in latency and processing overhead in cloud server which in turn degrades the real time performance of the system. Real time decision making and real time clinical data management requires techniques such as edge computing and distributed ledgers to provide fast computation decision making and data integrity of patient's electronic health records. Since most of the data processing computations is done at the edge which is nearer to the patient's home there is no raw data transfer and hence the security and privacy of patient is maintained.

6.4.1 CHALLENGES IN DEPLOYING EDGE COMPUTING

6.4.1.1 TRUST MANAGEMENT

Due to lack of security and privacy preserving mechanisms trust management with the consumers is a major concern. To manage and calculate trust values, Kamvar et al. [46] proposed a distributed model that assigns each individual EC node an exclusive universal trust value based on its upload history. This universal trust value is used for selecting a node so that the management system can meritoriously find malicious edge nodes and avoid them from transactions. A consistent trust management system known as GroupTrust proposed by Fan et al. [48] proposed reliable trust in case of dishonest ratings, malicious masquerading, and malicious collusion. It relies on the feedback credibility of pairwise similarity to improve the resiliency of trust value calculations for the case of dishonest ratings, defining trust propagation thresholds to control how trust is propagated. Optimization of network resource sharing and enhancing security in a mobile edge computing environment is proposed in Ref. [47]. A social trust framework based on deep reinforcement learning methodology which allocates the network resources is proposed in this paper. Objective information entropy theory is proposed in Ref. [49] where a feedback mechanism is used for universal trust calculation among the devices. A lightweight adaptive trust calculation algorithm is suitable for large scale IoMT devices with heterogeneous features and also offers fast trust calculation and low computational overhead.

6.4.1.2   HETEROGENEITY OF DEVICES

Providing a uniform interface over the heterogeneous edge devices is a perplexing task. Globalization of resources is enabled only when all the IoMT devices in the system are compatible with the network and trust management services. Authors in Ref. [50] proposed a social sensing-based edge computing model which hides the device details of computing nodes in the network and shares the resources however it assumes that there is no malicious nodes in the system and thus has its limitation. An ontology-based device identification model is proposed in Ref. [51] which provide a unified protocol for communication between diverse set of computing devices. Since edge devices with low power and low processing capacities are not capable of processing real time data such as live video stream and signals that requires complex computations for processing, such data will be sent through a network channel to cloud platform where the data are analyzed and processed. Hence heterogeneity of edge devices is a major challenge in incorporating IoMT in edge network.

6.4.1.3   QOS REQUIREMENTS

High Quality of Service (QoS) is an unavoidable feature in IoMT environment, since it deals with human life. Applications that are delay sensitive are highly recommended in real-time situations. Delay in transmission, transmission power, rate of signal transmission, jitter, and energy efficiency are the features to be considered while transmitting medical data over the network to enable remote healthcare services. Till date considering medical QoS features is essential but is less focused. Authors in Ref. [32] proposed an elevated QoS model based on mobile edge computing for remote healthcare applications. The rate of transmission is organized by a window-based rate control algorithm in this paper.

6.4.1.4   SECURITY AND PRIVACY

Remote medical services require to be highly secured and to preserve the privacy of patients by protecting their sensitive data. Authentication mechanisms and blockchain are the possible solutions in IoMT environment. There are three, four and five layered architectures in the literature for deployment of blockchain in IoMT for security. Rather than public blockchain which provides access to every device in the network [58] private blockchain is suitable for a smart hospital environment. Private Blockchain abstracts the medical data in every layer of architecture [59]. Hybrid architecture named Consortium Blockchain which incorporates two or more institutions in the system and will provide security and privacy of medical data from data tampering [60]. Due to the decentralized nature of blockchain tampering of data, single point of failure and denial of service are eliminated thereby providing a better QoS. Global data analysis in a cloud environment is done with encryption of medical database and cluster-based mining is proposed in Ref. [57]. The Brakerski-Gentry-Vaikuntanathan (BGV) Cryptosystem is employed with the conversion of floating point representation with equivalent integer representation is proposed to provide a secure and privacy preserving cloud computing environment for healthcare. Edge of medical things is also a crucial paradigm in Ref. [57] for providing the security and privacy of patients.

6.4.1.4 LATENCY

Edge computing environment that leverages IoMT in which most of computing and analysis of electronic health data, such as live video stream, IoMT signals, Images and sound signals, are done in edge devices can reduce the Latency to a greater extent [54]. A fast detection of covid positive is proposed in the work of [56] and also provides a higher rate of accuracy up to 96%. Manual diagnosis is replaced here and average time required for diagnosis is 20 seconds and it effectively differentiates the regular pneumonia and a novel corona viral infection. Deployment of 5G technology in tackling the pandemic can result in a reduction of latency [37]. Edge computing that leverages deep learning and a fast 5G technology is proposed in Ref. [57].

6.4.2 EDGE COMPUTING IN TACKLING COVID-19:

Since this pandemic situation requires computation of data in real time, greater accuracy with low latency, edge computing is such a solution which provides state of the art performance with location sensitivity and mobility. EC incorporated in IoMT has a vast application worldwide during the pandemic. Easy access of devices in the network enables patients who are home quarantine to access their medical services. Data integrity is provided through globalization of local medical data and blockchain since any change of data without consent of all the deciding authorities is not possible in the network. Enforcing public to follow proper guideline of pandemic situation, remote healthcare services, monitoring the containment area of high dense covid-19 cases and surveillance are the major applications of IoMT and edge computing in Covid pandemic and are presented in Table 6.1.

TABLE 6.1   Applications of IoMT in Covid-19

Authors	Proposed methodology	Inference
A. Ksentini and B. Brik [39]	Multi-access edge computing incorporated in IoT is proposed to ensure the social distancing between persons. The GPS coordinates of user location is gathered using a smart device, the user is carrying and distance between two users is calculated to ensure the social distancing.	The proposed algorithm which involves the collection of GPS coordinates and computation of distance between two individuals is done at the remote server to alleviate computational latency.
M. A. Rahman, et al. [37]	Covid-19 management framework with DNN running at both edge and cloud server. Edge layer does all the computations of IoMT signals with the local Deep Learning algorithm and then sent to the Cloud layer which runs Global DL to reconcile with local DL.	Distributed DL methodology allows the local edge servers share datasets with global DL environments.
X. Kong, et al. [40]	Proposed ECMask: an edge computing-based video processing model. Accuracy of face detection is achieved through video restoration with Laplacian operator.	Deep learning model for video restoration is optimized and running in local edge computing devices. Based on Face detection Wearing of mask is identified from the given dataset.
P. Ranaweera, et al. [41]	Multi-access edge computing model for contact-less treatment of Covid-19	Incorporated augmented reality for monitoring robots and remote surgery. Applicable in smart hospitals that incorporated IT infrastructure for processing.

TABLE 6.1 *(Continued)*

Authors	Proposed methodology	Inference
Shuai Ding, et al. [52]	Three layered architecture namely (i) Robot layer (ii) Edge Layer (iii) Cloud Layer. Remote healthcare services provided with the help of robots as data collectors.	Data is collected by robots and processed in the edge layer with fully convolutional Siamese (SiameseFC) network. Decision support is deployed at the cloud layer.
Ghayvat H, et al. [61]	Location information and points of contact of infected subjects is backtracked by the privacy preserving high processing edge devices.	Proposed COUNTERACT provides information about infected subject's location and point of contact with infected, suspected subjects for infection forecasting of COVID-19.

6.5 CONCLUSION

Mobility, location sensitivity, and low latency are the key factors of edge computing that enable fast and accurate analysis of healthcare data and has lead the future research directions towards optimization of edge and IoMT devices and ensuring accuracy, security, and privacy of candidates in IoMT-based health monitoring systems. In this chapter, we surveyed about the technologies used in smart healthcare systems, such as AI, IoMT, and edge computing, and their challenges of deployment in a real-time environment. Data classification is crucial while diagnosing and screening covid diseases. Differentiation of symptoms in regular pneumonia with COVID will improve the classification better. Artificial intelligence systems are to be employed in such situations.

KEYWORDS

- **artificial intelligence**
- **edge computing**
- **IoMT**
- **IoT**
- **Quality of Service**
- **remote health monitoring**

REFERENCES

1. Santosh, K. C., (2020). AI-driven tools for coronavirus outbreak: Need of active learning and cross-population train/test models on multitudinal/multimodal data. *J. Med. Syst., 44*(5), 1–5.

2. Maghdid, H. S., Ghafoor, K. Z., Sadiq, A. S., Curran, K., & Rabie, K., (2020). *A Novel AI-Enabled Framework to Diagnose Coronavirus COVID-19 Using Smartphone Embedded Sensors: Design Study* (pp. 180–187). arXiv Preprint arXiv:2003.07434. https://arxiv.org/abs/2003.07434.

3. https://www.cnbc.com/2020/03/03/bluedot-used-artificial-intelligence-to-predict-coronavirus-spread.html (accessed on 11 January 2022).

4. Bay, J., Kek, J., Tan, A., Hau, C. S., Yongquan, L., Tan, J., & Quy, T. A. (2020). BlueTrace: A privacy-preserving protocol for community-driven contact tracing across borders. *Government Technology Agency-Singapore, Tech. Rep, 18*, 1.

5. Rivest, R. L., Callas, J., Canetti, R., et al., (2020). *The Pact Protocol Specifications* (Vol. 1). Technical report.

6. Taiwoa, O., & Ezugwub, A. E., (2020). Smart healthcare support for remote patient monitoring during COVID-19 quarantine. *Informatics in Medicine Unlocked, 20*, 100428. https://doi.org/10.1016/j.imu.2020.100428.

7. Abou-Ismail, A., (2020). Compartmental models of the COVID-19 pandemic for physicians and physician-scientists. *SN Compr. Clin. Med., 2*, 852–858. https://doi.org/10.1007/s42399-020-00330-z.

8. Shapiro, M., Karim, F., Muscioni, G., & Augustine, A., (2021). Adaptive susceptible-infectious-removed model for continuous estimation of the COVID-19 infection rate and reproduction number in the United States: Modeling study. *J. Med. Internet. Res., 23*(4), e24389 URL: https://www.jmir.org/2021/4/e24389. doi: 10.2196/24389.

9. Greco, L., Percannella, G., Ritrovato, P., Tortorella, F., & Vento, M., (2020). Trends in IoT-based solutions for health care: Moving AI to the edge. *Pattern Recognition Letters, 135*, 346–353. ISSN 0167-8655. https://doi.org/10.1016/j.patrec.2020.05.016.

10. Magaña, E. P., Aquino-Santos, R., Cárdenas-Benitez, N., Aguilar-Velasco, J., Buenrostro-Segura, C., Edwards-Block, A., et al., (2014). WiSPH: A wireless sensor network-based home care monitoring system. *Sensors, 14*(4), 7096–7119.

11. Villarrubia, G., Bajo, J., Paz, D., Juan, F., & Corchado, J. M., (2014). Monitoring and detection platform to prevent anomalous situations in home care. *Sensors, 14*(6), 9900–9921.

12. Kaur, A., & Jasuja, A., (2017). Health monitoring based on IoT using raspberry PI. In: *2017 International Conference on Computing, Communication and Automation (ICCCA)* (pp. 1335–1340). Greater Noida.

13. Mathur, N., Paul, G., Irvine, J., Abuhelala, M., Buis, A., & Glesk, I., (2016). A practical design and implementation of a low cost platform for remote monitoring of lower limb health of amputees in the developing world. *IEEE Access, 4*, 7440–7451.

14. Aleksandar, K., Natasa, K., & Saso, K., (2016). E-health monitoring system. In: *International Conference on Applied Internet and Information Technologies*.

15. Rohmetra, H., Raghunath, N., Narang, P., et al., (2021). AI-enabled remote monitoring of vital signs for COVID-19: Methods, prospects and challenges. *Computing*. https://doi.org/10.1007/s00607-021-00937-7.

16. Yan, L., Zhang, H. T., Xiao, Y., et al. (2020). *Prediction of Criticality in Patients with Severe COVID-19 Infection Using Three Clinical Features: A Machine Learning-Based Prognostic Model with Clinical Data in Wuhan.* medRxiv preprint. doi: 10.1101/2020.02.27.20028027.

17. Wang, L., Lin, Z. Q., & Wong, A. (2020). Covid-net: A tailored deep convolutional neural network design for detection of covid-19 cases from chest x-ray images. *Scientific reports, 10*(1), 1–12.

18. Chen, J., Wu, L., Zhang, J., et al. (2020). *Deep Learning-Based Model for Detecting 2019 Novel Coronavirus Pneumonia on High-Resolution Computed Tomography: A Prospective Study.* medRxiv preprint. doi: 10.1101/2020.02.25.20021568.

19. https://deepmind.com/research/open-source/computational-predictions-of-protein-structures-associated-with-COVID-19 (accessed on 11 January 2022).

20. Jumper, J., Evans, R., Pritzel, A., Green, T., Figurnov, M., Ronneberger, O., ... & Hassabis, D. (2021). Highly accurate protein structure prediction with AlphaFold. *Nature, 596*(7873), 583–589.

21. Jonas, P., Nhut, M. P., & Dong, S., (2021). DeepTracer for fast de novo cryo-EM protein structure modeling and special studies on CoV-related complexes. *Proceedings of the National Academy of Sciences, 118*(2), e2017525118. doi: 10.1073/pnas.2017525118.

22. Mahapatra, S., Nath, P., Chatterjee, M., et al., (2020). *Repurposing Therapeutics for COVID-19: Rapid Prediction of Commercially Available Drugs Through Machine Learning and Docking.* MedRxiv.

23. Muratov, E., & Zakharov, A., (2020). *Viribus Unitis: Drug Combinations as a Treatment Against COVID-19.* ChemRxiv.

24. Moskal, M., Beker, W., Roszak, R., et al., (2020). *Suggestions for Second-Pass Anti-COVID-19 Drugs Based on the Artificial Intelligence Measures of Molecular Similarity, Shape and Pharmacophore Distribution.* ChemRxiv.

25. Ong, E., Wong, M. U., Huffman, A., & He, Y., (2020). COVID-19 coronavirus vaccine design using reverse vaccinology and machine learning. *Front. Immunol., 11*, 158.

26. Hu, F., Jiang, J., & Yin, P., (2020). *Prediction of Potential Commercially Inhibitors Against SARS-CoV-2 by Multi-Task Deep Model.* arXiv preprint arXiv:2003.00728.

27. Patrick, W. W., & Regina, B., (2021). Critical assessment of AI in drug discovery. *Expert Opinion on Drug Discovery.* doi: 10.1080/17460441.2021.1915982.

28. Dolui, K., & Datta, S. K., (2017). Comparison of edge computing implementations: Fog computing, cloudlet and mobile edge computing. In: *2017 Global Internet of Things Summit (GIoTS)* (pp. 1–6). doi: 10.1109/GIOTS.2017.8016213.

29. Sufian, A., Jat, D. S., & Banerjee, A. (2020). Insights of artificial intelligence to stop spread of covid-19. *Big Data Analytics and Artificial Intelligence Against COVID-19: Innovation Vision and Approach*, 177–190.

30. Hegde, C., Suresha, P. B., Zelko, J., Jiang, Z., Kamaleswaran, R., Reyna, M. A., Clifford, G. D. (2020). *Autotriage-an Open Source Edge Computing Raspberry Pi-Based Clinical Screening System.* medRxiv.

31. Abdellatif, A. A., Mohamed, A., Chiasserini, C. F., Erbad, A., & Guizani, M., (2020). Edge computing for energy-efficient smart health systems: Data and application-specific approaches. In: *Energy Efficiency of Medical Devices and Healthcare Applications* (pp. 53–67). Elsevier.

32. Sodhro, A. H., Luo, Z., Sangaiah, A. K., & Baik, S. W., (2019). Mobile edge computing based QoS optimization in medical healthcare applications. *International Journal of Information Management, 45*, 308–318.

33. Chen, M., Li, W., Hao, Y., Qian, Y., & Humar, I., (2018). Edge cognitive computing based smart healthcare system. *Future Generation Computer Systems, 86*, 403–411.

34. Pace, P., Aloi, G., Gravina, R., Caliciuri, G., Fortino, G., & Liotta, A., (2019). An edge-based architecture to support efficient applications for healthcare industry 4.0. *IEEE Transactions on Industrial Informatics, 15*(1), 481–489.

35. Zhang, H., Li, J., Wen, B., Xun, Y., & Liu, J., (2018). Connecting intelligent things in smart hospitals using Nb-IoT. *IEEE Internet of Things Journal, 5*(3), 1550–1560.

36. Han, T., Zhang, L., Pirbhulal, S., Wu, W., & Hugo, C. De. A. V., (2019). A novel cluster head selection technique for edge-computing based IoMT systems. *Computer Networks, 158,* 114–122, ISSN 1389-1286. https://doi.org/10.1016/j.comnet.2019.04.021.

37. Rahman, M. A., Hossain, M. S., Alrajeh, N. A., & Guizani, N., (2020). B5G and explainable deep learning assisted healthcare vertical at the edge: COVID-I9 perspective. In: *IEEE Network* (Vol. 34, No. 4, pp. 98–105). doi: 10.1109/MNET.011.2000353.

38. Hornyak, T., (2020). *What America Can Learn from China's Use of Robots and Telemedicine to Combat the Coronavirus [Internet].* CNBC. https://www.cnbc.com/2020/03/18/how-china-is-using-robots-and-telemedicine-to-combat-the-coronavirus.html (accessed on 11 January 2022).

39. Ksentini, A., & Brik, B., (2020). An edge-based social distancing detection service to mitigate COVID-19 propagation. In: *IEEE Internet of Things Magazine* (Vol. 3, No. 3, pp. 35–39). doi: 10.1109/IOTM.0001.2000138.

40. Kong, X., et al. (2021). Real-time mask identification for COVID-19: An edge computing-based deep learning framework. In: *IEEE Internet of Things Journal.* doi: 10.1109/JIOT.2021.3051844.

41. Ranaweera, P., Liyanage, M., & Jurcut, A. D., (2021). Novel MEC based approaches for smart hospitals to combat COVID-19 pandemic. In: *IEEE Consumer Electronics Magazine* (Vol. 10, No. 2, pp. 80–91). doi: 10.1109/MCE.2020.3031261.

42. Das, D., Santosh, K. C., & Pal, U., (2020). *Truncated Inception Net: COVID-19 Outbreak Screening Using Chest X-Rays.* doi: https://doi.org/10.21203/rs.3.rs-20795/v1.

43. Mukherjee, H., Ghosh, S., Dhar, A., Obaidullah, S. M., Santosh, K. C., & Roy, K., (2020). *Shallow Convolutional Neural Network for COVID-19 Outbreak Screening Using Chest X-Rays.* https://doi.org/10.36227/techrxiv.12156522.v1.

44. Rajinikanth, V., Dey, N., Raj, A. N. J., Hassanien, A. E., Santosh, K. C., & Raja, N., (2020). *Harmony-Search and Otsu Based System for Coronavirus Disease (COVID-19) Detection Using Lung CT Scan Images.* arXiv preprint arXiv:2004.03431.

45. Wang, B., Li, M., Jin, X., & Guo, C., (2020). A reliable IoT edge computing trust management mechanism for smart cities. In: *IEEE Access* (Vol. 8, pp. 46373–46399). doi: 10.1109/ACCESS.2020.297902.

46. Kamvar, S. D., Schlosser, M. T., & Garcia-Molina, H., (2003). The eigenTrust algorithm for reputation management in P2P networks. In: *Proc. 12th Int. Conf. World Wide Web (WWW)* (pp. 640–651). Budapest, Hungary.

47. He, Y., Yu, F. R., Zhao, N., & Yin, H., (2018). Secure social networks in 5G systems with mobile edge computing, caching, and device-to-device communications. *IEEE Wireless Commun., 25*(3), 103–109.

48. Fan, X., Liu, L., Li, M., & Su, Z., (2017). GroupTrust: Dependable trust management. *IEEE Trans. Parallel Distrib. Syst., 28*(4), 1076–1090.

49. Yuan, J., & Li, X., (2018). A reliable and lightweight trust computing mechanism for IoT edge devices based on multi-source feedback information fusion. *IEEE Access, 6*, 23626–23638.

50. Daniel (Yue), Z., Tahmid, R., Xukun, L., Nathan, V., & Dong, W., (2019). HeteroEdge: Taming the heterogeneity of edge computing system in social sensing. In: *Proceedings of the International Conference on Internet of Things Design and Implementation (IoTDI '19)* (pp. 37–48). Association for computing machinery, New York, NY, USA. doi: https://doi.org/10.1145/3302505.3310067.

51. Lan, L., Shi, R., Wang, B., & Zhang, L., (2019). An IoT unified access platform for heterogeneity sensing devices based on edge computing. In: *IEEE Access* (Vol. 7, pp. 44199–44211). doi: 10.1109/ACCESS.2019.2908684.

52. Mo, H., Ding, S., Yang, S., Zheng, X., & Vasilakos, A. V., (2020). *The Role of Edge Robotics As-a-Service in Monitoring COVID-19 Infection.* arXiv.

53. Hossain, M. S., Muhammad, G., & Guizani, N., (2020). Explainable AI and mass surveillance system-based healthcare framework to combat COVID-I9 like pandemics. In: *IEEE Network* (Vol. 34, No. 4, pp. 126–132). doi: 10.1109/MNET.011.2000458.

54. Rahman, M. A., & Hossain, M. S., (2021). An internet-of-medical-things-enabled edge computing framework for tackling COVID-19. In: *IEEE Internet of Things Journal* (Vol. 8, No. 21, pp. 15847–15854). doi: 10.1109/JIOT.2021.3051080.

55. Wang, H., (2020). IoT based clinical sensor data management and transfer using blockchain technology. In: *Journal of ISMAC* (Vol. 02, No. 03, pp. 154–159). http://irojournals.com/iroismac/ doi: https://doi.org/10.36548/jismac.2020.3.003 (accessed on 11 January 2022).

56. https://www.technology.org/2020/03/01/aialgorithm-detects-coronavirus-infections-in-patients-from-ctscans-with-96-accuracy/ (accessed on 11 January 2022).

57. Alabdulatif, A., Khalil, I., Yi, X., & Guizani, M., (2019). Secure edge of things for smart healthcare surveillance framework. In: *IEEE Access* (Vol. 7, pp. 31010–31021). doi: 10.1109/ACCESS.2019.2899323.

58. Nimra, D., Muhammad, R., Fahad, A., & Saima, A., (2019). Blockchain: Securing internet of medical things (IoMT). In: *(IJACSA) International Journal of Advanced Computer Science and Applications* (Vol. 10, No. 1).

59. Kumari, K. A., Padmashani, R., Varsha, R., et al., (2020). Securing the internet of medical things (IoMT) using private blockchain network. In: *Principles of Internet of Things (IoT) Ecosystem: Insight Paradigm* (pp. 305–326).

60. Aslam, B., Javed, A. R., Chakraborty, C., et al., (2021). Blockchain and ANFIS empowered IoMT application for privacy preserved contact tracing in COVID-19 pandemic. *Pers. Ubiquit Comput.* https://doi.org/10.1007/s00779-021-01596-3.

61. Ghayvat, H., Awais, M., Gope, P., Pandya, S., & Majumdar, S., (2021). Recognizing suspect and predicting the spread of contagion based on mobile phone location data (counteract): A system of identifying COVID-19 infectious and hazardous sites, detecting disease outbreaks based on the internet of things, edge computing, and artificial intelligence. *Sustainable Cities and Society, 69*(12), 102798.

62. https://covid19.who.int/ (accessed on 11 January 2022).

63. https://www.ecdc.europa.eu/en/geographical-distribution-2019-ncov-cases (accessed on 11 January 2022).

64. https://coronavirus.jhu.edu/map.html (accessed on 11 January 2022).

65. Dong, P., et al., (2020). Edge computing-based healthcare systems: Enabling decentralized health monitoring in internet of medical things. In: *IEEE Network* (Vol. 34, No. 5, pp. 254–261). doi: 10.1109/MNET.011.1900636.

CHAPTER 7

Decision Support and Knowledge Representation in Healthcare

C. MURALIDHARAN,[1] Y. MOHAMED SIRAJUDEEN,[2] and
R. SOMASUNDARAM[3]

[1]*Department of Computing Technologies, SRM Institute of Science and Technology, Kattankulathur, Tamil Nadu, India*

[2]*Assistant Professor, School of Computer Science and Engineering, VIT-AP University, Amaravati, Andhra Pradesh, India*

[3]*Faculty of Engineering and Technology, Sri Ramachandra Institute of Higher Education and Research, Chennai, Tamil Nadu, India*

ABSTRACT

The volume of medical data increases drastically day by day, which depends on the qualitative decision support system for analyzing and gaining knowledge from the data. Decision support systems (DSS) are the tools that are designed for examining the digital medical data for suggesting the next steps that need to be followed for treatments, extraction of dangerous or unfair medications, detection of symptoms, and so on. It is impossible by the physicians to analyze the clinical data manually and extract the knowledge from the data available. Hence, there is a need for the decision support system to analyze and integrate the useful information from the available data for effective decision support. The integration of DSS in the medial field improves the quality of medical care, eradication

Internet of Medical Things in Smart Healthcare: Post-COVID-19 Pandemic Scenario.
Saravanan Krishnan, PhD and Aboobucker Ilmudeen, PhD (Eds.)
© 2024 Apple Academic Press, Inc. Co-published with CRC Press (Taylor & Francis)

of adversarial events there by supporting the medical team members to provide efficient medications. The HealthIT.gov states that the clinical decision support system supports variety of decision support in the healthcare such as auto reminder and alert to the care taker of the patients, condition specific guidelines for medications, report summarization, diagnostic support, and so on. This chapter discusses about the decision support system and the knowledge representation in healthcare which plays a vital role in obtaining the proper knowledge and decision support on the wide range of available medical data.

7.1   INTRODUCTION

Healthcare is the field where medical care is provided to all communities based on their need. The healthcare personnel serves with intellectual efforts to safeguard the life of every living being. But the increasing number of diseases and changes acquired in the existing disease seems to be the hardest part [2]. Hence there is a need for us to collect and store the patient's report for further improvement in the healthcare. Chief Medical Officer Dr. Joe Kimura, who works at Atrius Health, says that it is too difficult for the average clinician to understand or integrate the multiple information into an effective decision as the amount of information is increasing tremendously. In the era of digital and innovative healthcare system, the clinical support system becomes a vital role for acquiring the effective and reliable decisions [8]. One of the essential tools for healthcare providers is Clinical Decision Support (CDS) systems as the data volume increases thereby increasing the responsibility for the healthcare personnel for delivering value-based healthcare. This can be enabled through the help of the Internet of Medical Things (IoMT) where every medical equipment are connected through the internet.

An electronic health record (EHR) is the data about the patient's record in a digitized form. The record will be a real-time data of the respective patients that are collected through the use of the IoMT that is permissible to access by the authorized users. The entire treatment history of the patients throughout their time will be collected and stored in a standard clinical data format thereby enabling a broader view of the patient [4]. Hence it is a vital part of healthcare unit which records the patient's clinical history, treatment plans, medications provided, immunization details, scanned images, laboratory test results, diagnosis, allergies, and so on. The evidence-based tools are allowed to access the records for making the decisions for enlightening the patient's care [8, 10]. Another important fact is to support the provider for streamlining and automation

In the modern environment, the healthcare system highly concentrates on reducing the variations in the clinical support, safety of patients and reduction in duplicative testing. For acquiring and enriching such an environment, it is necessary to harness the different perceptions of big data. For this purpose, IoMT-based different clinical decision support tools are designed, which helps in sifting large amount of existing digital data thereby predicting the alternate or next process for the treatment [7]. The IoMT is an infrastructure where multiple healthcare or medical devices, healthcare services, healthcare systems, and software applications get connected with one another. This enables the automatic collection of data from the medical environment. Since this is a real time collection of data from both the users and the environment, it is much useful in finding the insights and facts for better improvement of the medicare treatment.

This decision support system further supports the healthcare by providing the information that does not exist and finds the unpredictable dangers that might occur due to the interactions in the medications. If one needs the ensured medical care to human beings they there is needs to get assisted with the advanced technology like CDS. The electronic health record (EHR) modules are used in the CDS tools for streamlining the workflows of healthcare by using the previous medical data. Still, many organizations are working on it and facing significant challenges as it is user friendly which is provided with effective protocols for alerting the healthcare domain through multiple decision making pathways.

It is found that during 2016, the users of EHR spends much time in processing the notifications and it is estimated that approximately 76 notifications are received by the primary care providers [16]. But not all the notifications received are because of the clinical decision support system, but it is acquired from the physicians, laboratory results and many others. Another fact with this is collection of information from the patients because without the data, no information can be predicted. This CDS system has many subsystems such as knowledge-based and non-knowledge-based decision support system. The knowledge-based decision support system is usually called as expert systems which are created using the biomedical experts for identifying the relationship between the dependent and independent variables. Here the independent variables are symptoms and signs, whereas the dependent variable denotes the diseases underlying the independent variables. It includes the information such as patient data, information on the local hospitals and other compiled data that is compiled using a predefined set of rules as if, else, and then statements for making the decisions. Various decision tree structures are also used for decision making. This rule-based clinical decision support system is used predominantly in clinical applications. For example, based on age, height, weight, sex, etc., it predicts the risk of the patients and alerts the users for providing possible doses to patients. The non-knowledge-based clinical decision support system will not use any data that is available based on the knowledge base rather it uses the machine learning methods for prediction. Hence in this model the system by itself will do the process by learning the previous experience. Thus the patterns are found by learning the previous clinical data. This system is also trained based on the relationship between the independent and dependent variables, i.e., the signs and symptoms (independent variable) and the diseases (dependent variable). This chapter discusses more about the need for clinical decision support system and its variability such as knowledge-based decision support system and non-knowledge-based decision support systems.

7.2   NEED FOR DECISION SUPPORT SYSTEM

A decision support system (DSS) is an information system that works with a computer program which is used for judgments, support for new determinations and the subject of actions for a business or organization [6]. It sifts large amount of data and compiles massive information comprehensively for solving the problems thereby supporting decision making process. Usually the information used by the DSS is revenue targeted, past information for a particular period and other operation related data [10]. The DSS collects the data, analyzes and synthesizes it for producing the information report comprehensively, thus it differs from the other operations applications. It may be powered up through human or might be completely computerized and in few cases both may be combined for supporting the human users to be informed with the decisions quickly. For example, the DSS might be used for predicting the organization's revenue for the upcoming year through the assumptions on the organization's sales. A large number of factors are related to the projected revenue; hence it cannot be calculated manually. Based on the organization's past transactions, the DSS predicts the outcomes.

In the era of technology advancements, the data analysis is not essential to be fit to the large computing devices but can be used as small applications in the personal computer as DSS that even can make available as mobile applications. Thus the flexibility of the decision support system enhances the data analysis, exploratory and prediction in an effective and tiny manner for supporting the users in making the best decisions for their personal use or for their organizations.

The emergence of clinical decision support system intend to enhance the healthcare decisions by enhancing the proper clinical knowledge, patient health information, and so on. Usually the clinical decision support system is software designed which directly supports for clinical decision making where the individual patient data will be matched to the knowledge base and the assessments the particular patients which then be intimated to the clinicians for making the decisions. Whereas the current CDSS is used at the point of care and for the physicians to combine the suggestions or predictions provided by the CDSS with their knowledge. This is now been extended with increasing the data leveraging with human uninterruptable system.

The clinical decision support system is used for many purposes in the field of healthcare, such as:

- calculation on drug dosing;
- analyzing the standard drug usage guidelines;
- analyzing the severity indexes for the particular diseases;
- formulating templates for particular diseases;
- report identification based on the electronic health record input;
- timely triggers for delivering the medications or to imply the changes in the dosage;
- identifying the gaps for the patient care;
- identifying the preventive care screening.

7.3   CLINICAL DECISION SUPPORT SYSTEM USING IOMT

The clinical decision support systems are developed with the IoMT which may be computerized or non-computerized and includes a variety of interventions and tools that analyzes the different data, thereby supporting the physicians in making the proper decisions [11]. The guidelines of clinical or the support resources such as clinical key are included in non-computerized tools, and such systems are characterized as tools for managing the information. Another type of CDS system targets on focus attention. Some of the examples includes laboratory information system that might highlight the values of critical care data or pharmacy information systems that involves in ordering the drug and suggesting a new drug-drug interactions. Although most of them are developed possibly, an advanced clinical decision support system is developed where the recommendations are based on the patient specific scheme. Few are some of the example as, analyzing the interactions of drug disease, analyzing the dosage of drugs during the impairment of renal, laboratory test recommendations and so on.

Due to the increase in the electronic health record, surveys on patients, disease registries, the quality and quantity of the clinical data tends to increase tremendously [12, 13]. It is not mean that if the data are digitalized, the patient care would be better. Few studies shows that compilation of electronic health record and the computer-based physician order entry consistently decreases the error rate [14]. Hence for analyzing the electronic health records and computer-based physician order entry, a high quality clinical decision support system is required. In the current scenario, it is not clear that how to access the patient data, how to access the data, no sufficient time to search for the data or not aware of the medical insights, hence a precise and automated CDSS is needed for handling such cases.

7.3.1 APPROACHES OF IOMT-BASED DECISION SUPPORT SYSTEM

There are two different approaches in decision support system, such as:

1. knowledge-based clinical decision support system; and
2. non-knowledge-based clinical decision support system.

7.3.1.1 KNOWLEDGE-BASED DECISION SUPPORT SYSTEM

The knowledge-based decision support systems support in making the decisions by establishing a set of rules which is based on the judged medical conditions that are interpreted in the medical literature [15]. The knowledge-based clinical decision support systems are the systems that are designed so as to ensure the decision-making process more precise. This model uses the timely and appropriate data that are collected using the IoMT and knowledge management for satisfying the needed prediction. These systems are usually based on the relevant knowledge; hence it works based on the concept of artificial intelligence and communication technologies. These systems support the physicians in making the decisions through prediction and recommendation techniques.

7.3.1.2   NON- KNOWLEDGE-BASED DECISION SUPPORT SYSTEM

The non-knowledge-based clinical decision support system does not use predefined rules, rather uses the artificial intelligence algorithms for inducing the set of rules through the machine learning methods [16]. This allows the system to learn by itself from the n-number of encounters that rebuilds the set of rules as changes in the environment variable. Since the machine learning techniques such as genetic algorithms, decision trees, support vector machines, neural networks, and so on are used, it learns by itself for recognizing the patterns from the data sets case by case.

7.3.2   EFFECTIVENESS OF CLINICAL DECISION SUPPORT SYSTEM

Many of the research studies state that the examination on CDSS has its strong internal and external validity. Also, the Community Preventive Services Task Force has concluded that CDSS is more effective, and the trials on CDSS have resulted with more positive results. A review provided by the Community Preventive Services Task Force states that on analyzing the cardiovascular data, the improvement of CDSS is observed in three different quality of care practices [7].

- Screening recommendations (cholesterol or blood pressure) and other preventive care (e.g., smoking cessation).
- Clinical test based on evidences that are related to cardiovascular disease.
- Cardiovascular related treatments.

On the whole, the evidence on the above system shows that the CDSS is been tied up with cholesterol and the blood pressure. Thus the CDSS is been used to find the useful information based on the available data thereby making the useful decisions at right time.

7.4   KNOWLEDGE REPRESENTATION

Knowledge representation (KR) is one of the important parts of artificial intelligence (AI) that depicts the real-world problems in a simple computer understandable representation. It plays a major role in healthcare domain to diagnose a patient's health conditions and to recommend better medication support to healthcare workers [17]. KR uses human psychology patterns to solve complex problems. Human beings are best at understanding, reasoning, and interpreting any knowledge. These things can be done through machines by incorporating different machine learning and deep learning algorithms which is further known as knowledge representation and reasoning. KR is the process of understanding, interpret the knowledge, and reasoning by machines in an AI system. The representation of KR consists of various characteristics that are discussed in the following subsections.

7.4.1   CHARACTERISTICS OF KNOWLEDGE REPRESENTATION

KR is the representation of machines thinking or AI agent's intelligent behavior as a response to a particular situation [17]. Real-world knowledge is expressed by KR. This represented knowledge is used by computers for natural language processing and the method of medical diagnosis. Information representation not only preserves data in a database but also helps an intelligent machine to benefit from that knowledge and experience so it can act like humans intelligently [18, 19].

7.4.2   TYPES OF KNOWLEDGE

Knowledge is understanding or knowledge acquired through the experience of facts, situations, and information. The knowledge base is the core component of knowledge-based agents. It is expressed in the form of KB (Table 7.1; Figure 7.1).

TABLE 7.1   Knowledge in AI System

Knowledge	Description
Object	All the facts about objects in the context of our world.
Facts	Facts are the real-world realities and what we represent.
Events	Events are the behavior of our environment that occur.
Performance	Performance describes conduct that requires knowledge of how to do things.
Meta-knowledge	It is an understanding of what we know.

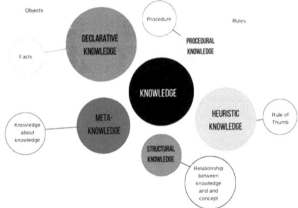

FIGURE 7.1   Types of knowledge in AI.

There are various types of knowledge representation in AI as mentioned in the following subsections.

7.4.2.1   DECLARATIVE KNOWLEDGE REPRESENTATION

The process of understanding something that includes facts, objects, and concepts is declarative knowledge (DK). It is also represented in sentences which are declarative. DK is easier than the language for procedures. It is part of the knowledge that stores the facts about the situation in the memory. This representation can be used for finding the relations between the things and different events.

7.4.2.2 PROCEDURAL KNOWLEDGE REPRESENTATION

Procedural knowledge (PK) is a form of knowledge that is responsible for understanding how to carry out something [20]. It discuss about how to do a particular task. Any activity involving rules, methods, procedures, ideologues, etc., may be applied directly to it. PK depends on the assignment on which it can be applied. It is also called as task, practical or imperative knowledge.

7.4.2.3 META-KNOWLEDGE REPRESENTATION

Meta-knowledge is called knowledge representation about the knowledge. The word is used to explain objects that identify information, such as tags, models, and taxonomies. Not only it discuss about the acquisition of knowledge about the task, it also deals about its origin, where it can be applied, what all the necessities for the task, what are all the information needed by others and how to utilize one's own knowledge. Several scholarly fields including bibliography, and epistemology are also called meta-knowledge.

7.4.2.4 HEURISTIC KNOWLEDGE REPRESENTATION

Heuristic knowledge represents the knowledge of certain experts in a case or subject. It is a method that is most probably faster than the classic methods. It is used to find approximate solutions for the problems. This is because one among accuracy, optimality, precision or completeness is the tradeoff for speed. Heuristic expertise is thumb rules based on prior experiences, approach understanding, and which are fine to work but not guaranteed.

7.4.2.5 *STRUCTURAL KNOWLEDGE REPRESENTATION*

Structural knowledge (SK) is a fundamental problem-solving knowledge. It defines relationships between different concepts, such as something's group, type, and part. The upcoming section describes the relationship between Decision support and Knowledge representation.

7.4.3 *DECISION SUPPORT SYSTEM*

A decision support system (DSS) is an information system that works with software programs which is used to facilitate judgments, courses of action, and a support system for an organization [9, 10]. DSS acts via data analysis and compiling the information inferred from it. Medical data includes various medical information about the patient's health conditions (Figure 7.2).

FIGURE 7.2 Decision support system (DSS).

DSS is targeted at low organized problems that are traditionally faced by high-level officials. DSS aims to combine the use of models or computational approaches with conventional functions for accessing and retrieving data. In particular, DSS focuses on characteristics that make them easy to use in an interactive mode by non-computer individuals. DSS stresses versatility and adaptability to accommodate environmental shifts and user-oriented decisions.

7.4.4 RELATIONSHIP BETWEEN DECISION SUPPORT AND KNOWLEDGE REPRESENTATION

Numerous researchers are investigating the structure of decision support and representation of knowledge. In Table 7.2, the relationship between the decision support and knowledge representation is given.

TABLE 7.2   Relationship between the Decision Support and Knowledge Representation

DSS	KR	References
CDSSs form part of a toolkit for information management that a healthcare organization may use to provide the "right knowledge to the right people in the right form at the right time."	Information management in healthcare organizations is a practice that promotes the competitive advantage of an organization through more productive use of its knowledge assets in a highly dynamic environment, where medical knowledge changes rapidly and where clinicians and patients engage in dispersed and collaborative processes.	[1, 2]
CDSSs have two tasks of knowledge management: one is a process-oriented activity that clarifies the priorities of the organization, the flow of information and the workflow, the roles and responsibilities, and the patterns of contact and alignment of the care process under which a CDSS system must function.	The role of information-modeling in which modelers represent the medical knowledge that helps the CDSS during the care process to provide effective decision-support services.	[3, 4]
In introducing CDS, the key challenge is not so much to try to incorporate CDS into the current workflow as it is to handle the ongoing organizational development process caused by the CDS intervention.	The knowledge-modeling task includes elicitation, representation, sharing, evolution, and distribution of knowledge (or knowledge-based DS) to users.	[5]

TABLE 7.2 *(Continued)*

DSS	KR	References
A significant purpose of CDSSs is to generate strategies that improve the behaviors of clinicians, with the ultimate aim of helping clinicians internalize these changes—an explicit-to-tacit transition.	It is a complicated method to extract information from experts. A variety of methodologies focused on personal construct psychology, such as the repertory grid method.	[6]

7.4.5   FUNDAMENTALS OF KNOWLEDGE REPRESENTATION

The following components of an artificial intelligence system are used to display intelligent behavior: learning, perception, representation of information and reasoning, planning, and execution.

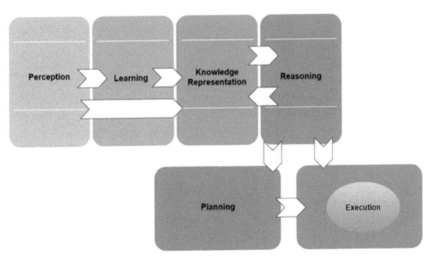

FIGURE 7.3   Knowledge representation process.

Figure 7.3 demonstrates how an AI system can communicate with the real world and what elements enable it to demonstrate intelligence. The perception portion of the AI system retrieves data from its environment. It may be visual, audio, or sensory feedback in another type. The learning aspect is responsible for learning from data obtained by the actions of perception. The key components of the complete cycle are the expression of knowledge and reasoning. Such two elements are involved in showing the intelligence of man-like computers. These two elements are independent of each other, but they are also combined. Planning and execution rely on evaluating the representation and reasoning of knowledge.

7.5   CLINICAL DECISIONAL SUPPORT SYSTEM WITH ELECTRONIC HEALTH RECORDS (EHR)

Due to the need for automation, there is an increase in the utilization of IoT healthcare devices, handheld devices, smart watches, the volume of Electronic Health Records (EHR) are increasing exponentially. Electronic Medical Record (EMR) is an electronic version of a patient's medical history, which automates the access to personal clinical information and streamlines the clinician's workflow. The track record of the patients and the availability of healthcare data helps in making better clinical decisions and provide better care for the patients.

To reduce the clinical variations, duplicative results, and to avoid clinical complications, a machine learning-based Clinical Decision Support (CDS) tools are used. This helps in sifting large amount of HER data which helps in suggesting the treatment steps, alert the caretakers regarding the patients which they fail to see and supports in reducing the problems that occurs due to the medication interactions. This CDS improves the quality of the care there by reducing the errors and the clinical adverse problems. EHR and medical data set given as an input to the CDS tools to streamline the workflow of the treatment. CDS tools not only helps in clinical decision makings, it also provides a path to user-friendly, effective protocols for alarm alerts.

False alarm and the burnout that occurs in the clinical trials are seems to be the drawbacks that may occur in few cases when CDS is implemented which obviously have the direct impact over the patients as they may be handled with false information.

The CDS tool supports all the clinicians, patients, caretakers of patients and administrative personnel in providing the useful information about the particular person or patient on time which aids in providing the right decision at the right time. This includes reminders for the caretakers for medicating the patients at the right time, guideline support for the clinical trials, data report making and summary producing in the prescribed format.

The main advantage of giving EHR data to the CDS tools are:

- Drug suggestion, allergy prediction, and prior clinical error detection reduces the medication errors and improve the quality of healthcare services.
- EHR helps to physicians to identify and access the most current information about the patient's problem before giving treatment.
- Clinical scoring tools and pre-test calculators that are embedded inside the EHR provides the patient specific information or medical record which can be utilized by the physicians for making the clinical decisions for the particular patients.
- EHR data are used to create an efficient alarm/alerts to notify the physicians or helps in triggering the predetermined orders. A recent study that is done on pediatric patients reveals that the patients who are between 10 and 17 years undergone usual care and the care using the EHR-based CDS and the blood pressures are measured at both the cases. It is observed that out of 31,579 patients who were undergone care 1.7% were identified with hypertension and they were experiencing about 2 years. Also, 17.1% of patients are hypertensive and are referred for controlling the weight through regular exercise. Whereas in usual care only 3.9% of patients were found to be with hypertension who were referred for counseling.
- Providing EHR data to CDS at the time of testing or diagnostician reduces the false positive and true negative errors.

7.6   USE CASES OF CLINICAL DECISION SUPPORT SYSTEM

The basic principles of the clinical decision support system is applied for caretaking the patients through different number of ways; right from the detection of disease or infection to the prediction on all the insights of cancer therapies through personal care.

1.   A hospital in Alabama states that the sepsis mortality rates in their hospital is been reduced approximately 53% when surveillance

algorithm is implemented. The real-time analytics used in the hospital have alerted the providers in finding the new diagnoses of sepsis or finding the vital signs, and also the system provides the alert/reminders to the physicians about the optimal treatment practices for treating the deadly patients.

2. Mayo Clinic uses the clinical decision support tool that supports the hospital nurses in delivering complete as well as accurate screenings of the patients through phone for seeking advice or appointments. This computerized decision software completely guides the nurses by using a series of standardized questions that are based on the current healthcare guidelines thereby ensuring that they will not miss any information regarding the patient's health.

3. Medical Center named Harding University and Unity Health-White County has combined the clinical decision support system software with the genetic test data and found that the hospital readmissions are reduced by 52%, which further reduces the visits of ED by 42%. They have also tested drug-drug and drug-gene interaction on high-risk patients and found that they were save around $43K per capita.

4. The CDS application developed by Yale and Mayo Clinic is used for patients who are presenting with head injuries uses the industry guidelines for providing the useful information to patients during the evaluation of the injury. This application explains the decision treatments to the respective patients thereby reducing the count of unnecessary CT scans.

7.7 CONCLUSION

Thus this chapter discuss about the decision support system and the knowledge representation in healthcare which plays a vital role in obtaining the proper knowledge and decision support on the wide range of available medical data. Also, it is observed that the integration of DSS in the medical field improves the quality of medical care, eradication of adversarial events thereby supporting the medical team members to provide efficient medications.

KEYWORDS

- clinical decision support
- decision support
- decision support system
- electronic health records
- electronic medical record
- healthcare
- knowledge representation

REFERENCES

1. Stefanelli, M., (2004). Knowledge and process management in health care organizations. *Methods of Information in Medicine, 43*(5), 525–535.

2. Berg, M., & Toussaint, P., (2003). The mantra of modeling and the forgotten powers of paper: A sociotechnical view on the development of process-oriented ICT in health care. *International Journal of Medical Informatics, 69*(2, 3), 223–234.

3. Gaines, B. R., & Shaw, M. L. G., (1996). WebGrid: Knowledge modeling and inference through the world wide web. In: *Proceedings of the Tenth Knowledge Acquisition for Knowledge-Based Systems Workshop, 65*, pp. 1–14.

4. Martinez-Franco, A. I., Sanchez-Mendiola, M., Mazon-Ramirez, J. J., Hernandez-Torres, I., Rivero-Lopez, C., Spicer, T., & Martinez-Gonzalez, A., (2018). Diagnostic accuracy in family medicine residents using a clinical decision support system (DXplain): A randomized-controlled trial. *Diagnosis (Berlin, Germany), 5*(2), 71–76. https://doi.org/10.1515/dx-2017-0045.

5. Haberman, S., Feldman, J., Merhi, Z. O., Markenson, G., Cohen, W., & Minkoff, H., (2009). Effect of clinical-decision support on documentation compliance in an electronic medical record. *Obstetrics and Gynecology, 114*(2), 311–317. https://doi.org/10.1097/AOG.0b013e3181af2cb0.

6. Cook, D. A., Teixeira, M. T., Heale, B. S., Cimino, J. J., & Del Fiol, G., (2017). Context-sensitive decision support (info buttons) in electronic health records: A systematic review. *Journal of the American Medical Informatics Association: JAMIA, 24*(2), 460–468. https://doi.org/10.1093/jamia/ocw104.

7. Jacob, V., Thota, A. B., Chattopadhyay, S. K., Njie, G. J., Proia, K. K., Hopkins, D. P., Ross, M. N., et al., (2017). Cost and economic benefit of clinical decision support systems for cardiovascular disease prevention: A community guide systematic review. *Journal of the American Medical Informatics Association: JAMIA, 24*(3), 669–676. https://doi.org/10.1093/jamia/ocw160.

8. Kilsdonk, E., Peute, L. W., & Jaspers, M. W., (2017). Factors influencing implementation success of guideline-based clinical decision support systems: A

systematic review and gaps analysis. *International Journal of Medical Informatics, 98*, 56–64. https://doi.org/10.1016/j.ijmedinf.2016.12.001.

9. Laka, M., Milazzo, A., & Merlin, T., (2021). Factors that impact the adoption of clinical decision support systems (CDSS) for antibiotic management. *International Journal of Environmental Research and Public Health, 18*(4), 1901. https://doi.org/10.3390/ijerph18041901.

10. Guo, X., Swenor, B. K., Smith, K., Boland, M. V., & Goldstein, J. E., (2021). Developing an ophthalmology clinical decision support system to identify patients for low vision rehabilitation. *Translational Vision Science & Technology, 10*(3), 24. https://doi.org/10.1167/tvst.10.3.24.

11. Schaarup, C., Pape-Haugaard, L. B., & Hejlesen, O. K., (2018). Models used in clinical decision support systems supporting healthcare professionals treating chronic wounds: Systematic literature review. *JMIR Diabetes, 3*(2), e11.

12. Contreras, I., & Vehi, J., (2018). Artificial intelligence for diabetes management and decision support: Literature review. *Journal of Medical Internet Research, 20*(5), e10775.

13. Sutton, R. T., Pincock, D., Baumgart, D. C., Sadowski, D. C., Fedorak, R. N., & Kroeker, K. I., (2020). An overview of clinical decision support systems: Benefits, risks, and strategies for success. *NPJ Digital Medicine, 3*(1), 1–10.

14. Mehta, N., & Pandit, A., (2018). Concurrence of big data analytics and healthcare: A systematic review. *International Journal of Medical Informatics, 114*, 57–65.

15. Shahmoradi, L., Safadari, R., & Jimma, W., (2017). Knowledge management implementation and the tools utilized in healthcare for evidence-based decision making: A systematic review. *Ethiopian Journal of Health Sciences, 27*(5), 541–558.

16. Jayaratne, M., Nallaperuma, D., De Silva, D., Alahakoon, D., Devitt, B., Webster, K. E., & Chilamkurti, N., (2019). A data integration platform for patient-centered e-healthcare and clinical decision support. *Future Generation Computer Systems, 92*, 996–2008.

17. Sohail, M. N., Jiadong, R., Uba, M. M., & Irshad, M., (2019). A comprehensive looks at data mining techniques contributing to medical data growth: A survey of researcher reviews. In: *Recent Developments in Intelligent Computing, Communication and Devices* (pp. 21–26).

18. Wu, W. T., Li, Y. J., Feng, A. Z., et al., (2021). Data mining in clinical big data: The frequently used databases, steps, and methodological models. *Military Med. Res., 8*, 44. https://doi.org/10.1186/s40779-021-00338-z.

19. Maikel, L. K., Leonardo, B. F., Michele, K. S., Bruna, R., Pedro, H. U., Nicola, L. B., & Leonel, P. C. T., (2021). Data mining in healthcare: Applying strategic intelligence techniques to depict 25 years of research development. *International Journal of Environmental Research and Public Health, 18*, 1–20.

20. Jayaraman, P. P., Forkan, A. R. M., Morshed, A., Haghighi, P. D., & Kang, Y., (2020). Healthcare 4.0: A review of frontiers in digital health. In: *Wiley Interdisciplinary Reviews: Data Mining and Knowledge Discovery* (Vol. 10, p. e1350). Wiley: Hoboken, NJ, USA.

CHAPTER 8

Roadmap of AI and IoMT in Smart Healthcare: Current Applications and Future Perspectives

SWAMYNATHAN RAMAKRISHNAN,[1] S. JIJITHA,[2] and T. AMUDHA[2]

[1]*Amity University Dubai, Dubai International Academic City, Dubai, UAE*

[2]*Department of Computer Applications, Bharathiar University, Coimbatore, Tamil Nadu, India*

ABSTRACT

Artificial intelligence (AI) refers to the field of science aimed at providing machines with the capability to behave smart and perform functionalities. In the healthcare industry, AI is indulged in diverse applications such as recommendations for treatments, diagnosis and prediction, personalized treatments, surgical assistance and engagements with patients. The IoMT ecosystem is focused on the generation, collection, analysis, and transmission of healthcare data to medical professionals, enabling remote connectivity between patients and physicians. IoMT offers excellent remote patient management solutions with greater accuracy in diagnosis and lowered costs as well. The coexistence of AI and IoMT can play a better role in providing Smart Healthcare services to society. This chapter discusses the strength of the two powerful technologies, AI and IoMT in improving healthcare services and presents a Smart healthcare framework using AI and IoMT.

Internet of Medical Things in Smart Healthcare: Post-COVID-19 Pandemic Scenario.
Saravanan Krishnan, PhD and Aboobucker Ilmudeen, PhD (Eds.)

8.1   INTRODUCTION

Artificial intelligence (AI) refers to the field of science aimed at providing machines with the capability to behave smart and perform functionalities such as logic, perception, reasoning, learning, planning, and decision-making. AI is emerged from the idea 'Can machines think?' by Alan Turing. Even though Turing dismissed the philosophical idea of thinking machines, the idea persisted and developed into a stage where machines are capable of learning, predicting, and reasoning and can be trained with the help of data. There are very few streams AI did not indulge into, like where there is a bulk of data, AI can be entertained. AI is flourished in the branches of Robotics, Machine Learning (ML), Neural Networks (NN), Expert Systems, Fuzzy Logic, and Natural Language Processing (NLP) [21, 33].

Internet of Things (IoT) has drawn a wide reputation in society, as it is a breakthrough in the life of humans by realizing the fact of communication among any type of objects, machines, and everything. IoT symbolizes the infrastructure of physical things in the real world and associated sensors with seamless connectivity over the World Wide Web. IoT-enabled things will continuously collect and share the information perceived from the environment with the software systems and designated experts. AI and IoT together focus on creating a super-smart world, as these state-of-the-art technologies open new horizons for smart healthcare, smart homes, smart cities, and also in many other vital domains such as smart vehicles and transport, smart energy systems, smart agriculture, water resources management, pollution monitoring and control and so on.

Internet of Medical Things (IoMT) is a well-connected network of medical appliances, wearable gadgets, healthcare systems, software tools, and medical services. The IoMT ecosystem is focused on the generation, collection, analysis, and transmission of healthcare data to medical professionals, enabling remote connectivity between patients and physicians. IoMT offers excellent remote patient management solutions with greater accuracy in diagnosis and lowered costs as well. Powered with a 24x7 patient monitoring capability and live communication of health-related information to the required specialists, IoMT opens up promising avenues in the field of healthcare. The coexistence of AI and IoMT can play a better role in providing Smart Healthcare services to society. AI can understand and act upon a very big amount of data generated, stored, and streamed from the connected 'Medical Things.'

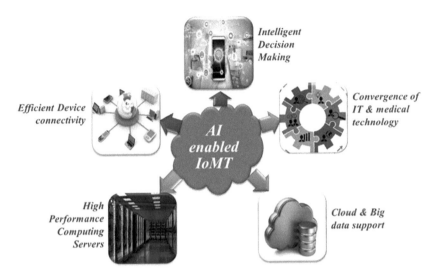

FIGURE 8.1   AI-enabled IoMT.

Figure 8.1 depicts the characteristics of IoMT environment empowered by AI. The environment provides seamless connectivity among smart medical devices with cloud services, high performance computing facility for real-time data processing, intelligent computing and decision making by machine learning algorithms. This chapter aims to discuss the strength of the two potential technologies, AI and IoMT in improving healthcare services. It provides an extensive review of the connected healthcare applications backed up by Artificial Intelligence, highlights the need for a conglomeration of AI and IoMT in further improving the medical services, and presents certain viewpoints about the paradigm shift in healthcare services through technological advancements and smart infrastructure.

8.2   REVIEW ON AI AND IOMT

Meherwar et al. [15] have surveyed the machine learning algorithms for disease diagnostics and provide a comparison of different machine learning algorithms involved in disease diagnosis and tries to identify the suitability of machine learning algorithms in disease diagnosis and decision making. Different diseases are considered and for each disease, machine learning techniques are applied and with the estimated accuracy.

It is concluded that for Support Vector Machine method is found suitable for detection of heart disease, functional tree for liver disease diagnosis, Naïve Bayes for diabetes, and rough set theory for dengue disease.

On intelligent patient monitoring, the importance of smart medical devices in monitoring the patients admitted in acute care environments like ICU or with ventilator support. The primary challenges noted are the legal and ethical concerns about data security and privacy in providing access to patient information, which requires strict guidelines and regulations. Debleena et al. [4] reviewed a chapter on AI in drug discovery and development and highlights the revolutionary aspects of AI in pharmaceuticals. The chapter addressed AI applied to different streams of pharma industries, comprising novel drug discovery, development, repurposing, productivity, clinical trials, and also discussed the AI tools in the field of pharmaceuticals and allied disciplines.

Olga et al. [16] discussed the methods involved in drug discovery of antifungal, anti-tropical, and antibacterial diseases, sensing of antiquorum, antibiofilm, anticancer, and neuroprotectors. Two various complementary approaches to be implemented in drug discovery are classical pharmacology and reverse pharmacology. Conventional pharmacology is termed phenotypic drug discovery that forms the foundation for drug discovery and reverse pharmacology and called as designated target-based drug discovery. Xin et al. [22] reviewed the concepts of AI in computer-based drug discovery. It includes the description of machine learning principles and their application in medical chemistry. Along with the basic techniques and notes for application, a review was also carried out on the current scenario of AI in assisting pharmaceuticals in drug discovery. The major challenges pointed out are quality enhancement, acquisition of relevant data, and improving the utility and fidelity of molecular representation of drugs. Paolo et al. [17] published a survey paper about smart surgical tools and augmenting devices. The chapter describes the overall composition of robotic systems for computer-assisted surgeries and gives examples of various classes of devices.

Vishnu et al. [19] presented a detailed outline of IoMT based on mobile health, smart medical centers, smart treatment of chronic diseases, remote healthcare, and tracking sensors. Also, states that emerge of IoT leads to the boom of IoMT in the personalized healthcare sector. The main concerns dealt with are security and privacy since the medical data is extra sensitive compared with other data. Ravi et al. [18] wrote an article on the challenges, roles, and application of IoMT orthopedic in COVID-19 pandemic. The background check on various services of IoMT and the application of those services for orthopedic patients are mentioned. Maria et al. [14] drew up a study on security threats and their prevention in IoMT edge network infrastructure. The prominent challenges of technology in any stream are security, privacy, and safety. Novel standards for security measures are essential for the safety of any network, and the try is to lay a platform for the research advances in safeguarding IoMT edge networks. The objectives addressed in the chapter are confidentiality, integrity, non-repudiation, authentication, authorization, and availability.

Adarsha et al. [1] discussed user experience, IoMT, current trends in healthcare, and the limitations in the connected health ecosystem. The adoption of IoT in the medical field is also a part of this study. The user group includes patients, doctors, administrators, nurses, policy providers, etc., and their user experience should be positive for the connected health ecosystem to grow. Security concerns, patient privacy, nonexistence of standards, banning unwanted exchange of data are the challenges pointed out. Fadi et al. [7] published a survey on the present and forthcoming trends of intelligence in the IoMT era. IoMT applications are generically divided into object-centric and body-centric applications with each subdivision of indoor and outdoor activity monitoring. The IoMT components discussed are data acquisition from IoMT components, IoMT gateway, and server/cloud service. Open research issues discussed are energy utilization, secured storage of data, data privacy, intelligent decision support systems, and effective networking.

Ikram et al. [9] published an analysis of a decade of IoT in health-care applications. Aimed to portray the existing picture of IoMT and the enhancements needed for critical diseases and some challenges which are not resolved in IoMT. IoMT was used for monitoring of limbs for restless leg syndrome in 2010; monitoring and control of rural healthcare in 2011; the identification of E-health apps in 2012; IoT-based M-health and secure remote monitoring in 2013; heart sound classification in 2014; stress detection in drivers in 2015; cardiac health monitoring in 2016; decision making system (DMS) for heart attack in 2017; M-healthcare for human activity recognition (HAR) in 2018; and the timeline ended in 2019 with breast cancer classification framework in the analysis. The challenges pointed out are personal data security, reinforcing patient privacy, sustaining connectivity, moderating personnel error.

Gulraiz et al. [8] discussed the applications, advantages, and challenges of IoMT in healthcare purview. The benefaction of IoT in the healthcare domain, its application and challenges in the medical field are noted along with future challenges. With references to the review, the challenges described are flexibility of IoT and security. There is also a point mentioned to close the gap between doctors, patients, and healthcare services and the introduction of IoMT is a good way to reduce that gap.

8.3 AI APPLICATIONS IN HEALTHCARE

In the healthcare industry, AI is indulged in diverse applications such as recommendations for treatments, diagnosis, and prediction, personalized treatments, surgical assistance, engagements with patients, etc. In this pandemic situation, the AI-Machine Learning-Deep Learning combo is proven to be successful in drug discovery, drug repurposing, and treatment planning. AI device applications amalgamate well with the IoMT, which includes remote patient monitoring, tracking medication orders, administrations, wearable health devices, hospital beds with sensors, etc. The collection of smart medical devices, from fitness wearable to smart hospital devices to implantable medical devices [21, 27, 33] in IoMT forms a network helpful for both the patients and doctors. Some of the streams where AI is flourished in the fields of healthcare are given in Figure 8.2 and discussed in the following subsections.

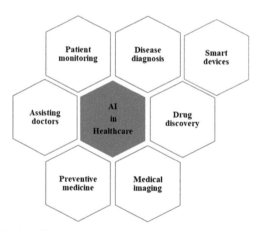

FIGURE 8.2   AI in healthcare.

8.3.1 ARTIFICIAL INTELLIGENCE IN DISEASE DIAGNOSIS

Disease diagnosis is one of the major areas of AI in the medical field. AI disease prediction and diagnosis techniques help in improving precision in diagnostic procedures and also enable autodiagnosis with better accuracy [10, 20]. Some of the AI disease diagnosis and prediction techniques include Machine Learning algorithms, Fuzzy Logic, etc. In most AI techniques, the diagnosis is based on structured and unstructured data. In the case of structured data, analysis is generally performed using ML techniques/algorithms, whereas unstructured data are analyzed by NLP. The credibility of ML in the medical industry is that it can handle huge datasets better than the capability of humans and also convert the analyzed data into better insights for the medical practitioners [13]. The most commonly used machine learning models are given in Figure 8.3. In the classification model, it simply determines either or not like a yes or no category. Clustering is used to find distinctive patterns in a dataset. Regression is used to find out the association between variables and predict the result. Regression and classification come under the supervised learning category, and clustering is in unsupervised learning.

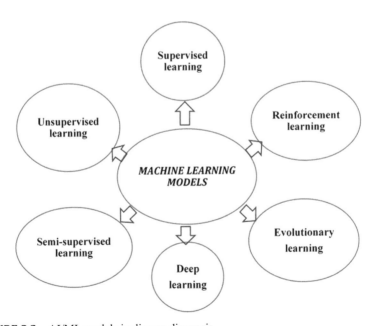

FIGURE 8.3   AI/ML models in disease diagnosis.

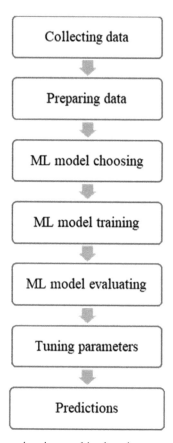

FIGURE 8.4   Medical diagnosis using machine learning.

The disease prediction includes various steps like collecting, analyzing, and preparing data, choosing the suitable ML model, training the model with the processed data, evaluation and tuning, and recording the predicted result [20], as given in Figure 8.4.

8.3.2   *ARTIFICIAL INTELLIGENCE IN PREVENTIVE MEDICINE*

Preventive medicine is the practice in the medical field to prevent disease, such as performing regular tests will help not to get caught off guard by disease. The application of AI in preventive medicine helps in early diagnosis and timely prevention. AI uses Deep Learning algorithms to meet the expectations of preventive medicine with Big Data [11]. There are so many applications that help in predicting types of cancers. In this pandemic situation, more people and hospitals in India prefer the telehealth system where the patients can call the doctor and share their health-related information, clarify queries and get recommendations from doctors. Some of the popular AI apps [26] are given in Table 8.1.

TABLE 8.1   AI Apps for Disease Prediction

AI app for Disease prediction	App Description
WebMD	It provides the features like a symptom checker, helps to locate a hospital or doctor using physician directory, can access medically reviewed information on a specific condition, and provide details of medicine/drugs, latest news, and medication reminders for patients.
ADA	It is a symptom checking and diagnosis app for any type of ailments.
Hucu.ai	It is a free messaging network with real-time risk reporting mostly used by nursing operators and post-acute care physicians.
SkinVision	This apps helps in detecting skin cancer.
Sens.ly	It is an avatar of a virtual reality nursing assistant. They ask the patients to carry out check-ups and report back to the respective medical practitioners.
Babylon	It is a doctor booking app.

8.3.3   ARTIFICIAL INTELLIGENCE IN PATIENT MONITORING

An intelligent patient monitoring system comprises all the details of the patients including current health status to latest lab results [5]. Sensors, smart machines, etc., can be used for patient monitoring. In this pandemic situation, people feel unsafe to go to hospitals. Remote patient monitoring looks like a better way to deal with such situations and many companies worldwide are developing different start-ups for patient monitoring [32].

- **London-based Babylon Health** introduced an AI chatbot that helps in providing information on the patients through Q&A sessions.
- **AiCure** provided a platform where the treatment progress can be measured by using facial expressions utilizing facial recognition and computer vision algorithms.

- **Eko** is a remote heart monitoring system using AI and sound.
- **Myia Labs** uses wearable devices like Apple Watch and Fitbit to monitor patients and then applies ML to predict relapses before it happens.
- **Current Health** has introduced an AI-powered arm band for remote patient monitoring.
- **Ten3T**, a Bengaluru-based company has developed a cicer patch for remote monitoring of patients.
- **NuvoAir** and **Hyfe** are AI-based applications for monitoring respiratory conditions of a patients.

The most commonly used tools in patient monitoring are wearable devices with sensors. There are [28]:

- Wearable fitness trackers like wrist bands which will keep an eye on the user's physical activity and heart rate.
- Smart health watches
- Wearable ECG monitors
- Wearable blood pressure monitors
- Biosensors – self-adhesive patch
- Glucose trackers for diabetic patients
- Wearable/implantable defibrillators for monitoring heart patients
- Q-collar is used to protect brain from sports traumas and concussions
- Electromyography (EMG) sensors are used for monitoring stroke patients
- Intelligent asthma monitoring wearable technology for asthma patients
- Patient's depression can be monitored through an app developed by Apple
- Smart contact lenses
- Pulse oximeter to measure the oxygen level of blood
- Pulse rate sensors
- Smart thermometer

8.3.4   ARTIFICIAL INTELLIGENCE IN DRUG DISCOVERY

Modern AI is the best prospect to be successful in the field of drug discovery since AI mixed its elements in the world of chemistry and biology. So the chances of AI having a major intervention in the pharmaceuticals field is inevitable. There are so many researches going on to disclose small molecular therapies in the fields of neural disorders, gastroenterology, oncology, etc. New drugs are under wraps for cardiovascular disease and diabetes. AI is learning through various ML techniques, like kernel ridge regression (KRR), Gaussian process regression (GPR), and neural networks (NN), about the atomistic potentials and other properties in quantum mechanical properties. Deep Learning is used in drug discovery which in turn uses the techniques of Artificial Neural Networks (ANN). ANN involves Multilayer Perception Network (MPN), Recurrent Neural Network (RNN), and Convolutional Neural Networks (CNN) [6].

AI is ready to ease the burden off the pharmaceutical industry too. From helping in drug design to increase in productivity, AI also helps in understanding the molecular structure of complex drugs easily. In the pharma industry, AI looks promising because it can address the main problem of clinical failure rates [10]. Due to the sensitive nature of the field, the pharmaceutical industry is expecting positive and promising signs from AI, to answer and solve some of the intricate problems in chemistry, to pull through. AI can be applied in different subfields in pharma like clinical trials, pharmaceutical manufacturing, pharmaceutical product management, drug discovery, and pharmaceutical product development. AI can contribute to several phases of drug discovery, which include drug design, chemical synthesis, polypharmacology, drug repurposing, drug screening, running trials, and testing. AI-based nano-robots are also being used for drug delivery. Figure 8.5 highlighted certain AI tools for drug discovery.

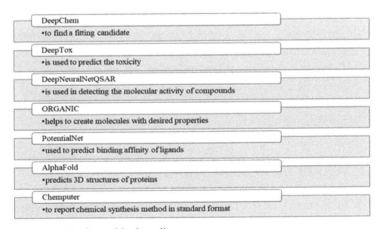

FIGURE 8.5   AI Tools used in drug discovery.

8.3.5 ARTIFICIAL INTELLIGENCE IN CLINICAL ASSISTANCE

AI helps the physicians by reducing misdiagnosis, summarizing patient records, suggesting procedures suitable for each patient like personalized medical care, monitoring the patients and their progress [34]. AI-enabled smart surgical instruments use an embedded or external controller to guide the surgery by sensing or using images. In much more complex cases robots or machines can carry out surgical techniques [24]. The most potential advances of AI in clinical assistance are:

- AI-assisted robotic surgery
- Virtual nursing/medical assistants
- Scan image analysis
- Maintaining electronic health records

AI virtual medical assistance applications [30] are:

- **Nuance and Suki** helps in medical record navigation
- **Robin Healthcare** helps in medical transcription
- **MedWhat** is an AI-based personal medical assistant app for searching medical information

AI applications in surgical robotics [31] are:

- **Raven Robot, PR2 Robot,** and **STAR robot** handles the Automation of Suturing
- **Surgical skills evaluation using ML** to analyze completion time of the surgery, speed, depth perception, path length, smoothness, and curvature.
- **ML for improved surgical robotics** – robots made up of flexible material and assist minimally invasive surgeries.
- **IDEAL-X system** is an ML for surgical workflow modeling and generating reports.

8.4 INTERNET OF MEDICAL THINGS

IoMT is the network of interconnected medical devices that can communicate with each other. IoMT is a collection of medical sensors/devices, software applications, healthcare systems, and services. It includes daily use wearables to stand-alone devices. The remote healthcare system of IoMT is much appreciated and stated as a "game-changer technology" [35]. The retail market of IoMT is very huge. Due to the rampant of the covid-19 virus, the market is down, that is not the case with IoMT. Since the hospital visits for other ailments are to be controlled due to the pandemic, people started taking care of their health by themselves. Even government suggests having a thermometer and a pulse-oximeter at every home for personal use. A wide range of IoMT devices can be used, for body use or home use, or community use, for hospital and clinical establishment correlated with real-time data, telehealth, etc., which in turn helps in reducing unnecessary visits to the hospital [25, 29]. Due to the rise in the availability of smart medical devices in the market, the imploration of having appropriate regulatory standards and monitoring systems is understandable.

8.4.1   WEARABLE DEVICES AND MEDICAL SENSORS

Sensors are more familiar with the Internet of Things. Since sensors can read different kinds of signals, it is a term widely used in IoMT. The versatility of sensor-embedded medical devices is that they can be used at homes and hospitals. Complicated sensors like implantable sensors are preferably carried out in hospitals. They are sensors embedded catheters, embedded sensors used to be implanted in body cavity and other embedded sensors which come in contact with body fluids [27]. Charles [3] published a paper on sensors in medicine in 1999. Since then, the practicality of sensors and their uses are quite relevant. The sensor developments were in the beginning stage but will go a long way. Some of the sensors are glucose sensor for diabetic patients, continuous monitoring system, weight and urine analyzing (glucose concentrations) toilets, microtool for reconstructing ultrasound images of heart, vessels, etc., automatic system for detecting bio-weapons, beginning of smart cardiac pacemakers, biochip photosensor as an artificial retina, electronic nose to catch odors of growing bacteria in ear, nose, throat, and auditory sensors. Figure 8.6 depicts wearable medical devices.

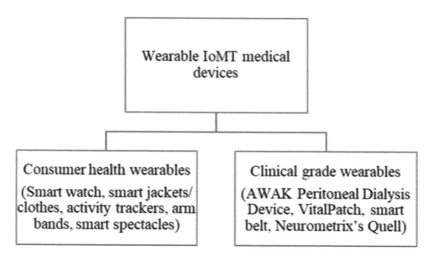

FIGURE 8.6   On-body wearable medical devices.

8.4.1.1   CONSUMER HEALTH WEARABLES

Consumer health wearables will help the user to stay checked about their BP, level of oxygen in the blood, water content in the body, etc. This will help the user to stay alert when the wearable gives notifications like "water content low in the body, chances of dehydration," and the user can immediately take steps to address the warning issued by the wearable device. These wearables are meant for personal use, for fitness tracking as well as health monitoring like smart armbands, smart watches, smart clothes/jackets, martial art vests, ski googles, activity trackers, etc.

8.4.1.2   CLINICAL GRADE WEARABLES

Clinical health wearables will help the doctors, nurses, and caretakers to keep an eye on the patients admitted to critical care units and also to those patients who require continuous monitoring and medical assistance. They are mainly for clinical/hospital uses. These wearables have to be certified and approved by the common medical standards available.

Implantable sensors are mostly used in hospitals under the guidance of medical practitioners, and they have to clear the common standards of medical assessment. Implantable sensors supposedly work with no power.

Sensors in catheters and body cavities are also to be inserted into the body using the tip of a catheter through an incision. They are less complex than implantable sensors. They can function for a maximum of two hours with an external power supply. Thermistors located in the catheter measure the blood flow in different locations of the heart. Figure 8.7 depicts the implantable medical devices and Table 8.2 describes the functionality of various medical sensors and devices.

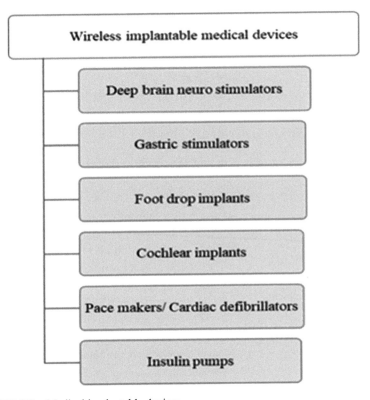

FIGURE 8.7   Medical implantable devices.

TABLE 8.2   Medical Sensors and Devices

Medical sensors / Devices	Description
Piezoelectric polymer sensors	Used in vibration detection and can be used in pacemakers.
Catheter ablation Sensors	Used to ablate or burn out dead tissue.

TABLE 8.2 *(Continued)*

Medical sensors / Devices	Description
Silicon MEMS-based disposable Pressure Intrauterine pressure (IUP) Sensors	Measures the contraction pressure exerted during child birth. They are inserted into the amniotic sac and removed during delivery.
Body cavity sensors	Measure the body temperature from oral as well as rectal probes.
Micro-thermocouple sensors	Used to get accurate temperature fast. They are flexible fine gauge thermocouples.
Disposable blood pressure sensors	Primarily employed in ICUs and during surgery to monitor blood flow and pressure
Magneto-resistive sensors in syringe pumps	For detection of medicine flow rate, full/empty syringe and occlusion
String pot position sensors	Used in the positioning of the remote surgical tool as well as patient beds while taking scans and x-rays
Very small MEMS-based accelerometers	For measuring tremors in patients with Parkinson's disease
Pyroelectric and Piezoelectric sensors	Used for study on sleep apnea
Piezo film receiver/transmitter	Detect the bubbles in infusion /syringe pumps
Piezo film sensors	Monitor patient limb activity and Rapid Eye Movement (REM), unexpected impacts, and fall detection
MEMS and load cell-based sensors	Conservation of oxygen and observe oxygen level in tanks
NTC temperature sensors	To observe body temperature
Force sensors	Measure dynamic and static loads on the prosthesis.
Position sensors	Monitor the body position of the patients.
Vibration sensors	Monitor the patient orientation and prosthetic parts.
Photo optic sensors	Measure heart rate and SpO_2 level
Smart belt	Used to detect the patient fall/slip and provides hip protection for senior citizens
Neurometrix's Quell	Neuromodulation device that pats the sensory nerves and relieves chronic pains.
VitalPatch	Monitor the patient's heart rate variations, ECG, body temperature, respiratory rate, physical activity, body posture, and fall detection.
AWAK Peritoneal Dialysis Device	A portable dialysis device for renal disease patients.

8.5   PROPOSED SMART HEALTHCARE ARCHITECTURE WITH AI AND IOMT

While IoT is establishing its root in everyday life, IoMT makes it possible in the medical field also and hence it will gradually become a non-negotiable part of people's life. IoT connects any type of generic device, and when it comes to IoMT, it connects various devices which are used in the medical and healthcare industry. Figure 8.8 depicts the smart healthcare scenario that can be realized by the effective utilization of AI and IoMT technologies. The difference in IoT with IoMT is that IoT is more focused on normal consumer grade, easy to use in day-to-day life while IoMT has its feet on clinical/hospital grade along with normal consumer grade. The notable trait is that the base of both IoT and IoMT is AI [21]. AI can collect and analyze a large amount of data which are produced with the help of IoMT devices like sensors. AI can then implement various algorithms and predict diseases at an early stage.

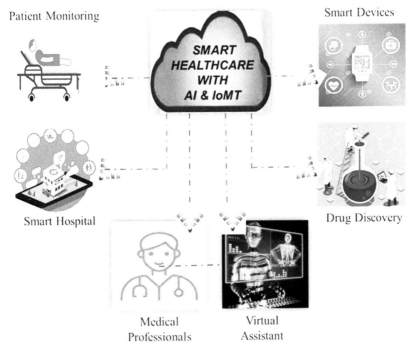

FIGURE 8.8   Smart Healthcare.

8.5.1 PROPOSED SMART HEALTHCARE ARCHITECTURE USING AI AND IOMT

It is imperative that with the help of IoMT and AI, the medical field can move forward in a much faster pitch with the technology. IoMT includes sensors and devices, which in turn collect medical data from the patient/ user. Since IoMT has its place in health maintenance and clinical care, the users have to be divided into patients and normal healthy users. AI and IoMT working together have greater advantages over the healthcare domain. People can reduce unnecessary visits to the hospital. When a person feels like having a rise in body temperature, having a smart thermometer in hand will enable the person to sense the temperature and send it to the doctor and get the medical observation at home through the IoMT network. This facility can be made easier by using Telehealth applications alongside smart medical devices. Figure 8.9 depicts the proposed AI and IoMT smart healthcare architecture with various layers and essential components in each layer.

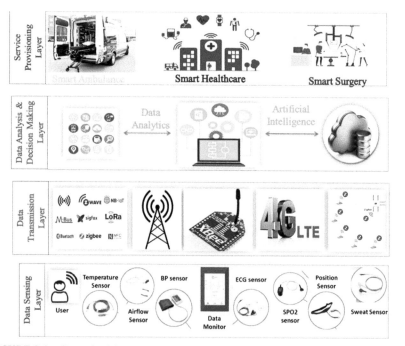

FIGURE 8.9   Smart healthcare architecture using AI and IoMT.

8.5.1.1 DATA SENSING LAYER

It is the main layer in the smart healthcare infrastructure that interacts with the physical environment. This layer collects data from the various medical sensors and devices that are inter-connected over the wired or wireless networks. Heterogenous data streaming from these connected IoMT sensors are collected and analyzed by intelligent AI techniques, which is quite challenging.

8.5.1.2 DATA TRANSMISSION LAYER

This layer in the smart healthcare infrastructure takes responsibility in performing the data communication between individual devices and sensors in IoMT environment. The users can be connected with wired broadband connections or mobile broadband connections like 3G, 4G/LTE or Wi-Fi. Short range communications can be made by using Bluetooth, M2M, RFID, Zig-Bee, and WAN.

8.5.1.3 DATA ANALYSIS AND DECISION MAKING LAYER

This layer is the core of smart healthcare using IoMT, which carries out data integration, manipulation, preprocessing, analysis and analytics, and decision making. Data analytics, machine learning, and artificial intelligence are applied here upon the huge data generated by the IoMT devices and intelligently processed to extract meaningful information, automate certain tasks, perform predictions and modeling to exhibit smart health-care solutions.

8.5.1.4 SERVICE PROVISIONING LAYER

Service provisioning layer provides as well as connects all the healthcare services such as smart hospital, smart ambulance, smart surgical provisioning, smart patient assistance and so on. The integrated healthcare data is maintained in Electronic Health Records (EHR), that can be accessed by the patients, physicians and other medical professionals, hospital networks, and other authorized members. public, organizations, corporations and they can be made aware of the operations of the smart city.

8.6   FUTURE PERSPECTIVES OF AI AND IOMT

In the future, AI and IoMT technologies are expected to have a very positive influence on the patients as well as the physicians. There will be a greater change in the healthcare practices, whereas the technology will orient towards personalized treatment planning as per the individual requirement. AI and IoMT together has a huge potential in healthcare from initial diagnosis, to patient treatment, to surgical care, to post maintenance of health. The improved benefits in the healthcare domain include the following.

- Improved quality and productivity in healthcare
- Improved patient engagement in self care
- Streamlined medical procedures and practices
- Quicker decision making
- Reduced treatment costs
- Personalized treatments

Machine Learning and Natural Language Processing provide great support in AI for handling the Bigdata generated by the IoMT devices. The advantage of ML is that it is not necessary to program a computer each time to perform a particular task. A model will be created by using the data archive for training and a well-trained model will make predictions with the real-time data provided [2]. The various ML techniques that can assist AI in healthcare-related predictions are Bayesian methods, artificial neural networks, logic programming, natural language processing, decision trees, and reinforcement learning [2]. Dimensionality reduction and feature extraction can also be applied wherever needed, in order to select only the significant attributes from the available data. Various analytics methods that can be used with healthcare data are:

- *Descriptive Analytics* – to analyze the past data of the patient and the disease history.
- *Diagnostic Analytics* – to diagnose or examine data and answer to the why question.

- *Predictive Analytics* – uses learning algorithms to understand and predict the future health concerns.
- *Prescriptive Analytics* – to make intelligent decisions with optimal outcomes.

In the future, remote patient monitoring systems will gain utmost importance where AI and IoMT will greatly help the medical practitioners to keep an eye on the discharged patients or patients with acute diseases. Over the years, specialized robots will be more common in assisting surgeons in complex surgeries and also can help the surgeons by monitoring the patients during the surgery and give notifications by using IoMT devices and sensors. AI helps in reducing the chances of getting human errors during diagnosis and also in surgical procedures. AI can also help the hospital administration in collecting patient details and maintain electronic health records of the patients. Since every component is connected in the IoMT network, it becomes quite easier to integrate the patient's previous medical history and current health information.

Smart technologies find their applications in almost every known field. They provide more flexibility and autonomy and at the same time, pose heavy challenges that are yet to be addressed.

- The data security challenges faced by IoT are much more intense with IoMT as all the data are related to patients, which requires a high level of privacy, confidentiality, integrity, authentication, and credibility of data.
- Higher chances of self-medication is a key challenge. For example, easy access to smart devices such as thermometers and pulse oximeter makes the user informative and may give the tendency to the users to opt for self-medication rather than consulting a doctor.
- Data storage is an issue related to IoMT. Devices in IoMT generate date in a 24x7 fashion, and hence handling such a huge and highly sensitive data requires enormous storage space. A clear distinction is needed to store only the essential data and discard unnecessary data, which is a difficult task in reality.
- The implementation of AI can be rather expensive considering with traditional medical practices.
- The lack of standards is still a problem in IoMT. IoMT requires appropriate regulation standards and policies and proper monitoring

systems, and these regulations have to be globally accepted and approved.

- Other challenges include data growth/size, lack of expertise, data source handling, data quality, resistance from customers and public, timeliness of analysis, ethics, etc.

8.7 CONCLUSION

AI is considered more of a kind of living intelligence. The AI terminology incorporates the conceptualization of an intelligent machine concerning operative as well as social significances. IoMT is aimed at networking medical devices and enabling the healthcare industry to move towards a more sophisticated ecosystem. Technology advancements have a huge impact on the medical field along with practiced medicine towards the public overview of health and staying healthy. This chapter has presented certain viewpoints on the capabilities of AI and IoMT, highlighted the need for the conglomeration of these two state-of-the-art technologies and portrayed a layered architecture of smart healthcare scenario. With all the glory of machine learning and deep learning technologies, AI is considered to be the future of healthcare solutions. The influence of AI and IoMT will have a significant progress and a promising future in the healthcare domain.

KEYWORDS

- **intelligent healthcare provisioning**
- **medical devices networking**
- **personalized treatment planning**
- **preventive healthcare**
- **smart health infrastructure**

REFERENCES

1. Adarsha, S. B., Kristen, R., & Stephen, E., (2019). User experience, IoMT, and healthcare. *AIS Transactions on Human-Computer Interaction*, 264–273. 10.17705/1thci.00125.

2. Arjun, P., (2019). *Machine Learning and AI for Healthcare: Big Data for Improved Health Outcomes.* 10.1007/978-1-4842-6537-6.

3. Charles, B. W., (1999). Sensors in medicine. *The Western Journal of Medicine, 171,* 322–325. 10.1136/bmj.319.7220.1288.

4. Debleena, P., Gaurav, S., Snehal, S., Dnyaneshwar, K., Kiran, K., & Rakesh, K. T., (2020). Artificial intelligence in drug discovery and development. *Drug Discovery Today, 26.* 10.1016/j.drudis.2020.10.010.

5. Dimitrios, I. F., Aristidis, L., & Vasilios, P., (2006). *Intelligent Patient Monitoring.* 10.1002/9780471740360.ebs0642.

6. Eric, S., (2017). AI-powered drug discovery captures pharma interest. *Nature Biotechnology, 35,* 604–205. 10.1038/nbt0717-604.

7. Al-Turjman, F., Muhammad, H. N., & Umit, D. U., (2017). Intelligence in the internet of medical things era: A systematic review of current and future trends. *Computer Communications*, 150. 10.1016/j.comcom.2019.12.030.

8. Gulraiz, J. J., Rao, M. L., Aftab, F., & Saad, R., (2017). Internet of medical things (IOMT): Applications, benefits and future challenges in healthcare domain. *Journal of Communications, 12,* 240–247. 10.12720/jcm.12.4.240-247.

9. Ikram Ud, D., Ahmad, A., Mohsen, G., & Mansour, Z., (2019). A decade of internet of things: Analysis in the light of healthcare applications. *IEEE Access, 7.* 1–13. 10.1109/ACCESS.2019.2927082.

10. Ilmudeen, A., (2021). Design and development of IoT-based decision support system for dengue analysis and prediction: Case study on Sri Lankan context. In: *Healthcare Paradigms in the Internet of Things Ecosystem* (pp. 363–380). Academic Press.

11. Ilmudeen, A., (2021). Big data-based frameworks for healthcare systems. In: *Demystifying Big Data, Machine Learning, and Deep Learning for Healthcare Analytics* (pp. 33–56). Academic Press.

12. Justin, S. S., Adrian, E. R., & Olexandr, I., (2018). Transforming computational drug discovery with machine learning and AI. *ACS Medicinal Chemistry Letters., 9.* 10.1021/acsmedchemlett.8b00437.

13. Kamdar, J. H., Jeba, P. J., & Georrge, J. J., (2020). Artificial intelligence in medical diagnosis: Methods, algorithms and applications. In: *Machine Learning with Health Care Perspective. Learning and Analytics in Intelligent Systems* (Vol. 13). Springer, Cham. https://doi.org/10.1007/978-3-030-40850-3_2.

14. Maria, P., Marina, K., Georgios, M., Victor, S., Ismael, E., Jonathan, R., & Dimitrios, L., (2020). A survey on security threats and countermeasures in the internet of medical things (IoMT). *Transactions on Emerging Telecommunications Technologies.* 10.1002/ett.4049.

15. Meherwar, F., & Maruf, P., (2017). Survey of machine learning algorithms for disease diagnostic. *Journal of Intelligent Learning Systems and Applications, 9,* 1–16. 10.4236/jilsa.2017.91001.

16. Olga, M. L., María, C. R., Rita, C., Eduarda, A., Vitor, V., & Francisca, V., (2018). Current screening methodologies in drug discovery for selected human diseases. *Marine Drugs, 16,* 279. 10.3390/md16080279.

17. Paolo, D., Blake, H., & Arianna, M., (2003). Smart surgical tools and augmenting devices. *IEEE Transactions on Robotics and Automation, 19,* 782–792. 10.1109/TRA.2003.817071.

18. Ravi, P. S., Mohd, J., Abid, H., Raju, V., & Shokat, A., (2020). Internet of medical things (IoMT) for orthopaedic in COVID-19 pandemic: Roles, challenges, and applications. *Journal of Clinical Orthopaedics and Trauma*, 11. 10.1016/j.jcot.2020.05.011.

19. Vishnu, S., Jino, R. S. R., & Jegan, R., (2020). *Internet of Medical Things (IoMT) – An Overview*, 101–104. 10.1109/ICDCS48716.2020.243558.

20. Simarjeet, K., Jimmy, S., Lewis, N., Sudan, J., Deepak, P., Gyanendra, P. J., Shaker El-Sappagh, S., et al., (2020). *Medical Diagnostic Systems Using Artificial Intelligence (AI) Algorithms: Principles and Perspectives* (pp. 228049–228069). IEEE. 10.1109/ACCESS.2020.3042273.

21. Thomas, D., & Ravi, K., (2019). The potential for artificial intelligence in healthcare. *Future Hospital Journal, 6*, 94–98. 10.7861/futurehosp.6-2-94.

22. Xin, Y., Yifei, W., Ryan, B., Gisbert, S., & Shengyong, Y., (2019). Concepts of artificial intelligence for computer-assisted drug discovery. *Chemical Reviews, 119*. 10.1021/acs.chemrev.8b00728.

23. Alex, D. *IoMT (Internet of Medical Things) or Healthcare IoT*. Available at: https://internetofthingsagenda.techtarget.com/definition/IoMT-Internet-of-Medical-Things (accessed on 11 January 2022).

24. Bernard, M. *How is AI Used in Healthcare – 5 Powerful Real-World Examples That Show the Latest Advances*. Available at: https://www.bernardmarr.com/default.asp?contentID=1542 (accessed on 11 January 2022).

25. Frost & Sullivan, *Internet of Medical Things Revolutionizing Healthcare*. Available at: https://aabme.asme.org/posts/internet-of-medical-things-revolutionizing-healthcare (accessed on 11 January 2022).

26. Hannah, J., (2020). 10 Healthcare Apps to Try in 2020. Available at:https://swisscognitive.ch/2020/03/27/10-best-ai-based-healthcare-apps-you-can-try-in-2020/ (accessed on 11 January 2022).

27. IEEE spectrum. *Choosing Sensors for Medical Applications*. Available at: https://spectrum.ieee.org/biomedical/devices/choosing-sensors-for-medical-applications (accessed on 11 January 2022).

28. Igor, K. *20 Examples of Wearables and IoT Disrupting Healthcare*. Available at: https://www.avenga.com/magazine/wearables-iot-healthcare/ (accessed on 11 January 2022).

29. What is IoMT? Available at: https://ordr.net/article/what-is-iomt/ (accessed on 11 January 2022).

30. Kumba, *AI for Virtual Medical Assistants – 4 Current Applications*. Available at: https://emerj.com/ai-sector-overviews/virtual-medical-assistants/ (accessed on 11 January 2022).

31. Kumba, *Machine Learning in Surgical Robotics – 4 Applications That Matter*. Available at: https://emerj.com/ai-sector-overviews/machine-learning-in-surgical-robotics-4-applications/ (accessed on 11 January 2022).

32. Nanalyze, *6 AI Healthcare Solutions for Remote Patient Monitoring*. Available at: https://www.nanalyze.com/2019/11/ai-remote-patient-monitoring/ (accessed on 11 January 2022).

33. Neelam, T. *6 Major Branches of Artificial Intelligence (AI)*. Available at: https://www.analyticssteps.com/blogs/6-major-branches-artificial-intelligence-ai (accessed on 11 January 2022).

34. Tanya, A. H. *4 ways Health Care AI Could Help Physicians' work*. Available at: https://www.ama-assn.org/practice-management/digital/4-ways-health-care-ai-could-help-physicians-work (accessed on 11 January 2022).
35. Vinati, K. *A Detailed Guide to IoMT Implementation in 2020*. Available at: https://arkenea.com/blog/iomt/ (accessed on 11 January 2022).

CHAPTER 9

Social, Professional, Ethical, and Security Issues Associated with IoMT and Smart Healthcare: Post-COVID-19 Pandemic Scenario

TRISHIT BANERJEE

Department of Basic Engineering and Sciences, Netaji Subhash Engineering College, Techno City, Garia, Kolkata, India

ABSTRACT

The IoMT has gained high levels of notoriety in the modern world with advanced solutions being deployed in multiple treatment facilities along with care units. The methodology used in this research work is that existing scholarly articles with various case studies have been researched to bring out information about the topic. The secondary data researched will account for an inclination to the qualitative form of research, which will make the approach deal more in non-numerical data. This qualitative form of research will be backed by a further descriptive representation of the same in this research. The overall representation will thus blend the findings of various research works, bringing out a compilation of significant information about the topic. The information brought out in this research will be made subject to further critical analysis as a part of the preparation of this research work. The issues found in this research work is that the healthcare domain has been revamped to a great extent due to the introduction of such facilities

Internet of Medical Things in Smart Healthcare: Post-COVID-19 Pandemic Scenario.
Saravanan Krishnan, PhD and Aboobucker Ilmudeen, PhD (Eds.)
© 2024 Apple Academic Press, Inc. Co-published with CRC Press (Taylor & Francis)

and the real-world applications have changed architectural frameworks introducing modern design elements and heightened optimization at the same instance. The problems emerge from the fact that there are several security-based issues when it comes to dealing with these advanced smart devices. There can be social, ethical, and professional problems that remain quite associated with IoMT which is why smart healthcare solutions cannot be banked upon easily without prior concern. The research direction and potential solution to these issues are discussed in this chapter. The research brings out a clear understanding of issues about IoMT along with various solutions that are required to be used in the respective cases. In adjustment to the Internet of Things, the healthcare industry has lacked a consistent approach making the entire process slow. The COVID pandemic has however changed this scenario making almost every single industry opt for a mandatory technological advancement as a primary route of dealing with various job-related operations. While this can be said that these technological advancements cannot be a primary route, at least in the case of the healthcare industry, such advancements are indeed the need of the hour, making the processes change in accordance with the changing times. IoMT is coming up at present as a major solution for various issues changing the healthcare system and the protection ensured by the same on the life of people. IoMT is successfully providing aid in tracking various health issues while at the same time providing for a scope to the healthcare practitioners to detect issues at a faster rate achieving effectiveness by not allowing issues to get extended becoming worse with time. However, technological advancements do come with various issues concerning the threats to the system pertaining to the loss of valuable information leading to further problems in the security of healthcare systems and the data handled by the same. The present-day innovation is bringing up various innovations pertaining to these threats so as to act as solutions against the same. It is expected that by the end of 2025, more than 25 billion devices will come into action with a major section covered up by IoMT devices. The difficulty in the management of the same is required to have aid from the related protocols in the healthcare system. In the conclusion section, this chapter discusses the potential threats that might emerge while dealing with these smart devices in a post-covid world thereby guaranteeing better perspectives and heightened analysis necessary for adequate control.

9.1   INTRODUCTION

The Internet of Medical Things (IoMT) has emerged as a disrupting technology that is currently being utilized in medical care and market segments have been revolutionized to a great extent. Healthcare services powered by smart devices along with real-time connectivity have helped in decreasing expenses and providing advanced medical care thereby improving patient results and decreasing the number of readmissions as well. Real-time monitoring facilities can be guaranteed by the smart devices and the patients will not have to depend extensively upon traditional methods, thereby providing high levels of reliability upon IoT healthcare solutions.

IoMT guarantees heightened levels of advanced capabilities that can deliver accurate diagnosis and fewer mistakes at the same instance. These technical solutions offer low-cost treatment facilities and the entire IT infrastructure can be paired with smartphone applications and thereby allowing patients to send health information promptly. Studies conducted by authorities at UCLA demonstrated the ability of such advanced medical devices. One prominent example includes the Fitbit activity tracker that can evaluate the heartbeats of a patient and detect ischemic heart diseases by constantly recording heart rates.

Before the year 2025 more than 20 to 30 billion medical devices were connected to IoT are expected to be a dominant part of the healthcare ecosystem. There are certain social, ethical, professional, and security threats associated with the growing number of IoT devices that must be tackled in the best ways possible. The devices exchanging huge volumes of information and the absence of a standardized architecture paired with artificially intelligent systems utilizing faulty source code can backfire in more ways than one. It is necessary to understand the threats along with the challenges that can gain prominence should these situations go neglected. It will offer a cybercriminal a chance to misuse and profit from vulnerabilities in the worst ways possible. The cybersecurity market is expected to increase to US\$27 billion by 2025 and it shows the extent of threat available outside.

There are significant challenges that must be highlighted while dealing with IoMT devices and the prime one dwells upon the contamination and loss of valuable details that can lead to significant levels of disruption. Often these devices have exploitable vulnerabilities that can assist hackers and perpetrators to hijack networks along with sensitive details. The ransoming of a device will be the gradual outcome in such situations and it will not only result in clinical risk but also compromise the care facilities completely. Covid patients requiring ventilators can become primary targets if these devices are used with IoMT solutions. It will gradually lead to the loss of life which should be viewed as a national concern as cybersecurity attacks are often initiated in the form of Cyber Terrorism. As these devices will be engaging in patient tracking, information analysis along with collection, report monitoring, and data sharing huge volume of sensitive details will get accumulated promptly which will be more than just attractive to the malicious intentions of hackers and perpetrators lurking on the online domains. There can be social risks emerging in the form of stigma or professional risks where doctors along with physicians will be selling private information in exchange for privileges and financial gains from Covid-19 vaccine manufacturers. Ethical challenges can also gain prominence where the sensitive details will be mined for marketable knowledge that will be used in turn to manipulate the patients into certain advanced treatment options suggested by virologists posing as experts in a post-covid world.

9.2   METHODOLOGICAL APPROACH

There are various sorts of methodological approaches that were available for exploring issues relevant to IoMT. In this particular work, the most important methodological route that has been opted is on existing scholarly articles. This will help bring out insights into the topic from various existing researches combining and analyzing data at the same time. This process will, in turn, provide for an ideal combination of data bringing out different aspects pertaining to the topic. The research will be mostly qualitative in nature studying non-numerical data brought forward by other researchers. Various case studies have been explored to derive the facts in the preparation of this research work. Based on the defined requirements, various case studies have been researched for and thereby selected. The qualitative form of research primarily undertaken in this case will bring out insights from secondary data in a descriptive approach. The descriptive approach taken up for this research will provide for an ideal blend of facts in this case. Such descriptive approaches are required for the overall understanding of the topic along with a detailed comprehension of other associated issues. The selection of case studies will follow a study conducted on the same so as to identify and bring out required information subject to further analysis. This analysis will aim to bring a critical perspective on the topic leading to the findings of the project. The social, professional, ethical as well as security issues will be identified with the help of the mentioned methodological approaches.

9.3 ANALYSIS

9.3.1 IOMT ISSUES THAT MUST BE MONITORED

The range of issues experienced can be categorized into four segments: social, professional, security, and ethical issues.

FIGURE 9.1   Analysis of IoMT issues.

9.3.1.1 SOCIAL ISSUES

IoMT devices have social and privacy-related issues in certain instances where an attack can emerge from hackers and perpetrators who can utilize the vulnerabilities and loopholes present in multiple devices. These devices having the capacity to communicate with each other have the low resource power necessary for adequate levels of security. As understood by Abdulraheem et al. [2], as a consequence, the attacker will have multiple access points that can include one vulnerability or another leading to a plethora of avenues that can be targeted. Improperly protecting the privacy-related details can lead to stigmatization and community members might end up marginalizing Covid-19 afflicted patients based on the health conditions sighted through the IoT devices. Lack of information confidentiality will be misused in society.

9.3.1.1.1 *Wearable Technologies Deployed*

IoMT guarantees the utility of wearable sensor technology that can monitor multiple variables along with health parameters providing high levels of monitoring services to doctors along with nurses who might not be within range. These wearable sensor networks utilize cloud computing services along with real-time network facilities to deliver intelligent healthcare to the end patients. One of the dominant forms of such devices includes the Apple Watch, Motiv, Kardia Mobile, Gym Watch, and Ava. Companies such as iBeat provide smartwatches that can prevent heart-related conditions by continuously evaluating heart rates thereby ultimately designed to save lives within patients. The wearables will have the potency to detect virus contraction in multiple individuals thereby providing authorities with a chance to isolate them appropriately thereby preventing future contraction.

There are a lot of black marketers peddling faulty vaccines who will be able to target these patients easily thereby selling them dubious medical solutions. The sensors will help in identifying the patients among the public and the lack of information confidentiality will backfire tremendously. In the words of Ali & Askar [1], the moderators need these smart devices to detect if virus contraction remains present, but the same information can be misused by marketers as well. Marketers will be legitimately and legally targeting these patients outside the boundaries of traditional care so that new solutions can be sold that do not remain well approved.

9.3.1.1.2 *IoMT Ecosystem in a Post-Pandemic World*

The IoMT can be deployed in a post-pandemic world where multiple systems along with devices should be capable of working in tandem. The ecosystem will include state-of-the-art applications, revamped IT infrastructure, advanced technologies, and heightened security that in combination will be capable of handling most of the health-related and medical threats experienced by vulnerable patients. Most of the devices will be dedicated to ensuring the safety of frontline personnel by continuously increasing efficacy and lessening the spread of diseases. It will ultimately help in decreasing mortality rates. The development of these systems will merge with artificially intelligent systems, blockchain, big data, and quantum computing if possible. All of these systems in combination will be able to intelligently analyze the extent of health threats experienced by front-line workers and patients as well. In the words of Khurana, Singh, & Choudhury [8], the ecosystem will only focus upon an extremely data-driven world that takes into account the advantages of 5G technology, Cloud Computing, and real-time information tracking to deliver the best solutions thereby reducing the time needed to become ready and deploy solutions. The best technological solutions that this advanced ecosystem will be able to guarantee to include Systems for Symptoms Decoding and Symptoms for Spread Tracing. The capacity to collect biomarkers, thereby identifying the symptoms of SARS Cov-2 infection will increase the likelihood of detecting the traces easily.

There are tremendous social issues that can gain dominance whenever such advanced information remains available for everyone to visualize and interpret. Society has been a victim of discrimination to a great extent where abusers and controllers need excuses to discriminate against certain community members, thereby undermining their lifestyles in the worst ways possible. The extent of social unrest rising due to the levels of racism, ageism, and sexism will get revamped when such information remains available. In the words of Zhu et al. [20], the end-users and the discriminators will utilize such advanced health information to segregate between multiple groups of people and a legitimate excuse will be presented to support this marginalization practice. It will be extremely undetectable and the loss of opportunities that are usually expected by threatened community members will become dominant. It is extremely crucial to understand the drawbacks of such high information availability.

9.3.1.1.3   *Advanced Vaccine Screening*

Vaccine screening will also become highly easy and with intelligent biomarkers, detection devices and scanners available at multiple facilities authorities will be able to utilize the potency of the same biomarkers to track if certain patients have the virus within themselves. It will speed up detection to the greatest extent possible, which will ultimately help in isolating the vulnerable people. According to Jha, Anumotu, & Soni [6], these streamlined detection methods are more than just crucial to identify the importance of vaccine tracking technologies. Vaccine passports will also be given to an individual based on the level of this detection which can also protect nations not yet vulnerable.

There can be other significant problems when vaccine passports and advanced screening methods emerge at the forefront. Expats, individuals utilizing and depending upon student or work visas will be targeted in the worst ways possible. In countries that remain extremely diversified, these solutions cannot work promisingly at all which is why how the new international laws will end up eliminating the efficacy of human rights needs to be monitored to a great extent. As per the words of Thangamani et al. [18], there has been an increased number of reports showcasing how governments in various countries have shut down borders showcasing a dominant sign of discriminatory practices against individuals of certain nations even though they remain vaccinated. The question of vaccinating with the right product also gains prominence where vaccine passports are only given to individuals who have been given one particular company shot. A similar case was seen in the case of Europe when countries black-listed the Covishield dose.

9.3.1.2   *PROFESSIONAL ISSUES*

Certain professional issues can also emerge at the forefront when doctors and nurses engage in selling sensitive details procured from patients to potential marketers who will have the prime duty of manufacturing Covid-19 treatment solutions and streamlining performance at the same instance. Data mining activities are quite common in the modern world and marketable information once procured can be utilized to execute manipulative selling practices that can be more than just detrimental. In the words of Chatterjee & Hanawal [3], these professional issues must be tackled adequately with the use of codified contracts that must be formulated to control the activities of physicians and professionals in a given healthcare facility. Anyone with access to a covid patient data must be subjected to periodic verifications and monitoring.

9.3.1.2.1   Professional Challenges of Cloud Computing Framework Deployed

Cloud Computing frameworks have been highly effective when it came to projecting contraction in infected patients thereby providing high levels of control over infection rates. These cloud computing models help in creating decision trees that ultimately assess the potency of infection depending upon the symptoms shown by patients. Social network analysis gained prominence and it presented the state of the outbreak which was highly essential in the case of influenza epidemics. Proposed frameworks help in testing synthetic data to a great extent and evaluations were run on more than 2 million users. The cloud computing models help in providing 94% accuracy for high levels of classification and 81% of the resource utilization became necessary in the Amazon EC2 cloud.

The significant professional challenges that will be experienced while deploying cloud computing solutions for pandemic management include compliance violence, identity theft along high levels of malware infections that will give rise to data breaches. As understood by Hamou-Lhadj & Razgallah [5], it would propagate towards diminished customer trust and the social unrest will gain prominence as well. The data breaches will compromise the security of the patients, and denial of service attacks can also be launched upon multiple medical devices which will lead to tremendous issues. The insecure interfaces along with the APIs must be managed effectively to prevent the hijacking of accounts and the number of patients remains innumerable in this instance.

9.3.1.2.1.1   Fog Computing Deployed

When it comes to understanding the advantages of Fog computing organizations, such as Technavio provides heightened levels of solutions.

The global fog computing market as researched by this organization is expected to grow by $28.87 billion. In the words of Haji & Ameen [4], the up-to-date analysis gets delivered through this report regarding the market scenario and the latest drivers along with trends are ensured as well. Fog computing solutions developed by this company will help in in-depth research thereby having all the needs covered. The research reports will include foreseeable market scenarios and pre-along with post-Covid analysis will get delivered as well. The market remains fragmented and the degree of fragmentation increasing to a heightened extent will get accelerated during this forecast.

The dominant professional issues that will be experienced while deploying fog computing involves authentication-related problems and trust issues as well. Energy consumption remains quite high, which is why the business model will not become supportive while dealing with innumerable patients wanting to procure the services. As per the words of Jothi & Pushpalatha [7], the increased design complexity will help insider threats to grow to a great extent if talented programmers and technicians emerge at the forefront. Physical security considerations are also high, and a decentralized design will not be able to support such high post-pandemic needs thereby making the patients vulnerable to privacy loss and information leakage.

9.3.1.2.1.2 IoMT Architecture and Professional Challenges

The IoMT architecture includes an application layer, data processing layer, network layer, sensing layers. These layers in combination will be capable of delivering the right architecture necessary which is why it is crucial to evaluate the importance of vulnerabilities that might be present at every significant segment. The sensors and the physical objects at the base level might remain extremely vulnerable to abusive attacks which can compromise the physical security of these devices. In the words of Mahak & Singh [9], at the network layer, the Internet gateways having low levels of encryption and faulty network technologies that do not follow promising cryptographic solutions will remain vulnerable to a great extent thereby attacking the business model in the worst ways possible. In a post-pandemic world, data processing will increase to a tremendous extent which will not be possible without dedicated servers and it will create a business load that will be difficult to manage. Smart applications at the application layer must have hardwired source code capable of impenetrable source code thereby providing the best levels of security to a heightened extent without which patient care will get compromised extensively leading to high mortality rates because of professional failure.

9.3.1.3   ETHICAL ISSUES

There can be ethical challenges paired with the utility of IoMT devices. The devices generating a lot of information will be paired with artificially intelligent systems that can have faulty source code. As understood by Mohanty et al. [10], discrimination and inequality will be quite dominant in these systems and informed consent might not have the proper codified structure. The privacy of the covid-19 afflicted patients can be lost and treatment facilities will include bias or unverified decision-making leading to more complications than what can be accounted for. As understood by Mothukuri et al. [11], the transparency and trust from the source code will be lost completely and people having access to the software will be capable of engaging in malicious practices as well.

9.3.1.3.1   Big Data and AI Systems Deployed in IoMT

Big data has the potential to provide huge volumes of information to help workers, frontline defense teams, epidemiologists, and scientists at the same instance as well so that they can make informed decisions when it comes to fighting the coronavirus. The data can be utilized to track the virus on a global scale, thereby creating innovation in every single medical arena. With the help of big data, decision-making systems will get revamped to the best extent possible, and the best solutions will get guaranteed as an outcome. In the time of a pandemic when the volumes of information remain too much to control such solutions can provide the right levels of efficiency in the best ways possible. As identified by Najmi et al. [12], artificially intelligent systems can work with big data to process the information in the most positive manner. These artificially intelligent systems will be capable of detecting patterns faster than most business intelligence tools which is why vaccine delivery, medical treatment structure, and other healthcare-related solutions will be identified at the fastest note. The IoMT utilizing all of these advantages in a combined manner will be able to guarantee more benefits than what can be needed which is why in a post-pandemic world a combined solution will become important.

9.3.1.3.2 Ethical Challenges of Big Data in IoMT

There are significant challenges when it comes to deploying big data in IoMT to manage the pandemic in a post-Covid world. In the words of NICULA & ZOTA [13], big data will be capable of procuring huge volumes of information from the smart devices and patterns will be extracted from these systems to identify suitable solutions along with other necessary measures to be taken. Protecting the sensitive details in the big data systems from insider and outsider threats will be the central challenge in this situation. There will be issues with data rights along with ownership when multiple companies emerge at the forefront sharing smart devices, and if there remains an absence of standardized systems, then the problems will grow. According to the words of Obradovic [14], this will lead to more complications while engaging in e-discovery to find out where the issues originated from. Insider threats will gain high levels of prominence in such situations where the patterns and the marketable information can get sold, leading to huge levels of problems for the patients who purchase these solutions for themselves. Big data will be able to procure information during the pandemic and in a post-Covid world, this information can be in turn used for other marketing ventures that might focus upon entertainment, job opportunities, or other sectors as well. Information procured insensitive and disruptive times due to health pressures can get misused in the distant future extensively. The data will not change in several aspects such as names, contact numbers, Social Security numbers, and even addresses which is why this information can be repurposed later unethically.

9.3.1.3.3 Ethical Challenges of AI Systems in IoMT

Artificially intelligent systems depend extensively upon source code and the big data tools will be supplying high levels of information to these Intelligent Systems. The developers often include bias along with prejudice while creating the source code intentionally or unintentionally. The faulty source code present in the Intelligent Systems dealing with Covid patients will lead to more problems than what can be handled. Hospital admissions, primary care, availability of vaccines, and post-recovery measures will get compromised to heightened extents which is why the right solutions must be delivered by tweaking the source code in the most objective manner possible. It can be highly impossible to ensure such better levels of transparency because developers often engage in such practices unintentionally, thereby making the detection process more than just difficult. In the words of Saini [15], an artificially intelligent system with faulty code in IoMT will compromise the treatment solutions present thereby leading to more problems than what can be handled. Artificially intelligent systems not working objectively in a post-pandemic world will compromise patient quality care and case examples can be noticed easily. There is a lot of AI recruitment software scanning through profiles to find candidates which show biased selection. This can get mimicked horribly in a post covid world within IoMT devices where certain communities will get oppressed. The smart devices will not be able to guarantee the right solutions and the projection of wrong numbers will increase mortality rates in certain communities.

9.3.1.4   SECURITY ISSUES

Certain security issues were also must be accounted for to the fullest extent as insufficient testing and updating-related issues can emerge when there are network challenges. IoMT malware and ransomware attacks are extremely devastating and if botnets emerge at the forefront, then the sensitive details belonging to patients will get compromised completely. The data security and privacy concerns will extend to mobile, web, and cloud platforms. Small IoMT attacks can easily evade detection which the intrusion detection and intrusion prevention systems will not be able to capture at all. Faulty artificially intelligent systems deployed in Covid wards that implement improper automated functionalities can lead to disturbing results. As understood by Zhang et al. [19], even different organizations will follow different security standards while making the IoMT devices and it will backfire in certain situations when a standardized security solution does not remain enabled. Smart devices provided by one company can be secured enough to stop the malicious intent of hackers and perpetrators, but when paired with weaker IoMT devices, the entire infrastructure can get compromised.

9.3.1.4.1 IoMT-Based Sensor Technologies

Smart devices have sensor technologies present within them that can be achieved through miniaturization and other advancements in the avenues of digital signal processing. It gets embedded into various applications in our lives through which data can be collected, and professionals will have the capacity to evaluate critical situations in the worst manners possible. An informed improvement will gain prominence in blood equipment monitoring, noninvasive sensors, heart rate monitors along with diabetes measurement devices all miniaturized providing the best solutions in the medical industry.

There are significant challenges that will gain prominence if the miniaturized sensors do not have adequate levels of security-enabled within them. Physical barriers will be quite weak in the sensors due to the lack of resources because there is a need to make them as small as possible. According to Shepherd & Apeh [16], medical devices will have weak security in such situations and the availability of advanced cryptography will be quite impossible due to the low computing power generated from time to time. It will help hackers and perpetrators break the barrier easily thereby compromising the life of a patient. It can lead to political issues of assassination and even civil wars in certain instances if cyber terrorists get details. There have been tremendous virus contraction rates among members of the parliament to even Presidents as seen in the cases of Donald J. Trump, Boris Johnson, and Jair Bolsonaro.

9.3.1.4.2 Internet of Medical Things and Real Cases

When it comes to examining the application of the IoMT in real cases during a post-pandemic world, one must take into account at 1st the quickest ways through which virus contraction can be scanned. In the words of Shreenidhi, Prabakar, & Kumar [17], the ever-increasing population subjected to such a highly transmittable virus spreading at an alarming rate must be monitored in real-time. The absence of real-time monitoring has led to vaccine supply shortages because the numbers are wrong which IoMT can fix. The new sensors along with technological solutions will be able to guarantee instant recognition of positive patients so that the best solutions are availed. The sensors might be present in hospitals, airports, and even within cell phones in the distant future. It would be quite feasible to include such IoMT devices in smartphones so that patients can instantly recognize if they need professional care. There have been smartphone-based Covid tests that give results in less than 30 minutes s which must be tapped into in the best ways possible. CRISPR-based COVID-19 smartphone test will be utilized for these detections in the post-pandemic world. The smartphone camera will be capable of detecting the signal directly without amplifying the viral genome utilized in most genetic tests. These tests usually quantify the amount of virus in the sample and the viral load increases, which can be eliminated perfectly in smartphone-based testing methods.

There are serious challenges when it comes to utilizing these state-of-the-art solutions while detecting the coronavirus contraction rates within patients. As identified by Zhang et al. [19], the extent of cybersecurity problems already existing on smartphone platforms such as android or even iOS makes it extremely challenging to deploy such devices on these models. In the United States alone last year there were a total of 1001 massive data breaches that clearly shows that deploying medical devices on smartphones will be extremely challenging. It will collect enormous volumes of information and eliminate privacy, confidentiality, and even availability of data especially if the DDoS attacks are launched.

9.4   RESEARCH DIRECTIONS AND SOLUTIONS FOR ISSUES

The research pertains to the issues related to IoMT and various solutions pertaining to the same. The pandemic has made it a necessity for the healthcare industry to get more technologically advanced so as to maintain consistency in its operations in the post-pandemic world. This has made the IoMT a necessary route for the healthcare industry to opt for. IoMT has provided for a major solution while leading to obvious issues rising up as drawbacks of the system. The solutions for such drawbacks are given below. This has to be realized that the IoMT is significantly contributing to the fast detection of problems in order to act upon them in an effective manner.

Findings of Potential Issues and Solution
Social Issues

Issues	Solutions
Loss of patient confidentiality due to the use of wearable sensor technology.	The only solution is for developing anti-malware software and factor authentication processes for this kind of technology.
Marginalization and discrimination due to COVID detection information.	Awareness about the treatment facilities.

Professional Issues

Issues	Solutions
Cloud attacks.	Cyber-attacks can be prevented with the help of IoT analytics which can help to review the information from several data. Encryption of communication has to be ensured by using applications like AES 256.
Privacy loss with authentication-related problems of fog computing.	Betterment of authentication approaches.

Ethical Issues

Issues	Solutions
Lack of standardization leads to issues regarding data rights with BIG DATA in IoMT.	Wi-Fi should be used for healthcare units to have a good network. Bluetooth gateway is much needed. This will secure standardization.
Faulty source code will compromise the quality of care of patients.	Bettering the source code. Bettering the transparency levels.

Security Issues

Issues	Solutions
Vulnerability of IoMT-based sensor technologies to get hacked.	Enabling adequate security levels.
Vulnerability to virus attacks.	Enabling adequate anti-malware levels.

9.5 CONCLUSION

There are several layers when it comes to understanding the design elements and foundations or architectures of medical devices. At the

1st layer, we have devices and at the second layer, we have data. The 3rd layer is analytics whereas the 4th layer is connectivity. These layers in combination guarantee efficiency in smartphones and the integrated solution become possible. The device will be capable of transmitting data from one location to another and sensors record this information. Vast amounts of data collected by the sensors are transmitted over cloud servers which get delivered through the connectivity layer. Analytics help in understanding patterns where intelligence tools are often utilized to initiate predictive or descriptive analytics showing possible scenarios.

The IoMT will be able to revamp the entire medical infrastructure in the best manner possible, and the devastating shortage of supplies and personnel witnessed in the middle of the pandemic will get eliminated in the distant future. These devices will relieve the burden and prevent burnout experienced by nurses and physicians that can have the capacity to destabilize the entire health industry. Patients with chronic diseases who cannot shift from one location to another will require the advancement of such technologies. They will be given wearables, biosensors, and electronic medicines combined with smartphone connectivity thereby guaranteeing better levels of health monitoring. Unethical marketing practices are best implemented on such vulnerable Covid patients thereby showing the challenges of IoMT. The devices will guarantee cheaper solutions in a streamlined manner which will be highly crucial in a post-pandemic world but care must be taken to adequately handle the related threats.

There are significant disadvantages when it comes to deploying all of these solutions in an integrated manner. At the connectivity level, there can be encryption-based issues or cryptographic problems that will easily lead to the leakage of valuable patient information in the post-pandemic world. According to the words of Ali & Askar [1], the analytics might have faulty data categorization issues that make systems generate false results or even design flaws that will backfire in terms of wrong automated implementations increasing mortality rates horribly. Oxygen flow increment and decrement rates connected to such faulty IoMT devices will get compromised. The data collected from the sensors will stand incapable of improving application functionality if poor sources remain available. Data often gets compromised when leakages occur through spying tools. The devices will have lower physical security which can also be jailbroken thereby assisting insider threats. The authorities in the organization will have to look out for personnel who might want to damage the devices to procure sensitive data about a patient.

It is highly crucial to understand the importance of deploying IoMT devices in a post-pandemic world due to the multitude of advantages available. Failure to do that can backfire tremendously because the huge volumes of workload getting generated by healthcare workers and frontline teams remain more than just incomparable. It is crucial to not only deploy these options but also optimize them efficiently. Optimizing them will include eliminating the social, security, ethical and professional threats in the most streamlined manner possible. It is important to understand that with the presence of these threats, it would be twice as dangerous to deploy the smart devices that will be used as weapons instead of medical solutions. Understanding the applications of these devices in an integrated form in a threat-free world is imminent that can be only delivered by cybersecurity experts working collaboratively.

KEYWORDS

- **5G technology**
- **Amazon EC2 cloud**
- **APIs**
- **cloud computing**
- **COVID-19**
- **CRISPR**
- **cyber terrorism**
- **DDoS**
- **ethical issues**
- **intelligent systems**
- **IoMT**
- **professional issues**
- **SARS Cov-2**
- **security issues**

REFERENCES

1. Ali, K., & Askar, S., (2021). Security issues and vulnerability of IoT devices. *International Journal of Science and Business, 5*(3), 101–115.

2. Abdulraheem, M., Awotunde, J. B., Jimoh, R. G., & Oladipo, I. D., (2021). An efficient lightweight cryptographic algorithm for IoT security. *Communications in Computer and Information Science, 1350*, 444–456.

3. Chatterjee, S., & Hanawal, M. K., (2021). *Federated Learning for Intrusion Detection in IoT Security: A Hybrid Ensemble Approach*. arXiv preprint arXiv:2106.15349.

4. Haji, S. H., & Ameen, S. Y., (2021). Attack and anomaly detection in IoT networks using machine learning techniques: A review. *Asian Journal of Research in Computer Science*, 30–46.

5. Hamou-Lhadj, A., & Razgallah, A., (2021). An analysis of the use of CVEs by IoT malware. In: *Foundations and Practice of Security: 13th International Symposium, FPS 2020* (Vol. 12637, p. 47). Montreal, QC, Canada, Revised Selected Papers. Springer Nature.

6. Jha, K., Anumotu, S., & Soni, K., (2021). Security issues and architecture of IoT. In: *2021 International Conference on Artificial Intelligence and Smart Systems (ICAIS)* (pp. 1381–1385). IEEE.

7. Jothi, B., & Pushpalatha, M., (2021). WILS-TRS—A novel optimized deep learning-based intrusion detection framework for IoT networks. *Personal and Ubiquitous Computing*, 1–17.

8. Khurana, M., Singh, T. P., & Choudhury, T., (2021). Effective threat and security modeling approach to devise security rating of diverse IoT devices. In: *Data Driven Approach Towards Disruptive Technologies: Proceedings of MIDAS 2020* (pp. 583–593). Springer Singapore.

9. Mahak, M., & Singh, Y., (2021). Threat modeling and risk assessment in Internet of things: A review. In: *Proceedings of Second International Conference on Computing, Communications, and Cyber-Security* (pp. 293–305). Springer, Singapore.

10. Mohanty, J., Mishra, S., Patra, S., Pati, B., & Panigrahi, C. R., (2021). IoT security, challenges, and solutions: A review. *Progress in Advanced Computing and Intelligent Engineering*, 493–504.

11. Mothukuri, V., Khare, P., Parizi, R. M., Pouriyeh, S., Dehghantanha, A., & Srivastava, G., (2021). Federated learning-based anomaly detection for IoT security attacks. *IEEE Internet of Things Journal*.

12. Najmi, K. Y., AlZain, M. A., Masud, M., Jhanji, N. Z., Al-Amri, J., & Baz, M., (2021). A survey on security threats and countermeasures in IoT to achieve users confidentiality and reliability. *Materials Today: Proceedings*.

13. NICULA, S., & ZOTA, R. D., (2021). Technical and economical evaluation of IoT attacks and their corresponding vulnerabilities. *Informatica Economica, 25*(1).

14. Obradovic, D., (2021). *Cybersecurity of IoT Systems: Analyzing Security Vulnerabilities in a Cloud Supported Embedded System Environment*. Page 8, https://urn.fi/URN:NBN:fi:amk-202104195122 (accessed on 15 May 2021).

15. Saini, G., (2021). Security vulnerabilities and mitigation challenges in IoT based healthcare systems. *International Journal of Modern Agriculture, 10*(2), 495–508.

16. Shepherd, A., & Apeh, E., (2021). An IoT security awareness and system hardening advisory platform for smart home devices. In: *International Conference on Human–Computer Interaction* (pp. 439–446). Springer, Cham.

17. Shreenidhi, H. S., Prabakar, S., & Kumar, P. A., (2021). Intrusion detection system using IoT device for safety and security. In: *2021 International Conference on Computational Intelligence and Knowledge Economy (ICCIKE)* (pp. 340–344). IEEE.

18. Thangamani, T., Prabha, R., Prasad, M., Kumari, U., Raghavender, K. V., & Abidin, S., (2021). IoT defense machine learning: Emerging solutions and future problems. *Microprocessors and Microsystems*, 104043.

19. Zhang, H., Anilkumar, A., Fredrikson, M., & Agarwal, Y., (2021). Capture: Centralized library management for heterogeneous IoT devices. In: *USENIX Security Symposium*.

20. Zhu, Z., Lan, K., Rao, Z., & Zhang, Y., (2021). Risk assessment method for IoT software supply chain vulnerabilities. In: *Journal of Physics: Conference Series* (Vol. 1732, No. 1, p. 012051). IOP Publishing.

CHAPTER 10

Smart Healthcare: Impacts, Implications, and Challenges for Future Healthcare Delivery

KUNAL RAWAL,[1] ANUSHREE ACHARYA,[2] and SHWETA SONI[3]

[1]*Senior Faculty Hospital Administration, SGT University, Gurugram, Haryana, India*

[2]*Assistant Professor, Hospital Administration, SGT University, Haryana, India*

[3]*Assistant Professor, SGT University, Gurugram, Haryana, India*

10.1 INTRODUCTION

The healthcare sector is undoubtedly undergoing advancements and transformation due to COVID-19 scenario. It is being shifted from a conventional physician-focused approach to a patient-centric approach [1]. The aftermath of COVID-19 resulted in multi-morbidities, multi-mortalities, deterioration of resources and devastation of healthcare systems around the globe which directly impacted the rise of the quality health service delivery in the population. The requirement for more healthcare utilities, incorporation of technology, accessibility to the healthcare services and updated system is being raised with the time where smart healthcare is proven to be the solution to all these problems being faced by the healthcare sector.

Internet of Medical Things in Smart Healthcare: Post-COVID-19 Pandemic Scenario.
Saravanan Krishnan, PhD and Aboobucker Ilmudeen, PhD (Eds.)
© 2024 Apple Academic Press, Inc. Co-published with CRC Press (Taylor & Francis)

The smart healthcare is a sustainable system that can be retained and practiced in any real-time where Internet of Medical Things (IoMT) plays a crucial role [1]. IoMT can be considered as the foundational component of Smart healthcare which involves the combination of medical devices and applications that can connect to healthcare information technology systems using networking technologies. The sudden outbreak of COVID-19 enhanced the transformation towards the healthcare system incorporation with IoMT, Artificial intelligence, robotics, precision medicine, 3-D printing, augmented and virtual reality, genomics, telemedicine, and many more. These services assist healthcare system to access the patient, establish the communication between the consultant and patient, mobility of healthcare and maintain the patient record through healthcare information systems such as physical devices, like a measuring system, weight scale and patient's health indicators like glucose, force per unit area, vital signs, and activity watching, etc., to connect with the web and transforms data from the physical to the digital world. Through IoMT, smart healthcare integrated the patient along with healthcare infrastructure to achieve a common set of goals. The digitalization of medical services provokes the ease of delivery of healthcare services to the population [2].

These various services are used by governments to collect medical data regarding public health to serve the population with the intent of covering a large population. Hospitals are adopting digital applications and software to connect with fellow hospitals, diagnostic centers, blood banks, pharmaceutical shops, community health centers, district hospitals [3] to refer the patients to one another. This networking also helps healthcare units to understand the need of the patient and create a distinguished image in the healthcare world. The technological advancements in healthcare came up with the modified approach of recent diagnostic techniques including radiology services, laboratory services and pathology units. The advanced imaging system allows clinicians to diagnose the disease to the great extent. Reports of these tests can be provided digitally to the patients, doctor, or any other consulting healthcare professionals and can be easily accessed by the patients and physician anywhere in the world through digital technics and with gadgets. The healthcare sector always gets occupied with dealing with different unrecognized diseases. A recent example of such a life-threatening disease is COVID-19 laid the whole healthcare system down. Hence in current time medical science needs to be concentrated on research and development activities. Smart healthcare catalyzes the medical research activities, experiments, development of drugs and vaccines through digital medical devices and telecommunication technologies.

With the help of IoMT, tele-education is being used to educate healthcare professionals throughout the world regarding diseases and their new developments. A healthy lifestyle is now becoming a part of every individual. Patients are more concerned about their own health status, diets, physical activities, lifestyle changes, psychological and mental health. Hence healthcare is now undergone to provide various health applications and software where the patient can now assess his own health status and connect with a physician for further reference. These applications also involve the follow-up and feedback mechanism of the patient to improve the services of the concerned hospital, healthcare unit and medical professionals. Smart healthcare also incorporates advanced laboratory setups to provide the services to the patients without any error. All these advancements lead the healthcare industry towards smart healthcare which not only facilitates the processes but also enhances patient satisfaction. The integration of smart healthcare into traditional healthcare practices is a new challenge to the industry [22]. Many developed countries have accepted smart healthcare with comfort, but developing countries are still struggling to incorporate these modifications due to challenging adaptation, lack of resources, the response of population, future challenges, technicality of the concept, hiring skilled and qualified medical staff, and many more. Hence these challenges need to cope with time to establish a better healthcare system in the world.

The pandemic brought up numerous opportunities towards a bright healthcare system and life-threatening challenges at the same time. The concept of Smart healthcare benefitted the medical and paramedical workforce of the healthcare sector to utilize their potential in learning new ways of delivering healthcare services with adequate efficiency [4]. The IoMT stimulates the development of smart hospitals, smart power networks, smart transport, and smart infrastructure, smart buildings (intelligent solutions for a living), and many more. On the other hand, the technology always comes up with the uncertainty of future and risk which influence the social, cultural, economic, and legal aspects of any healthcare setup. Hence the smart healthcare is the need of the hour which will make lives convenient as well as contribute solutions for challenges in the healthcare system.

10.1.1 SMART HEALTHCARE'S CORE TECHNOLOGY

Doctors, nurses, technicians, patients, hospitals, nursing homes, diagnostic centers, and research organizations all play a significant role in smart healthcare. It's a multi-dimensional entity that includes illness prevention and monitoring, diagnosis and treatment, hospital management, health decision-making, and medical research [27]. Smart healthcare is built on the foundation of information technologies such as the IoT, cellular technologies, cloud computing, cognitive technologies, 5G, microelectronics, and artificial intelligence, as well as contemporary biotech. In all facets of smart healthcare, these technologies are frequently utilized. Patients can utilize wearable gadgets to keep track of their health at all moments, seek medical care through digital assistants, and use virtual houses to implement remote services; doctors can employ a variety of sophisticated clinical decision support systems to assist and improve diagnosis [22]. Doctors can handle medical data using an integrated information platform that incorporates tools like the Laboratory Information Management System (LIMS), Picture Archiving and Communication Systems (PACS), and the Electronic Medical Record (EMR). Robotic surgery and mixed reality technology can help with more accurate surgery. Radio-frequency identification (RFID) technology can be used to administer people materials and the distribution network in healthcare facilities, with integrated management platforms collecting data and assisting decision-making. From the standpoint of scientific research organizations, it is conceivable to employ techniques such as machine learning instead of manual drug screening and to discover eligible subjects utilizing big data by leveraging mobile medical platforms [27].

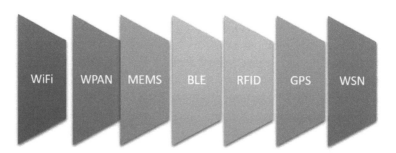

FIGURE 10.1   Different modes of delivery of smart healthcare technology.

Smart healthcare can efficaciously lower the cost and hazard of medical interventions, improve the utilization efficiency of medical resources, encourage local exchanges and cooperation, push the development of telemedicine and self-service medical attention, and eventually make personalized medical services widespread using these technologies.

10.1.2 THE IMPACTS OVER HEALTHCARE (FIGURE 10.2)

FIGURE 10.2 The Impacts over healthcare.

10.1.2.1 REDUCED HUMAN FALLACY

Technological advancements proactively help clinicians to prevent, diagnose, and treat patients. The devices like ventilators, drug infusers, pulse rate monitors, etc., provide the human health information digitally to assist the healthcare workforce to define the line of treatment for the disease [14]. Human processes are obvious to have errors due to analytical complications, but the technology can be trusted with fewer errors and more accuracy to develop a well-organized system in healthcare. Moreover, the integration of human processes with IoMT technology gives effective and efficient output for patient satisfaction and convenience to healthcare professionals. According to the report of India under COVID lockdown published in 2021, Table 10.1 data are obtained.

TABLE 10.1   Reduced Human Fallacy

S. No.	Year	Sentinel Events	Adverse Events	Near Miss
1	2017	10.3 %	65.5%	24.1%
2	2018	8.3%	54.5%	37.2%
3	2019	8.6%	55.0%	36.4%

10.2.1.2   THE REMOTE HEALTHCARE

Now, the doctors and hospitals are not far away to approach. They can be contacted with the use of mobile applications and software. This convenience of communication is guided by the integration of information technology and telecommunication with the catalyzation of IoMT technology. Along with mobile applications, mobile transportation is also an emerging concept through which the patients can be traced with their location, whether urban or rural and may treat the patient. Tele-education is one of the most important components of healthcare where thousands of medical and paramedical professionals are being taught about the treatment of disease, prevention, drugs usage, and vaccination during the COVID-19 period. Video conferencing and virtual platforms provide communication between patients, physicians, and healthcare setups.

10.2.1.3   REPORTING, MONITORING, AND MEDICAL RESEARCH

Smart healthcare involves the medical devices that collect and transfer health data such as blood pressure, oxygen, and blood sugar levels, weight, and ECGs with reference to IoMT. These data are stored in the cloud and can be shared with a physician, insurance company, a participating health firm, or an external consultant, to allow them to look at the collected data regardless of their place, time, or device which assists the clinicians, healthcare givers, and health insurance companies to regulate monitor the patient's data to draw the line of treatment, healthcare facility needed and health insurance cover of the patient. These collected data are used to generate the statistics of the healthcare status. The technological and IoMT perspective of healthcare involves the medical research domain as well. The discovery of drugs and vaccines is a great success to control the disease spread and reduce the mortality rates in the population which could be achieved by advanced technology. Even the existing devices are now being updated with IoMT by simply using embedding chips of smart devices. This chip enhances the assistance and cares that a patient requires.

10.1.2.4 PREEMPTIVE AND SYNCHRONIZED HEALTHCARE AT THE SECONDARY AND TERTIARY LEVELS

An IoMT-based medical system allows total healthcare systems to move away from a reactive, inconsistent, and uncoordinated paradigm of service delivery and toward a preemptive, consistent, and coordinated approach. Such a strategy is advantageous since it allows patients and healthcare professionals to earn excellent care in a less invasive and pleasant manner. This shift in the healthcare scenery towards IoMT is also alluring to decision-makers because it has the potential to greatly increases the effectiveness (and thus reduce resource use) of the healthcare system, as well as provide the versatility to shift care models and service delivery as needed on a personal or community basis [18].

10.1.3 IMPLICATIONS OVER FUTURE HEALTHCARE DELIVERY (FIGURE 10.3)

FIGURE 10.3 Implications over future healthcare delivery.

10.1.3.1   DELIGHTFUL EXPERIENCE OF HEALTHCARE

The healthcare sector is now being patient-focused and putting efforts to accomplish the addition of positive experience for patients in the health-care setting up. The goal is to fulfill the patient's expectations and not only provide him satisfactory services but to make his experience delightful. The COVID-19 altered the healthcare service delivery approach and developed new challenges to deliver the healthcare services in physical mode. Therefore, the evolution of IoMT and smart healthcare assisted healthcare professionals to provide healthcare services in remote mode to enhance the positive feedback of the patients. Smart healthcare engaged the patients in creative ways with less effort and least time, such as the history of the patients are being taken by robots after the exposure of COVID-19. The vitals are being captured with the help of digital health indicators and devices. Smart parking is being used by patients to free the spot-on time and many more to make a delightful experience for the patients.

TABLE 10.2   The Differences Between Traditional and Modern Healthcare Following the Digital Health Transformation

S. No.	Characteristics	Traditional Medicine	Modern Medicine
1	Point of Care	Clinic or Lab	Patient
2	Based On	Population	Individual
3	Unit Structure	Hierarchy	Partnership
4	Treatment through	Prescription and Medicine	Collaboration
5	Data owned by	Institutions	Patient
6	Experience	Individual Experience dominates	Limitless data analyzes
7	Physician's Role	As authority	As guide
8	Practice	Ivory tower	Social Media
9	Cost derived by	Physician	Technology

10.1.3.2   EXTENDED PATIENT CARE AND ACCESSIBILITY

The outbreak of COVID-19 improvised the criteria of patient care with major attention to the quality healthcare services with their maximum utility. These services persisted not only till the time of hospitalization but with the post-discharge follow-ups. The pandemic scenario caused severe damage to the respiratory systems of the patients who have chronic diseases such as diabetes, hypertension, cardiological disorders, respiratory diseases, neurological disorders, etc., for a long time [30]. Hence more care to be expected and fulfilled by the healthcare systems which became easier with the use of IoMT technology. For instance, patients can easily monitor their blood sugar levels at home through glucometers. Smart healthcare enabled the patients to access the healthcare services from anywhere in the world with the help of tele-consultations. Electronic Medical Records (EMR) of patients can be stored and can be communicated to the physicians with the help of tele-communication to deliver better healthcare services to the patients.

10.1.3.3   IMPROVED ACCESS TO PRIMARY HEALTHCARE

The mortality and morbidity attributed to modifiable risk factors are greater than ever before, hence an emphasis on disease prevention must become a concern this decade. IoMT in healthcare coverage has the capacity to boost public health and shift our healthcare paradigm to a real hybrid approach of primary, secondary, and tertiary care, in which the healthcare system can make better use of its existing staff. Even among high healthcare users, more than 90% of lifestyle self-management is done by patients outside of hospitals and clinical settings, therefore reforming health delivery in this way is critical to improving self-management for people living with chronic disorders. A substantial public demand exists for widely obtainable health information. In a 2018 US survey, 58% (931/1604) of smartphone users said they have downloaded a health-related app to help them manage their lifestyle. Artificial intelligence has also accelerated the availability of moment in time health information, such as chatbots (AI clinicians) that can provide lifestyle and health opinions. With no official procedure for certifying applications or informing customer choice, more than half of the most highly rated applications make medical claims that are not permitted, and more work remains to be done to understand the potential of chatbots to enhance health. As a result, a trustworthy virtual care evidence base is critical. Digital prescriptions might become an enabler of further use of IoMT in healthcare and support a wider population focus on illness prevention if health providers have access to evidence-based digital resources, gadgets, and smartphone applications.

10.1.4 THE ENABLERS (FIGURE 10.4)

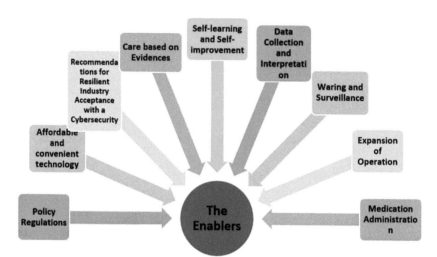

FIGURE 10.4   The enablers.

10.1.4.1 POLICY REGULATIONS

Healthcare system functions over the medical ethics, code of conduct, and laws which enables the system to work in an efficient manner. The procedures, operational activities, and their execution exist over these policies, regulations, and standards. Hence in the case of IoMT, policy support is very essential for their smooth implementation in the healthcare sector [4]. Developed countries already formulated the policies for e-Health (such as web-based and software programs to deliver health services) and either have or are in the process of developing policies for IoMT infrastructure, investment, and/or implementation in healthcare. For example, the countries like China, India, Indonesia, Japan, Malaysia, the Philippines, Singapore, Thailand, the European Union, the United States, and Vietnam currently have relevant policies for IoMT. Australia is also in the process of establishing a policy for IoMT development and investment. The policy formulation will help the healthcare sectors of these countries to prevent malpractices and enhanced form of patient accessibility towards the utilization of healthcare services [6].

10.1.4.2 AFFORDABLE AND CONVENIENT TECHNOLOGY

Because of the pervasiveness of technology, consumers and healthcare providers now have more access to digital materials than it has ever been. However, health systems must be conscious of the disparities that may arise because of widespread adoption of IoMT for healthcare, such as those who may not be able to purchase or access technology hardware or dependable internet services due to geographic location or financial hardship. Likewise, if people don't think the technology is user-friendly, have bad connections, or don't think the effort was built in consultation with them (both patients and health practitioners), they're likely to be frustrated and hesitant to adopt it.

10.1.4.3 RECOMMENDATIONS FOR STRONG AND RESILIENT INDUSTRY ACCEPTANCE WITH A CYBERSECURITY EMPHASIS

The threat of cyberattack is a serious hindrance to IoMT's mass acceptance. To avoid unlawful monitoring and classification, patients' confidentiality must be protected. From such a viewpoint, the greater the autonomy and intelligence of the things, the greater the issues for identity and privacy protection. According to a cyber defense analysis done by the Healthcare Information and Management Systems Society in 2019, 64% of healthcare businesses have been vulnerable to foreign intrusions in the previous 12 months [17]. According to Bloomer News, 90% of all healthcare systems have been targeted in the preceding two years [19]. Moreover, whether reflected in the financial, administrative, or academic sectors, healthcare, and clinical enterprises experience the highest data breaches [23].

10.1.4.4 CARE-BASED ON EVIDENCE

The augmented increase in the volume of healthcare data generated by IoMT devices makes data processing challenges. The digital devices provide evidence-based care by collecting data sets from different sources. The analysis of this data is performed to take out useful insights to detect errors and provide required treatments to patients. Intelligent analysis using new methods can save financial resources as well. When health-related information gets integration with efficient methods it promotes early identification of disease patterns, which expands public health surveillance. This ensures that safe and timely decisions on the treatment of a specific disease are being taken which assists to reduce patient mortality.

10.1.4.5 SELF-LEARNING AND SELF-IMPROVEMENT

IoMT sensors allow data to be gathered, but they cannot deliver rehabilitation therapies on their own. Based on rapid patient assessment and the development of rehabilitation techniques that correspond to medical research, timely and accurate therapies can be provided. To offer an accurate medication, many things must be addressed. Self-learning techniques can adaptively examine and offer novel treatment alternatives, whereas computer systems rely solely on data acquired by sensors and prior case reports. For data processing and extraction, a few self-learning methods [such as artificial neural networks (ANN), genetic algorithms (GA), ant colony optimization (ACO), and simulated annealing (SA)] are appropriate [32]. For big data analytics, a variety of distributed computing platforms are now in use. Apache Samza, Apache Spark, Hadoop MapReduce, Apache Storm, and Flink are among these platforms. The most extensively used platforms for huge data storage and analysis are Hadoop MapReduce and Apache Spark [21].

10.1.4.6 DATA COLLECTION AND INTERPRETATION

When a healthcare device's real-time application sends a large volume of data in a short amount of time, it's difficult to retain and manage if cloud connectivity is unavailable. As for healthcare providers, manually collecting data from many devices and sources and interpreting it is a risky proposition. IoMT devices can gather, transmit, and evaluate data in real-time, reducing the requirement for raw data storage. This can all be done on the cloud, with providers only seeing the final reports with graphs. Furthermore, hospitals and healthcare management enable firms to obtain critical healthcare analytics and information insights, allowing for faster decision-making and fewer failures.

10.1.4.7   WARING AND SURVEILLANCE

In the event of a life-threatening situation, prompt notification is essential. Medical IoMT devices collect crucial data and send it to clinicians in live time for tracking, as well as sending out warnings to individuals about critical parts via mobile applications and other smart devices [20]. Summaries and notifications provide a reliable assessment of a medical illness, regardless of location or time. It also aids in making well-informed judgments and providing prompt treatment. As a result, IoMT offers real-time alerting, tracking, and monitoring, allowing for hands-on remedies, improved accuracy, and appropriate medical intervention, as well as significantly improved patient healthcare service results.

10.1.4.8   EXPANSION OF OPERATIONS

Emergency rooms will be able to provide more accurate and excellent care because of the Internet of Things. For their emergency hospital workers, several institutions are building an Uber-like real-time monitoring system. Instead of sitting schedules all around hours, healthcare professionals would be able to be on the spot only when their services are required. Intern mentorship is another unique application of IoMT. Interns can view an operation in real-time without having to be present in the operating room thanks to Virtual Environments.

10.1.4.9   MEDICATION ADMINISTRATION

Smart pill containers allow a physician to monitor whether or not a patient is taking his prescriptions as prescribed and to assess the recommended course of action. Patients who fail to take their medicine on time can benefit from this.

10.1.5   THE APPLICATION STATUS OF SMART HEALTHCARE (FIGURE 10.5)

FIGURE 10.5   The application status of smart healthcare.

10.1.5.1   ADMINISTRATION OF HEALTH

Chronic illnesses have progressively climbed to the forefront of the human disease continuum and have become a new epidemic since the beginning of the twenty-first century. Chronic diseases have a protracted progression of illness, are incurable, and are expensive; therefore, chronic health management is critical. The conventional hospital- and physician-health management model, on the other hand, appears to be incapable of dealing appropriately with the growing number of patients and diseases. Patient self-management is emphasized more in the new smart healthcare health management model [26]. It focuses on patient self-monitoring in live time, instant review of health data, and prompt medical behavior intervention. IoMT-connected implantable/wearable smart devices, smart buildings, and smart health information platforms give a solution to this problem. Monitoring systems, microcontrollers, and wireless devices in third-generation wearable/implantable devices can smartly sense and monitor various physiological indicators of patients while saving energy, enhancing convenience, and allowing the data to be combined with health information from other streams. This method entails making the transition from context monitoring to continual observation and coordination care. It decreases the disease's related dangers while also making it easier for medical institutions to track the disease's prognosis.

10.1.5.2 PREVENTION OF ILLNESS AND RISK ASSESSMENT

Conventional illness risk prediction relies on medical experts taking the effort to gather patient data, comparing that data to official institution recommendations, and then publicize the prediction results. This method has a time delay and does not offer individuals correct recommendations. Illness assessment is dynamic and tailored in smart healthcare. It allows patients and doctors to take part, proactively monitor their illness risk, and implement targeted prevention strategies based on their own monitoring data [26]. The novel illness hazard forecasting model gathers information from smart devices and smart apps, transfer it to the cloud via a connection and evaluate the data using big data-based algorithms before sending the anticipated results to users via short message service in real-time. These strategies have been demonstrated to work. They assist physicians and patients in making changes to their health behaviors at any time, as well as judgment in developing regional health policies with the goal of lowering illness risk.

10.1.5.3 PERSONAL ASSISTANT

A virtual assistant is a program, not a person. Virtual assistants employ speech recognition to speak with users, rely on big data for information sources, and answer based on the user's preferences or needs after computations. Automated systems combine session experience and speech technology to assist users with a variety of activities, such as generating reminders and managing their homes. Virtual assistants in smart healthcare primarily serve as a communication link between physicians, care recipients, and medical institutions. It improves medical care more accessible. For users, the virtual assistant can effortlessly convert regular, daily English into medical terms via their smart IoMT device, allowing them to seek the proper medical care more accurately. For doctors, the virtual assistant may respond to pertinent details depending on the recipient's fundamental information, making it easier for them to manage patients and organize medical procedures, allowing them to save some hours.

10.1.5.4   SMART HOSPITALS

Area, institution, and family healthcare are the three main components of smart healthcare. To improve existing patient care procedures and add new features, smart hospitals rely on information and communication technology-based settings, particularly those based on IoMT optimization and automated operations. There are three main types of services for smart hospitals: services for medical staff, services for the care recipients, and services for administrators. In hospital managers, the needs of these service users must be considered. The communication system in hospital administration unites digital devices, smart buildings, and staff by combining different digital systems based on the Internet of Things. This technology can also be used to detect and control diseased persons in hospitals, manage hospital professionals daily, and track tools and biological material. Patients have access to a variety of activities, including clinical assessment systems, virtual scheduling, diagnosis, and physician contacts. These computerized systems shorten the time it takes for patients to receive medical treatment [20]. Patients wait less time and receive more personalized care.

10.1.5.5   SMART PHARMACEUTICAL INDUSTRY

In the pharmaceutical sector, smart healthcare is used for drug manufacture and supply, stock management, anti-counterfeiting, and other procedures. Using RFID technology, make adequate, dependable, reliable, and economical transit of healthcare products. In case of a decision, constructing an integrated management platform can enable functions like resource distribution, evaluation, and evaluation metrics, as well as reduce healthcare bills, achieve maximum resource consumption, and assist hospitals and the pharmaceutical industry in making development decisions.

10.1.5.6 ASSISTING DRUG RESEARCH

Pharmaceutical innovation will become more exact and convenient with the use of big data and artificial intelligence in scientific study. Receptor screening, drug development, clinical testing, and other aspects of the drug development process are all included. To uncover effective action points, conventional drug target testing physically crosses known medicines with numerous possible target molecules in the body. This strategy is not only time-consuming, but it is also frequently neglected. Furthermore, the artificial intelligence system can collect real-time data from the outside world and can improve or modify the scanning process [13]. This challenge can be effectively handled by using artificial intelligence for virtual clinical testing. The IoMT, big data, and artificial intelligence are all used in drug studies. To begin, employing artificial intelligence to assess and match several cases can help with screening for methodological limitations and identifying the most appropriate target individuals, as well as enhancing targeted audience targeting. All information is compiled and collected on the right occasion so that researchers can examine it.

10.1.6 THE CHALLENGES OF SMART HEALTHCARE (FIGURE 10.6)

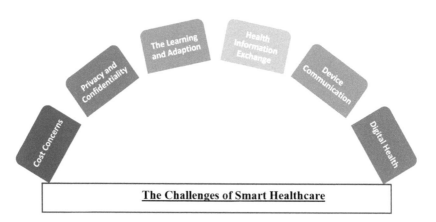

FIGURE 10.6 The challenges of smart healthcare.

10.1.6.1   COST CONCERNS

The development of new technology always faces challenges of adaptation by the healthcare sector due to its cost concerns. The enforcement of designing new healthcare delivery approaches with the involvement of medical devices, digitalization and new dimensions of technology is a challenging task for healthcare experts. The cost of development of such an automotive system cost higher than practicing the conventional system of healthcare. The development through research, trials and experiments, implementation, adaptation, training and retraining of healthcare workforce, maintenance of devices and appliances, and development of networks of hospital inculcate many funds, which is why the adaption of advancements is easier for developed countries as compared to developing ones. The utilization of smart healthcare services and IoMT devices depends on the financial capacity of the healthcare sector of the country.

10.1.6.2   PRIVACY AND CONFIDENTIALITY

IoMT-based systems are being utilized by the healthcare sector as long as it remains safe for its users. It involves the highest risk of privacy and security on both ends of the communication. In IoMT systems, all the tasks are being performed over the Internet. Thus, the personal data of clinicians and patients can be accessed at various stages for the purpose of data collection, transmission, and storage. Patients' safety is a considerable issue that needs to be prevented from leaking any or tracking or illegal identification. Providing more laser protections and security keys is an essential component to be considered to prevent mishaps and malpractices at the time of any telecommunications. The technical space is needed to store the patient data with safety so that privacy, trust, and security throughout the healthcare environment can be ensured. 10.1.6.3   The Learning and Adaption
The healthcare professionals practice their domains throughout their lives and keep updating their knowledge with the time to deliver the best healthcare services to the patients. Continuous learning is part of their professional skill. Many consultants, paramedical staff, and technicians are experienced and serving the population for more than 20 years. Hence the transformation of healthcare forces them to adapt the technological

advancements and IoMT devices which result in resistance or slow learning as they are trained with the conventional methods of healthcare delivery. This lack of interest to learn the new methods and modified modes of procedures create the complexities for adaption. Also, the lack of awareness for the benefits of these services in the population differs from country to country which directs the way towards the time taken for adaptation.

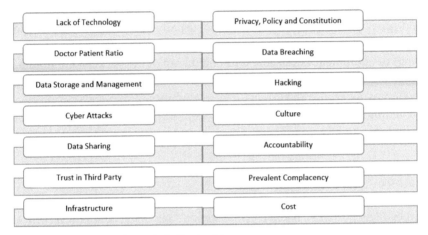

FIGURE 10.7   Privacy issues in Indian healthcare system.

10.1.6.4   HEALTH INFORMATION EXCHANGE

Health information exchange (HIE) improves healthcare provision by allowing varied healthcare entities to share healthcare information electronically safely and securely [16]. Presently, customer transfer directed transfer, and query-based transfer is the three approaches used to achieve HIE [28]. Patients can access their own electronic records through consumer-mediated communication, allowing them to follow their health complications, identify if there is any inaccurate invoicing or clinical data, and update existing self-reports. When a health agency communicates crucial information to other professionals involved in the same patient's care, such as laboratory tests and medication dose, it is known as a directed exchange. When a healthcare organization requires the past health records of a new patient, the query-based transfer is most used. This is accomplished by using the HIE system to seek access to this information.

10.1.6.5   DEVICE COMMUNICATION

Communication is one of the most difficult aspects of establishing smart or connected health. Several gadgets now have sensors for data collection, and they frequently communicate with the server in their very own language. Because each manufacturer has its own unique method, sensors from various manufacturers may or may not be able to communicate with one another. Because of the heterogeneous software environment and privacy concerns, valuable data is usually separated on data islands, undercutting the core reason behind IoMT [8]. The existence of multiple types of equipment raises concerns about employing wireless communication technology to connect medical devices. Clinicians may find it difficult to employ smart health systems. The availability of numerous features can sometimes make a system difficult, demoralizing healthcare personnel from learning how to utilize it [7].

10.1.6.6   DIGITAL HEALTH

Embedded systems, packet prioritization, big data, and bIoMTech are all used in the development of digital health (including linked and smart health). The formulation and construction of such a diverse system necessitate a broad understanding of multiple domains. To respond to continually changing requirements, the system must likewise adapt over time.

10.2   CONCLUSION

In the end, it can be concluded that smart healthcare is a growing domain of healthcare and has potential for more research. These developments in the field of smart healthcare provide a great opportunity for healthcare systems for the predictions of healthcare issues and diagnose, treat, and monitor patients without any bar of location. The adoption of technology-supported health services complements the healthcare system to ease the delivery of healthcare services and to enable health systems to deliver flexible models of patient care and replace the traditional health service delivery practices through IoMT. The implementation of smart healthcare relies on a clear and firm code of practice for the management of patient data, privacy, confidentiality, cybersecurity, and the use of IoMT devices in healthcare.

There are still important gaps for future research to get addressed, which relate to the IoMT technology itself, the health system, and the users of IoMT technology. Specific future research on IoMT technology needs to address designing the IoMT devices with standardized protocols and adaptability with international and cross-state health systems across the country. More work is also needed on the efficiency of the technology to resolve the issues and challenges of the healthcare system. From a health system perspective, there is a need for clinical guidelines on digital health prescriptions and policy regarding remuneration for primary and secondary care services provided through the IoMT. Hence, more effort is needed to determine the acceptability and digital literacy of patients and clinicians in the context of using IoMT to improve the delivery and overall experience of healthcare. The COVID-19 exposed the loopholes of the world healthcare system and provided alternatives to cope with these problems with the help of Smart Healthcare. In this changing world, smart healthcare may rise as the new hope towards the establishment of a quality healthcare system. Challenges may impact the implementation, but analytical strategies may provide a new era of healthcare.

KEYWORDS

- **artificial intelligence**
- **COVID-19**
- **IoMT in healthcare**
- **smart healthcare**
- **telemedicine**

REFERENCES

1. Bokhour, B. G., Gulraiz J. Joyia G. M., VanDeusen Lukas, C., Bolton, R. E., Hill, J. N., Mueller, S. L., & N., LaVela (2018). Patient-centered care is a way of doing things: How healthcare employees conceptualize patient-centered care. Health Expectations, 21(1), 300–307.
2. Kraus, S., Palmer, C., Kailer, N., Kallinger, F. L., & Spitzer, J. (2019). Digital entrepreneurship: A research agenda on new business models for the twenty-first century. International Journal of Entrepreneurial Behavior & Research, 25(2), 353–375.

3. Biermann, F., Kanie, N., & Kim, R. E. (2017). Global governance by goal-setting: the novel approach of the UN Sustainable Development Goals. Current Opinion in Environmental Sustainability, 26, 26–31.

4. Aayog, N. I. T. I. (2020). Empowered Group 6 Engages CSOs/NGOs/Industry/Intl Organizations in India's fight against COVID-19. Press Bureau of India.

5. Cheng, Y., Wei, W., Zhong, Y., & Zhang, L. (2021). The empowering role of hospitable telemedicine experience in reducing isolation and anxiety: evidence from the COVID-19 pandemic. International Journal of Contemporary Hospitality Management, 33(3), 851–872.

6. Cullen, W., Gulati, G., & Kelly, B. D. (2020). Mental health in the COVID-19 pandemic. QJM: An International Journal of Medicine, 113(5), 311–312.

7. De Grood, C., Raissi, A., Kwon, Y., & Santana, M. J. (2016). Adoption of e-health technology by physicians: a scoping review. Journal of Multidisciplinary Healthcare, 335–344.

8. Dimitrov, D. V. (2016). Medical internet of things and big data in healthcare. Healthcare Informatics Research, 22(3), 156–163.

9. Friedman, M., Hamilton, C., Samuelson, C. G., Lundgren, M. E., & Pott, T. (2013). Diagnostic value of the Friedman tongue position and Mallampati classification for obstructive sleep apnea: a meta-analysis. Otolaryngology-Head and Neck Surgery, 148(4), 540–547.

10. Joyia, G. J., Liaqat, R. M., Farooq, A., & Rehman, S. (2017). Internet of medical things (IoMT): Applications, benefits and future challenges in healthcare domain. J. Commun., 12(4), 240–247.

11. Kraus, S, Huang, H., Leone, D., & Caporuscio, A., . (2021). Managing intellectual capital in healthcare organizations. A conceptual proposal to promote innovation. Journal of Intellectual Capital, 22(2), 290–310.

12. Aggarwal, N., Ahmed, M., Basu, S., Curtin, J. J., Evans, B. J., Matheny, M. E., & Thadaney-Israni, S. (2020). Advancing artificial intelligence in health settings outside the hospital and clinic. NAM Perspectives, 2020.

13. Li, J. P. O., Liu, H., Ting, D. S., Jeon, S., Chan, R. P., Kim, J. E., S. Thomas ... & Ting, D. S. (2021). Digital technology, tele-medicine and artificial intelligence in ophthalmology: A global perspective. Progress in Retinal and Eye Research, 82, 100900.

14. Matheny, M., Israni, S. T., Ahmed, M., & Whicher, D. (2019). Artificial intelligence in health care: The hope, the hype, the promise, the peril. Washington, DC: National Academy of Medicine.

15. Mheidly, N., & Fares, J. (2020). Leveraging media and health communication strategies to overcome the COVID-19 infodemic. Journal of Public Health Policy, 41(4), 410–420.

16. Moore, T., Shapiro, J. S., Doles, L., Calman, N., Camhi, E., Check, T., ... & Kuperman, G. (2012). Event detection: a clinical notification service on a health information exchange platform. In AMIA Annual Symposium Proceedings (Vol. 2012, p. 635). American Medical Informatics Association.

17. Mutlag, A. A., Abd Ghani, M. K., Arunkumar, N. A., Mohammed, M. A., & Mohd, O. (2019). Enabling technologies for fog computing in healthcare IoT systems. Future Generation Computer Systems, 90, 62–78.

18. Nathani, N., & Khatri, V. K. (2021). A Review on Artificial Intelligence, Internet of Things and Wearable Technology for Smart Healthcare. International Journal of Distributed Computing and Technology, 7(1), 26–34.

19. Pettypiece, S. (2015). Rising cyberattacks costing health system $6 billion annually. The Bloomberg Business.

20. Pradhan, B., Bhattacharyya, S., & Pal, K. (2021). IoT-based applications in healthcare devices. Journal of Healthcare Engineering, 2021, 1–18.

21. Praveena, M. A., & Bharathi, B. (2017, February). A survey paper on big data analytics. In 2017 International Conference on Information Communication and Embedded Systems (ICICES) (pp. 1–9). IEEE.

22. Raykar, S. S. (2022). IoT Enabled Mobility Based Healthcare Monitoring and Implementation of Prediction Model (Doctoral dissertation, Goa University).

23. Ruckert, A., Schram, A., Labonté, R., Friel, S., Gleeson, D., & Thow, A. M. (2017). Policy coherence, health and the sustainable development goals: a health impact assessment of the Trans-Pacific Partnership. Critical Public Health, 27(1), 86–96.

24. Schram, A., Ruckert, A., VanDuzer, J. A., Friel, S., Gleeson, D., Thow, A. M., ... & Labonte, R. (2018). A conceptual framework for investigating the impacts of international trade and investment agreements on noncommunicable disease risk factors. Health Policy and Planning, 33(1), 123–136.

25. Self, W. H., Tenforde, M. W., Rhoads, J. P., Gaglani, M., Ginde, A. A., Douin, D. J., ... & Cass, C. (2021). Comparative effectiveness of Moderna, Pfizer-BioNTech, and Janssen (Johnson & Johnson) vaccines in preventing COVID-19 hospitalizations among adults without immunocompromising conditions—United States, March–August 2021. Morbidity and Mortality Weekly Report, 70(38), 1337.

26. Tian, S., Yang, W., Le Grange, J. M., Wang, P., Huang, W., & Ye, Z. (2019). Smart healthcare: making medical care more intelligent. Global Health Journal, 3(3), 62–65.

27. Wang, P., Chen, K., Zhu, S., Wang, P., & Zhang, H. (2020). Severe air pollution events not avoided by reduced anthropogenic activities during COVID-19 outbreak. Resources, Conservation and Recycling, 158, 104814.

28. Williams, C., Mostashari, F., Mertz, K., Hogin, E., & Atwal, P. (2012). From the Office of the National Coordinator: the strategy for advancing the exchange of health information. Health Affairs, 31(3), 527–536.

29. World Health Organization. (2019). Ebola Virus Disease Democratic Republic of Congo: External situation report 72.

30. World Health Organization. (2020). Mental Health and Psychosocial Considerations during the COVID-19 Outbreak, 18 March 2020 (No. WHO/2019-nCoV/MentalHealth/2020.1). World Health Organization.

31. Xue, A., Oros, V., La Marca-Ghaemmaghami, P., Scholkmann, F., Righini-Grunder, F., Natalucci, G., ... & Restin, T. (2021). New parents experienced lower parenting self-efficacy during the COVID-19 pandemic lockdown. Children, 8(2), 79.

32. Yuehong, Y. I. N., Zeng, Y., Chen, X., & Fan, Y. (2016). The internet of things in healthcare: An overview. Journal of Industrial Information Integration, 1, 3–13.

CHAPTER 11

IoMT-Based Caring System for Aged People in a Post-COVID Scenario

A. PONMALAR[1] and JOSE ANAND[2]

[1]*Department of CSE, Sri Sai Ram Institute of Technology, Chennai, Tamil Nadu, India*

[2]*Department of ECE, KCG College of Technology, Karapakkam, Chennai, Tamil Nadu, India*

ABSTRACT

Numerous aged people are living unaccompanied in their households. If the aged people tumble, it may be problematic for them to demand for help at this current scenario because of the Covid-19 pandemic situation. The foremost objective of this chapter is to design an android-based tumble detection device at a reasonable cost for the aged people. The technique describes the layout of the android-based totally fall detection sensor device with a pulse value tracking unit. The device is capable of well-known a falling incident to the touch individual such that the incident may be said to the ambulance branch to the soonest possible, and to offer essential scientific remedies for the injured aged in a quick span of time. The layout and implementation integrate each hardware and software program that paintings seamlessly in detecting and reporting a fall at domestic and still have an brought normal monitoring device. So each 10 mins as soon as their region could be shared to the caretaker. The hardware element includes the falling detection sensor and pulse sensor that detects the frame function of the person whether or not it's miles on a falling mode at

Internet of Medical Things in Smart Healthcare: Post-COVID-19 Pandemic Scenario.
Saravanan Krishnan, PhD and Aboobucker Ilmudeen, PhD (Eds.)

the same time as the software program aspect includes a few formulation that come across the fallings and triggers the alarm and sends notification thru Short Message Service (SMS) with the precise region via means of the usage of the Global Positioning System (GPS) in the smart Android phone.

11.1   INTRODUCTION

The global populations of aged humans in addition to folks that stay by myself were growing over the years [1]. The overall populace of older humans will increase from 8.2% in 2012 to 8.6% in 2013. By 2030 it is predicted to be the class of getting older international locations with aged constituting greater than 15% of the populace, approximating to 4.66 millions of people. Millions of older humans; 65 and older contain in collapse injuries. Actually, it's miles envisioned that 1 of 4 aged people fell down every year and about 2.8 million aged humans are handled in critical stage after their fall [2]. Fall coincidence end up pretty general amongst the aged and consider what could take place if no person is there to assist them while fall injuries take place. The fast improvement of Internet of Medical Things (IoMT) era marks it practicable for involving diverse clever gadgets cooperatively via the Internet and supplying greater information interoperability techniques for software purpose [3]. Recent studies suggest greater ability packages of IoMT in data extensive commercial sectors consisting of healthcare amenities. In this advanced sensor technology era, aged tracking takes by no means remained less difficult with the assist of IoMT. The deployment of digital gadgets have additionally been brought to locate any falling state of affairs. Wearable gadgets have additionally been said to apply to screen and permitting rapid size of fitness parameters [4]. The present day fashion in fitness tracking structures is to transport from the clinic to transportable non-public gadgets consisting of smartphone. However, those strategies have positive constrain for that reason restricting the gadgets to offer an wise and correct state of affairs of the aged state. By uniting this option collectively through IoT as podium, the data amassed via sensors may be united by a cloud-based product wherein information is saved and evaluated. At the same time, as a few packages are run, it might sincerely enhance and make existence a whole lot less difficult for aged condition [5].

11.1.1 CLOUD COMPUTING

Cloud computing is an on-demand-based resources available immediately on the PC, specifically records dumbs and calculating authority, without straight active governance through the user. The time period is usually used to explain records centers to be had to many customers over the Internet. An easy definition of cloud computing entails handing over specific varieties of offerings over the Internet. From software program and analytics to steady and secure records garage and networking resources, the entirety may be introduced thru the cloud. You can get admission to it from pretty much any pc that has net get admission to. Cloud computing is a huge time period which refers to a set of offerings that provide agencies a cost-powerful method to growth their information technology (IT) potential and functionality [6].

11.1.2 INTERNET OF THINGS

IoT defines the community of bodily substances, which are entrenched with sensing devices, software, and different technology aimed at the cause of joining and changing facts by different gadgets and structures using the global connectivity. Belongings have advanced since the merging of techniques, static analysis, learning, ubiquitous computing, product-based sensing devices, and integrated structures [7]. Customary arenas of entrenched structures, Wi-Fi sensing networking, manipulate edifices, computerization (consisting of domestic and constructing computerization), and various methodologies to connect to IoT [8]. In today's customer bazaar, IoT has supreme tantamount with commodities bearing on the concept of "clever domestic," consisting of devices and applications (inclusive of illuminations fittings, regulators, home protection edifices and photo devices, and diverse consumer applications). It assist one or more unusual places, and are controlled by devices connected to such application, inclusive of smart devices and clever loudspeakers. IoT concepts are utilized in healthcare structures. Some extreme issues approximately dangers within the boom of the IoT, mainly withinside the regions of privateness and protection, and therefore enterprise and governmental movements to cope with those issues have started consisting of the improvement of worldwide standards [9].

Primary utility of a clever domestic to offer people support with infirmities or aged individuals. These proposed domestic structures uses a smart generation to house an proprietor's precise incapacities. Vocal sound manages to help customers with vision and movement barriers whilst alert structures are linked immediately to cochlear transplants worn through hearing-impaired customers with extra protection capabilities. The additional functionalities and capabilities encompass sensing units that reveal for clinical traumas along with drops or seizures. Intelligent domestic generation carried out in this manner can offer customers with extra freedom and a better best of life.

11.1.3   SECURITY

Security is the most important difficulty in adopting IoMT technology, with worries that fast improvement is occurring without suitable attention of the profound safety demanding situations concerned and the supervisory adjustments that are probably essential. Majority of technological safety worries are just like the ones of traditional servers, workstations and smartphones. These worries consist of the use of susceptible verification, disremembering to alternate evasion authorizations, unencrypted communications dispatched among gadgets with SQL skills, man-in-the-center assaults, and negative coping with of safety apprises. Though, numerous IoMT gadgets take extreme operative boundaries at the computational energy to be had to them [10]. These constraints regularly lead them to not able to at once use primary security features along with enforcing firewalls or the use of robust crypto subsystems to encode the information using different gadgets and a minimum fee with customer attention of multiple gadgets kinds a strong safety repairing rare device. IoMT gadgets additionally have get admission to new regions of records, and might regularly manage bodily gadgets, in order that even with the aid of using it turned into viable to mention that many Internet-related home equipment should already "secret agent on human beings of their personal homes," which includes televisions, kitchen home equipment, cameras, and thermostats [11]. Computer-managed gadgets in vehicles along with footbrakes, locomotives, ringlets, cover and stem reliefs, horn, hotness, and console had proven to be prone to assailants and get admission to within the network. In a few circumstances, car PC structures with Internet-related, permitting are subjugated distantly. Safety investigators had proven the cap potential to distantly manage pacesetters without ability. Advanced hackers tested far flung manage of insulin impels and transplantable cardioverter defibrillators. Unwell tenable Internet-reachable IoMT gadgets also can be subverted to assault others [12]. A dispensed denial of carrier assault powered with the aid of using Internet of factors, devices that jogging the Mirai malware took down a domain name server issuer and fundamental net websites. This took inflamed more or less 65,000 IoT gadgets in just 20 hours. Ultimately the contaminations improved to around 200,000 to 300,000 infections. Brazil, Colombia and Vietnam had affected 41.5% and this had a particular IoT device consisted of DVRs, IP cameras, routers, and printing device. Highest carriers that limited the maximum inflamed devices have been documented as ZTE, MikroTik, etc. A researcher on workstation at Cloudflare stated that native DDoS susceptibilities be in IoT devices since of a negative implementation of the publish–subscribe pattern [13]. These kinds of attacks take about safety professionals to sight IoT as an actual chance to Internet amenities. The U.S. National Intelligence Council in an unsystematic file continues to be tough to reject "get admission to nets of devices and managed with remote gadgets with the aid of using opponents of the offenders, and disruption creators." An exposed marketplace for combined sensor records should serve the pursuits of trade and safety no much less than it allows offenders and detectives perceive prone boards. Therefore, vastly similar sensor synthesis also weaken communal consistency that proves to be basically mismatched with agreements ensures in opposition to irrational exploration. Generally, the intellect network perspectives the Internet of factors as a wealthy supply of records [14].

11.2   RELATED WORKS

The latest developments in miniaturized computing and hardware devices to Machine-to-Machine (M2M) infrastructures have permitted IoT systems to redesign numerous application domains. Healthcare structures are amongst those packages which are transformed with IoT, announcing an IoT department called the IoMT. IoMT structures permit faraway tracking of sufferers with persistent diseases [15]. This offers well timed diagnostics for the sufferers that relates their lifestyles in case of emergencies and protection are needed project for the consideration of the elders using a stable IoMT structures with records through a series of transmission and storage [16]. The state-of-the-artwork studies provides throughout the range of clinical imaging information, deliberates medical conversion, and offers destiny guidelines for proceeding medical repetition. Additionally, it precise developments in clinical imaging achievement technology for special functionalities, emphasizing the need for green clinical record control techniques within the setting of Artificial Intelligence (AI) in large healthcare records statically [17]. It offers an outline of present day and rising algorithmic techniques for sickness type and organ/tissue separation, that specialize in AI and deep learning knowledge of constructions to overcome the existing method. The medical advantages of in silicon technology and image processing developments related with developing 3D rebuilding and imaging packages are additionally recognized [18].

Targeting a stable protection development within the Wi-Fi conversation among current and destiny implantable clinical gadgets using Programmer Monitor Device (PMD) [19]. A public clinical server performing as a depended on authority is introduced. A devoted Pacemaker Proxy Device (PPD) is proposed to protect mediator among PMD and the gadgets are looking after all clinical protection, legal responsibility and duty issues [20]. The key concept is primarily based on embedding low complexity and resilient, the virtual body identities a brand new idea within the gadget to restrict bodily substitution/cloning attacks. A biometric identification extracted from the affected person's ECG (electrocardiogram) is helping the safety gadget via means of an alternative hard-to-clone affected person non-public fitness profile. A gadget gaining knowledge on a set of rules is deployed to extract such biometric identification [21]. Various hardware structures are evolved for packages which include ambulance control [22], automated irrigation gadget [23], and many others to the use of diverse microcontrollers as an embedded device. The improvement of a successful clinical product calls for now no longer best engineering layout efforts, additionally medical, regulatory, advertising and marketing and commercial enterprise expertise. The gadgets associated with the procedure of designing clinical gadgets discuss the stairs required to take a clinical product concept from idea, via improvement, verification and validation, regulatory approvals, and marketplace release [24].

Data series procedure, annotation schemas, and settlement consequences for extracting fitness desires from SMS conversations among a fitness instructor and the sufferers are discussed with initial consequences using robotically to detect the subject matter barriers in fitness training dialogs [25]. The worldwide populace has come to be a subject valued by all nations. During an identical period, it additionally varieties the problem of aged care became more and more critical; that specializes in aged care establishments and proposes four care signs such as physiological feature tracking, pastime area tracking, fall prevention, and emergency assist [26]. The IoT is a brand new truth this is absolutely converting our regular lifestyles, and guarantees to revolutionize current healthcare allowing a greater personalized, preventive and collaborative shape of care. Aiming to mix those critical topics, this offers an IoT-equipped answer for the aged residing who seek help that's capable of displaying and sufferers critical facts in addition to offer mechanisms to cause alarms in emergency situations [27]. The cause of this challenge is to combine the technology of Wi-Fi sensor networks and public conversation networks to assemble a healthcare gadget for senior residents at domestic without interfering with their everyday activities. This gadget offers four most important functionalities, which includes indoor tracking, outdoor tracking, pastime and fitness choice, emergency choice, and alarm [28].

The populace of elder humans is developing swiftly, and nowadays a lot of them must live alone, independently as opposed to antique age homes. With growing age, humans generally tend to neglect about matters which additionally create protection troubles. A Wireless Sensor Network (WSN) on clever domestic gadget for such senior humans to assist them comfort their daily activities and offer them benign, rigorous and stable residing is mentioned [29]. An optimization solution [30] for locating the excellent course to carry the sensed physiological parameters to the care taking center [31] is mentioned for a biomedical sensor network [32]. The aged is mainly worrying and hard for casual care takers. Computerized structures to help casual care givers will fill an incredible want. A gadget is evolved to offer pointers for aged care to casual care givers making use of case reasoning strategies. The pointers are separated into 4 parts, specifically, bodily treatment, food, emotional, and exercising management [33].

With the advent of latest era in each day lifestyles, this era is used for the useful resource of the aged. Aged people falling down is a common exercise for them under their current lifestyle. Attention is on what might be a useful resource for the aged. Surveys on concerning fall detection algorithms with diverse sensors deployed are discussed. Looking at wearable era, the era is reasonably-priced and correct however inconvenient and a handy and inexpensive device is developed [34]. With the efflux of the growing older populace, the want for looking after the aged widespread device is a needed one. The increase of assistive robots keeps increasing. Robots are poignant human lives, especially in the growing older populace. The inspiration at the back of the studies and improvement of those robots for the use of caring for the elder one is of greater use because of this societal want [35].

11.3   PROPOSED SOLUTION AND IMPLEMENTATION

Android is a Linux-primarily working gadget for Android gadgets like Smart devices. This has open supply platform to be had for customers to broaden Android packages the use of the Android Software Development Kit (SDK). The provision provided for the aged is an Android utility that video display units the phone's integrated sensing units, identifying downfalls and provide indicators on fall happening. The primary goal of this venture is to offer an smooth and person-pleasant manner to aware the customers all through an incidence. So quick and handy first-useful resource instrument. The Google Maps application programming interface suggests the vicinity at which the autumn took place and additionally the closest direction to the particular vicinity. The utility additionally brands it smooth for the person to arrange and offer it to the aged earlier than they come out.

The disadvantages are:

i.   There is no security and privacy.
ii. The performance is low.
iii. On a server-side, there is a possibility of server attack where the third party will access the data easily.
iv. There is less security in storage part where all the sequence are stored in a database can be easily retrieved by the third party.

11.3.1   PROPOSED SYSTEM

This works provides lots of issues and upgrades that had been included in to the capability of the tool with a purpose to replicate preferred functions which include cost, layout complexity, length, software program development, weight, loss of portability, etc. This layout makes use of a miniaturized pulse sensor as a IC sensor which has been optimized for terribly correct sensing and size of modifications withinside the heartbeat charge. The gadget calculates the pulse charge in beat in keeping with minute with the assist of the microcontroller, shows the measured coronary heart charge on a 16 x 2 person LCD and sends an SMS with modern BPM value, on every occasion the coronary heart charge is going above or beneath a hard and fast threshold, whilst on the equal time putting off a buzzer alarm connected to the affected person module to cause an alert. With small length and portability in mind, the selection of the LCD show and miniaturized sensor targets at doing away with the want for a PC show, whilst making it less complicated to hold the gadget about, for non-stop tracking. It accordingly guarantees flexibility in real-time faraway tracking irrespective of distance and location. Another exciting function of this specific layout is the reprogrammable and exposed supply situation of the device is less complex to represent a particular coronary heart charge to observe that to perform the device options, to fit the customers demand based on different natural parameters and affected person conditions. The advent of the exposed supply Arduino unit on this undertaking marks it fairly particular and accordingly unlocks entrance for extra examination and expansion of its fantastic suppleness purposes and the volume to which it is able to be carried out for lots of functions.

The merits are:

i.   Easy monitorization without any person.
ii.   Quick emergency detection.
iii. Time consuming.
iv.   Best accuracy Model helps in better treatment as early.
v.   Easy data storage through the cloud.

11.3.2   SYSTEM ARCHITECTURE

In the proposed system shown in Figure 11.1, we have built an android application where patient heart rate, pulse, fall detection are monitored and stored in the database. If any rise in their health issue a SMS will be sent to their guardians and if they have gone lost they can be easily tracked by GPS which gives the current location where they are in.

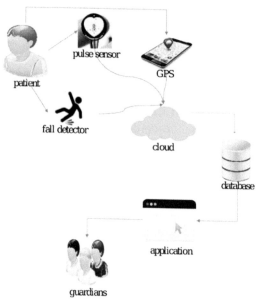

FIGURE 11.1   System architecture.

The advantages are:

i.   High security and more effective.
ii.   The performance and the accuracy is high.
iii. More flexibility and reliable.
iv.   Highly secured because of cryptographic technique.
v.   Time consuming.
vi.   Best accuracy Model helps in better treatment as early.

11.3.3   SOFTWARE REQUIREMENTS

A prerequisite stipulates an outside element with which a scheme or structure modules must intermingle, or that sets forth restraints on arrangements, judgment and other issues produced by an interface. The following software is used for the development of the system.

i.   Programming Software: Arduino IDE
ii.   Programming Language: Embedded C

iii. Android App Development: MIT App Inventor
iv. Android App Development Language: Graphical Programming Language

A cloud server is an electronic server (in place of a physical server) jogging in an utility service atmosphere, constructed, developed and brought into the utility service arena using the Internet to access the information from remote locations. This is referred to as digital servers. A cloud server is a pooled, centralized server useful resource this is hosted and brought over a network, usually the Internet, and accessed on call for through more than one users. Cloud servers can carry out all of the identical features of a conventional bodily server, turning in processing power, garage, and applications.

i. Login with cloud username and password
ii. View all new patient key generation the mail
iii. View all doctor details
iv. View all insurance details
v. View all report upload by patient
vi. Result
vii. Logout.

11.3.4 SYSTEM MODULES

The important modules for the system are:

- **Sensing Module** – In this module we used fall detection sensor and pulse sensor, this gives the large sector probability being proximity detection and range measurement.
- **Automatic GPS Control Module** – GPS receivers are commonly utilized in smartphones, fleet control system, navy, etc., for monitoring or locating location.
- **Alert Module** – Static time evaluation for fallen situation identification structures, specifically for business goods. Seeing that positive fallen may be deadly or unfavorable to fitness, it's far vital that the organized fallen situation identification structures are excessive co-operational competence, ideally working in realistic situations.

- **Health Detection Module** – In this, a heartbeat monitor sensor and pulse sensor is connected using the Arduino with proper interface.

Used a 204 LCD show panel to show all of the alert messages. This sensor is pretty clean to apply and operate. Place your finger on the pinnacle of the sensor, and it's going to feel the pulse via means of measuring the extrade in mild from the enlargement of capillary blood vessels. Sensor may be used with ESP8266 to add the BPM information to the Internet. When a heartbeat happens, blood is driven thru the body frame and receives embraced into the capillary tissues. Subsequently, the quantity of those capillary tissues upsurges. So among the two successive heartbeats, this quantity inner capillary tissues declines. The extrade in quantity among the heartbeats impacts the quantity of mild so that it will convey thru those tissues and is restrained by the contribution of a processor. The pulse sensor is one of the best pulse sensors for expertise the precept in the back of Pulse Rate Measurement. However, in relation to accuracy and balance, the sensor falls some distance in the back of. The higher opportunity of this sensor is the clean pulse sensor that's exceptionally stable. Apart from the clean pulse sensor, in case you need to degree the blood oxygen together with the coronary heart rate, you may use MAX30100 Pulse Oximeter Sensor. You can carry out facet assessment to evaluate the overall performance of various pulse sensors.

11.3.5 ACTIVITY DIAGRAM

The activity diagram details the workflow of the proposed IoMT-based alerting system for the aged people. Figure 11.2 shows the activity diagram for the proposed system which depicts the complete behavior of the architecture. The diagram has a starting control point and the flow of procedures or functions or activities carried out throughout the execution and finally the finishing point. The system continuously monitors the sensor connected to the aged people and if there is any up normal values on the physiological parameters or the aged person fall down, that also is monitored through the sensor value, immediate the system will send an alert message to the care taker stating the condition of the aged person and the current location of the aged person under care using the GPS present in the system. Thus this system is very useful for aged persons in the post covid situation where no direct human monitoring is required.

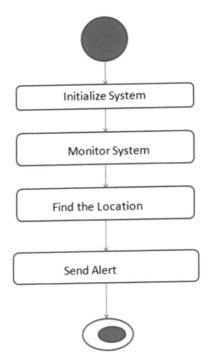

FIGURE 11.2   Activity diagram.

11.4   TESTING AND RESULTS

The motive of checking out is to catch up the errors. Testing is the system of looking for to catch up each possible responsibility spot in a piece device. It presents a manner to examine the competence of mechanisms, sub-assemblies, meetings and/or a finished device. It is the system of workout program with the reason of making sure that the gadget encounters its supplies and person expectancies and fixes now no longer flop in an intolerable manner. These are diverse kinds of take a look at. Each takes a look at kind cope with a particular checking out necessities. Figure 11.3 shows the screenshots of the developed App. The mode button to be enabled for sensing the parameters or the person under care. Once the device is on, it will sense the data and the location of the person and the sensed physiological parameters and displayed on the caretaker mobile, as shown in Figure 11.4.

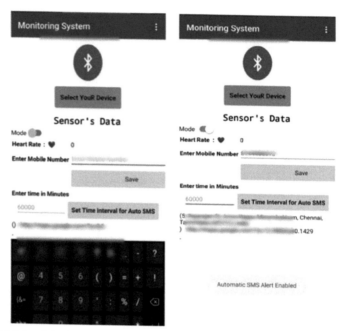

FIGURE 11.3   Selection of device for monitoring.

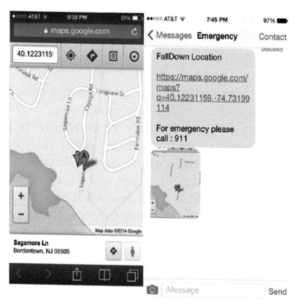

FIGURE 11.4   Location of the person.

11.5   CONCLUSIONS AND FUTURE WORK

The system was developed using an Android mobile application that gave to understand of the improvement and demanding situations worried in cellular utility improvement. The advanced gadget offers an easy, user-pleasant utility to assist the aged at some point of collapse. The utility is applied and examined on actual gadgets. Android is a working gadget; this is optionable and open source. A brand novel utility is advanced and consistent with one's necessities running on GPS, in-constructed sensors, and Google Maps V2 application programming interface for displaying places on Google Maps. More advancements can be made in the application for customer-specific needs.

KEYWORDS

- **Android application**
- **caring system**
- **hardware and software**
- **IoMT**
- **sensors**

REFERENCES

1. Kumata, A., Tsuda, Y., Pref, K., Suzuki, H., Ra, E., & Morishita, T., (2011). Advanced community model using daily life information transmitter for supporting welfare workers and senior citizens living alone in a welfare society. In: *2011 8th International Conference on Ubiquitous Robots and Ambient Intelligence* (URAI) (414–417). doi: 10.1109/URAI.2011.6145854.
2. Longitudinal ageing study in India, (2020). *An Investigation of Health, Economic, and Social Well-being of India's Growing Elderly Population.* India Report. https://www.iipsindia.ac.in/sites/default/files/LASI_India_Report_2020_compressed.pdf (accessed on 11 January 2022).
3. Forrest, S., Baker, K., & Ketel, M., (2021). Internet of medical things: Enabling key technologies. *Southeast Con., 2021,* 1–5. doi: 10.1109/SoutheastCon45413.2021.9401862.
4. Vajar, P., Emmanuel, A. L., Ghasemieh, A., Bahrami, P., & Kashef, R., (2021). The internet of medical things (IoMT): A vision on learning, privacy, and computing. In: *2021 International Conference on Electrical, Computer, Communications*

and Mechatronics Engineering (ICECCME) (pp. 1–7). doi: 10.1109/ICECCME52200.2021.9590881.

5. Jose, A., Gowtham, H., Lingeshwaran, R., Ajin, J., & Karthikeyan, J., (2021). IoT based smart electrolytic bottle monitoring. *Advances in Parallel Computing Technologies and Applications, 40*, 391–399. IOS Press.

6. Fazio, M., Ranjan, R., Girolami, M., Taheri, J., Dustdar, S., & Villari, M., (2018). A note on the convergence of IoT, edge, and cloud computing in smart cities. *IEEE Cloud Computing, 5*(5), 22–24. doi: 10.1109/MCC.2018.053711663.

7. Aditya, R. R., Ajay, H., Balavanan, M., Lalit, R., & Anand, J., (2017). A novel cardiac arrest alerting system using IoT. *International Journal of Science Technology & Engineering, 3*(10), 78–83.

8. Wang, P., Yang, L. T., & Li, J., (2018). An edge cloud-assisted CPSS framework for smart city. *IEEE Cloud Computing, 5*(5), 37–46.

9. Niranjana, S., Hareshaa, S. K., Irene, Z. B., & Anand, J., (2020). Smart monitoring system for asthma patients. *International Journal of Electronics and Communication Engineering, 7*(5), 5–9.

10. Alshamaseen, T., Althunibat, S., & Qaraqe, M., (2021). Secure key distribution for IoT networks based on physical layer security. In: *2021 IEEE 26th International Workshop on Computer Aided Modeling and Design of Communication Links and Networks* (pp. 1–6).

11. Vaishnavi, R., Anand, J., & Janarthanan, R., (2009). Efficient security for desktop data grid using cryptographic protocol. *Proceedings of the IEEE International Conference on Control, Automation, Communication and Energy Conservation (INCACEC'09), 1*, 305–311.

12. Verma, A., Surendra, R., Reddy, B. S., Chawla, P., & Soni, K., (2021). Cyber security in the digital sector. *2021 International Conference on Artificial Intelligence and Smart Systems (ICAIS)*, 703–710. doi: 10.1109/ICAIS50930.2021.9395933.

13. Srinath, D., Janet, J., & Anand, J., (2010). A survey of routing instability with IP spoofing on the internet. *Asian Journal of Information Technology, 9*(3), 154–158. Medwell Journals Scientific Research Publishing Company.

14. Fu, J., Shi, Z., & Zhang, Z., (2020). An edge computing framework for digital grid. In: *2020 IEEE 3rd International Conference on Electronic Information and Communication Technology*, 670–673.

15. Ghubaish, A., Salman, T., Zolanvari, M., Unal, D., Al-Ali, A., & Jain, R., (2021). Recent advances in the internet-of-medical-things (IoMT) systems security. *IEEE Internet of Things Journal, 8*(11), 8707–8718. doi: 10.1109/JIOT.2020.3045653.

16. Bennet, P. M. S., Sagari, S., Chailshi, C., & Divya, S., (2019). AI healthcare interactive talking agent using NLP. *International Journal of Innovative Technology and Exploring Engineering, 9*(1), 3470–3473.

17. Degadwala, S., Vyas, D., & Dave, H., (2021). Classification of COVID-19 cases using fine-tune convolution neural network (FT-CNN). In: *2021 International Conference on Artificial Intelligence and Smart Systems*, 609–613.

18. Panayides, A. S., et al., (2020). AI in medical imaging informatics: Current challenges and future directions. *IEEE Journal of Biomedical and Health Informatics, 24*(7), 1837–1857. doi: 10.1109/JBHI.2020.2991043.

19. Hamadaqa, E., Abadleh, A., Mars, A., & Adi, W., (2018). Highly secured implantable medical devices. In: *2018 International Conference on Innovations in Information Technology (IIT)* (pp. 7–12). doi: 10.1109/INNOVATIONS.2018.8605968.

20. Ponmalar, A., Anand, J., Dharshini, S., Aishwariya, K., & Mahalakshmi, S., (2021). Smartphone controlled fingerprint door look system. *Advances in Parallel Computing Technologies and Applications, 40*, 400–407. IOS Press.

21. Jose, A., Raja, P. P. J., & Meganathan, D., (2017). Q-learning-based optimized routing in biomedical wireless sensor networks. *IETE Journal of Research, 63*(1), 89–97.

22. Bali, V., Mathur, S., Sharma, V., & Gaur, D., (2020). Smart traffic management system using IoT enabled technology. In: *2020 2nd International Conference on Advances in Computing, Communication Control and Networking* (pp. 1–6).

23. Prakash, B. R., & Kulkarni, S. S., (2020). Super smart irrigation system using the internet of things. In: *2020 7th International Conference on Smart Structures and Systems* (pp. 1–5).

24. Panescu, D., (2009). Medical device development. In: *2009 Annual International Conference of the IEEE Engineering in Medicine and Biology Society* (pp. 5591–5594). doi: 10.1109/IEMBS.2009.5333490.

25. Gupta, I., et al., (2018). Towards building a virtual assistant health coach. In: *2018 IEEE International Conference on Healthcare Informatics (ICHI)* (pp. 419–421).

26. Lu, Y. H., & Lin, C. C., (2018). The study of smart elderly care system. In: *2018 Eighth International Conference on Information Science and Technology* (ICIST) (pp. 483–486). doi: 10.1109/ICIST.2018.8426110.

27. Pinto, S., Cabral, J., & Gomes, T., (2017). We-care: An IoT-based health care system for elderly people. In: *2017 IEEE International Conference on Industrial Technology (ICIT)* (pp. 1378–1383). doi: 10.1109/ICIT.2017.7915565.

28. Huo, H., Xu, Y., Yan, H., Mubeen, S., & Zhang, H., (2009). An elderly health care system using wireless sensor networks at home. In: *2009 Third International Conference on Sensor Technologies and Applications* (pp.158–163). doi: 10.1109/ SENSORCOMM.2009.32.

29. Ransing, R. S., & Rajput, M., (2015). Smart home for elderly care, based on wireless sensor network. In: *2015 International Conference on Nascent Technologies in the Engineering Field (ICNTE)* (pp. 1–5). doi: 10.1109/ICNTE.2015.7029932.

30. Anand, J., Raja, P. P. J., & Meganathan, D., (2015). Performance of optimized routing in biomedical wireless sensor networks using evolutionary algorithms. *Comptes Rendus de l'Academie Bulgare des Sciences, 68*(8), 1049–1054.

31. Anand, J., Raja, J., Paul, P., & Meganathan, D., (2015). Design of GA-based routing in biomedical wireless sensor networks. *International Journal of Applied Engineering Research, 10*(4), 9281–9292.

32. Nath, M. P., Mohanty, S. N., & Priyadarshini, S. B. B., (2021). Application of machine learning in wireless sensor network. In: *2021 8th International Conference on Computing for Sustainable Global Development* (pp. 7–12).

33. Wongpun, S., & Guha, S., (2017). Elderly care recommendation system for informal caregivers using case-based reasoning. In: *2017 IEEE 2nd Advanced Information Technology, Electronic and Automation Control Conference (IAEAC)* (pp. 548–552). doi: 10.1109/IAEAC.2017.8054075.

34. Mohamed, O., Choi, H., & Iraqi, Y., (2014). Fall detection systems for elderly care: A survey. In: *2014 6th International Conference on New Technologies, Mobility and Security (NTMS)* (pp. 1–4). doi: 10.1109/NTMS.2014.6814018.
35. Sharma, A., Rathi, Y., Patni, V., & Sinha, D. K., (2021). A systematic review of assistance robots for elderly care. In: *2021 International Conference on Communication Information and Computing Technology* (ICCICT) (pp. 1–6). doi: 10.1109/ICCICT50803.2021.9510142.

Index